JZ
SS34
EDU

Education and Reconciliation

Other titles in the Education as a Humanitarian Response series

Education as a Global Concern, Colin Brock

Education, Aid and Aid Agencies, Zuki Karpinska

Education and HIV/AIDS, Nalini Asha Biggs

Education, Refugees and Asylum Seekers, Lala Demirdijan

Also available from Continuum

Comparative and International Education: An Introduction to Theory, Method, and Practice, David Phillips and Michele Schweisfurth

Education and Reconciliation

Exploring Conflict and Post-Conflict Situations

Edited by
Julia Paulson

Education as a Humanitarian Response

continuum

Continuum International Publishing Group

The Tower Building   80 Maiden Lane
11 York Road   Suite 704
London SE1 7NX   New York NY 10038

www.continuumbooks.com

British Library Cataloguing-in-Publication Data
A catalogue record for this book is available from the British Library.

ISBN: 978-1-4411-5325-8 (paperback)
       978-1-4411-0136-5 (hardcover)

Library of Congress Cataloging-in-Publication Data
Education and reconciliation : exploring conflict and post-conflict situations / edited by Julia Paulson.
p. cm. -- (Education as a humanitarian response)
Includes bibliographical references.
ISBN: 978-1-4411-5325-8
ISBN: 978-1-4411-0136-5
1. War and education. 2. Conflict management–Study and teaching.
3. Conflict management. 4. Reconciliation–Political aspects.
I. Paulson, Julia.
JZ5534.E39 2011
303.6–dc22

                                        2010045140

Typeset by Newgen Imaging Systems Pvt Ltd, Chennai, India
Printed and bound in Great Britain

Contents

List of Illustrations

Figures

Image

Tables

Series Editor's Preface

Underlying this entire series on *Education as a Humanitarian Response* is the well known adage in education that 'if we get it right for those most in need we will likely get it right for all if we take the same approach'. That sentiment was born in relation to those with special educational needs within a full mainstream system of schooling. In relation to this series it is taken further to embrace the special educational needs of those experiencing disasters and their aftermath, whether natural or man made. Much can be learned of value to the provision of normal mainstream systems from the holistic approach that necessarily follows in response to situations of disaster. Sadly very little of this potential value is actually perceived, and even less is embraced. Consequently one of the aims of the series, both in the core volume *Education as a Global Concern,* and the contributing volumes, is to bring the notion of education as a humanitarian response to the mainstream, and those seeking to serve it as teachers, other educators, and politicians. The theme of this book in the series, *Education and Reconciliation: Exploring Conflict and Post-Conflict Situations*, and the fact that it is among the first of the volumes to be published, is particularly apposite in that the number of countries where education is afflicted by violent conflict has increased dramatically. This has led to the 2011 EFA Global Monitoring Report being focused on this issue. At the same time the frequency and scale of major natural disasters seems also to be rising. Both types of disaster and especially the educational response to them, so well documented and supported by the Inter-Agency Network for Education in Emergencies (INEE), should be in the forefront of wider thinking about the type of education we need to be fostering in order to be successful in the vital challenge of sustaining the human and physical environments on planet Earth.

Colin Brock
UNESCO Chair in Education as
a Humanitarian Response, University of Oxford, UK.

Notes on Contributors

Colin Brock is Senior Research Fellow at University of Oxford, UK, and specialises in Comparative and International Education. He holds a UNESCO Chair in the field of Education as a Humanitarian Response.

Sarah Dryden-Peterson is an SSHRC Post-Doctoral Fellow at the Ontario Institute for Studies in Education, University of Toronto, Canada.

Jason Hart is Lecturer in International Development in the Department of Social and Policy Sciences, University of Bath, UK and Research Associate at the Refugee Studies Centre, University of Oxford, UK.

David Johnson is Reader in Comparative and International Education at the University of Oxford, UK and Dean of St. Antony's College, Oxford, UK.

Briony Jones is Lecturer in International Development in the School of Environment and Development, University of Manchester, UK.

James Kearney is Head of Peace and Security at the United Nations Association UK. In addition, he is completing doctoral research on societal reconstruction in Rwanda at the University of Edinburgh, where he is also a member of the Edinburgh United Nations Association's Middle-East Working Group.

Julia Paulson is a Doctoral Researcher at the University of Oxford, UK and a part time Lecturer at Bath Spa University. She is Programme Officer at the NGO TREE AID.

Alan Smith is UNESCO Chair in Education at the University of Ulster, UK.

List of Abbreviations

ACT	All Children Together
BiH	Brčko, Bosnia-Herzegovina
CAC	Children and Armed Conflict
CHE	Council on Higher Education
CMAN	High-Level Multi-Sectoral Commission (Comisión Multisectoral de Alto Nivel)
CNE	National Education Council
DFID	UK Department for International Development
DPA	Dayton Peace Accords
EMU	Education for Mutual Understanding
EU	European Union
FBiH	Federation of Bosnia and Herzegovina
HBI	historically black institution
HWI	historically white institution
IDF	Israeli Defense Forces
LTTE	Liberation Tigers of Tamil Eelam
MED	Northern Ireland Council for Integrated Education
NPHE	National Plan for Higher Education
NURC	Rwandan National Unity and Reconciliation Commission
NWU	North West University
OECD PISA	Organisation for Economic Co-operation and Development, Programme for International Student Assessment
OHR	Office of the High Representative
PEN	National Education Project (Proyecto Educativo Nacional)
RS	Serb Republic
SACHR	Standing Advisory Commission on Human Rights
SDS	Serb Democratic Party
SFOR	Stabilisation Force in BiH
TRC	Truth and Reconciliation Commission
UNDP	United Nations Development Programme

Introduction: Education and Reconciliation

Julia Paulson

Chapter Outline

'That teacher used to belong to Shining Path', a colleague said to me as we left a meeting in the Andean town of Puquio, Peru, in 2004. We were working, together with local education authorities, on a project that used Peru's recent Truth and Reconciliation Commission (TRC) to promote reconciliation and human rights in schools. The teacher we had just met with, elected to the school human rights council, was sceptical about the possibilities for teaching human rights to his students since repercussions from the violence of Peru's recent armed conflict had entered into so many of their homes. 'Alcoholism and domestic violence are such problems in Puquio', the teacher reminded us. My colleagues were sceptical about the teacher's ability to promote human rights and reconciliation concepts for other reasons related to his personal experiences in Peru's armed conflict as a member of the insurgent group that waged war on the country for nearly two decades.

This brief vignette captures some of the complexities involved in working towards reconciliation through education. Many education initiatives, like human rights education, peace education and efforts to bring children from conflicting groups together in classrooms, aim to promote reconciliation in situations affected by conflict. These initiatives aim to foster integration, to teach peaceful values and attitudes via concepts like human rights and citizenship and to retell history in a manner that might help create a 'culture of peace'.

These initiatives do not, however, always contemplate the dynamics and legacies of conflict as exemplified in the meeting described above. The human rights councils, contemplated for national roll out in schools across Peru, assumed teacher facilitators with flawless human rights records and communities able to guarantee the rights of children. Neither of these assumptions were likely to hold in Puquio, a community that had been very much affected by and involved in conflict. In Puquio many teachers and former students were actors in the violence between state forces and Shining Path insurgents. The local police force was distrusted due to conflict-related injustice and harsh discrimination against women and children. Years of violent conflict, insecurity and poverty continued to affect the lives of children born after the 'official' end of the conflict in the mid-1990s through, for instance, elevated rates of domestic violence. Nonetheless, throughout the planning and implementation of our project community members, Ministry of Education officials and donors repeatedly agreed: education is crucial for reconciliation.

A crucial relationship

The individuals I spoke with in Peru years ago are not the only ones to think that education is an important component of, and means towards, reconciliation. Recent years have seen growing international attention turn towards both education in emergencies and transitional justice. That some form of truth-telling or transitional justice enterprise must occur following a period of violent conflict or massive human rights abuses has become an international norm (Kelsall, 2005). And, in 2010 the United Nations adopted a resolution on the right to education in emergency situations (United Nations General Assembly, 2010). Reconciliation is a common goal of these two international priorities and 'linking education and reconciliation' (Parmar et al., 2010, xxiii) is becoming a growing concern for international actors working in conflict and post-conflict situations.

Scholars and international practitioners alike consistently point to the crucial relationship between education and reconciliation (see for example: UNICEF Innocenti Research Center, 2009; Smith and Vaux, 2003; Minow, 1998). Various educational initiatives around the world, from citizenship education to curricular reform to the development of integrated schools, list reconciliation among their aims. Likewise, TRCs and other transitional justice initiatives in post-conflict situations increasingly make recommendations for educational reform and engage children in their work (Parmar et al., 2010). Indeed, that education contributes towards reconciliation is one of the 'foundational assumptions' that informs international work around education in emergencies (Barakat et al., 2008).

However, while reconciliation is 'a common place in political rhetoric', exactly what reconciliation 'means in practice is seldom clear'. (Hamber and Kelly, 2009, 287). There is a lack of agreement on the nature of reconciliation, on its necessary components, on its required participants and on how to gauge whether and when it has been achieved. For some, like Archbishop Desmond Tutu (1999) who led South Africa's TRC, forgiveness is central to reconciliation. Others argue that this roots reconciliation in the Judaeo-Christian tradition, irrelevant to many conflict and post-conflict situations (Wilson, 2001). Researchers suggest other ways to reconcile relationships between formerly conflicting groups; these include increasing opportunities for inter-group contact (education is an important venue here) (Donnelly and Hughes, 2009; Allport, 1954), fostering co-existence (Sampson, 2003), learning to live together (again education is key) (Sinclair, 2004) and encouraging dialogue (Tully, 2004). Critical scholars call for the acknowledgement and redress of pre-conflict inequalities and injustices before they see realistic possibilities for any of the above strategies to lead to the transformation of relationships and societies (Laplante, 2008).

With little clarity about what reconciliation is or how it might be pursued in practice, it is unsurprising that there is even less certainty about exactly how it can be fostered via education. While reconciliation and its methods remain murky and undefined in most situations affected by conflict, so too do the actual ways in which education might contribute. For Gita Steiner-Khamsi (2003), like all 'education-for' agendas, education for reconciliation can be read as a political signal indicating particular intentions and commitments. It is more an indication of an alignment with a specific international agenda than it is a concrete programme of actions towards a well-defined goal. Steiner-Khamsi describes education for reconciliation initiatives as the demonstration by post-conflict states of 'the political will to work towards the social integration of conflicting ethnic groups' (2003, 181). But what of actors beyond the post-conflict state who promote education for reconciliation? What of the parent groups who advocated for integrated schools during the Troubles in Northern Ireland? What of the TRC staff who recommended sweeping educational reform as an essential response to conflict in Peru? Or the international actors who sculpted the integration of segregated schools in Brčko, Bosnia-Herzegovina (BiH) with visions of international best practice in mind? And what of the students who responded in protest to those efforts? While Steiner-Khamsi's insight that reconciliatory educational intentions are likely political is important, the chapters in this volume demonstrate that this insight applies to a host of actors including, but not limited to, the state.

The contributors to this volume explore the complex, important and little understood relationship between education and reconciliation with a critical eye. They do not aim to disprove the assumption that education can (and does) contribute to reconciliation (indeed some chapters offer glimpses of reconciliation through education in action). Rather, contributors seek to understand how and in what ways education might foster, contribute towards or encourage reconciliation. They look at particular instances around the world in which education has been imagined to play a reconciliatory role and they explore what this has meant in the lives of those expected to reconcile, and in the broader conflict-affected context. In this way, contributors also uncover some of the ambiguities, unintended consequences and silences within the 'education leads to reconciliation' equation.

Some shared characteristics

Before introducing the chapters in this volume, it is important to highlight three features they share. The first has already been mentioned: these chapters approach both education and reconciliation as political processes. They are interested in actors, intentions, outcomes and omissions. They look at how the assumption that education can contribute to reconciliation has been embodied in specific contexts and through particular initiatives. They seek to understand the effects of these particular embodiments for children, young people and communities affected by violent conflict.

Second, no common definition of reconciliation guides the volume as a whole. This is consistent with other edited volumes on reconciliation (see for example Quinn, 2009) since, as mentioned above, scholars and practitioners have 'not settled on any one particular definition'. (5). Debate is lively not just on the definition of reconciliation, but also on its nature (is it a process or an end-point?), its constituents (does it involve a collective, conflicting groups or individuals?) and its components (here education is but one suggestion). While this volume does not resolve any of these definitional issues, contributors do investigate the implications of particular conceptions (or lack thereof) of reconciliation in the contexts they explore. The chapters together demonstrate that the murkiness around reconciliation as a concept (and around the potential of education to contribute towards it) matters in terms of enabling and disabling possibilities in situations affected by conflict. Where contributors are able to distil and describe reconciliatory processes at work in the contexts they explore, they make particularly valuable contributions towards better understanding the nature of this crucial process.

Finally, the chapters focus on a range of actors active in planning, promoting, participating in and indeed preventing reconciliation and/or education initiatives. The focus is not always or necessarily on conflicting individuals or groups and the challenges that they face in reconciling their experiences. Some chapters take this focus or include it within a broader exploration of conflict related dynamics; others identify international actors, state and education sector policy and politics, host communities uninvolved in past conflicts and young people (often not yet born when the conflict in question was ongoing) as key actors in the reconciliation / education relationship. In this way, the chapters expand the problem of how education might contribute towards reconciliation to include those who assume and imagine that it can, along with those groups and individuals who are imagined to be in need of reconciling.

The chapters

In Chapter 1, anthropologist Jason Hart draws on his research with young people of the Occupied Palestinian Territories and in Sri Lanka to explore how educational initiatives based more on international norms, so-called best practice, and assumptions about the universality of conflict experience affect the lives of the young people they intend to benefit. Rather than offering meaningful opportunities for reconciliation, Hart finds that such programmes are likely to bewilder, antagonize or disinterest young people. Their own experiences of conflict might not be easily reconciled with universalized perspectives of peace and human rights that are expected to apply without any transformation of inequalities or injustice. Likewise, young people might not identify with notions of the traumatized child exposed to conflict despite their own experiences with and proximity to violent conflict. Hart's eloquent and important assertion of the centrality of young people's own lived experience to any educational programming likely to be successful in responding to and transforming conflict experiences is an important one to bear in mind as subsequent chapters explore particular educational and/or reconciliation initiatives around the world.

In Chapter 2 Sarah Dryden-Peterson finds reconciliation in action at a primary school in the state of Massachusetts, in the United States. Dryden-Peterson's research with African migrants dislocated after various experiences of conflict and persecution offers a fresh insight into reconciliation not between previously conflicting groups but between individuals and families, their personal conflict-affected pasts, and their changed circumstances in a new country. Dryden-Peterson proposes an understanding of reconciliation as a process of building a new life and describes the practices of the primary school where she conducted ethnographic research as key in enabling this process. The school supported opportunities for reconciliation with oneself, the creation of relationships with others and the building of a new life in society. The ways in which the teachers and school environment at Merrimack Elementary School enabled these processes for African parents are fascinatingly detailed by Dryden-Peterson, who also draws attention to the disabling context of structural violence within the United States. This study offers important conceptual insights about the nature of reconciliation and usefully expands the concept beyond its usual confines. It also provides empirical evidence of the reconciliatory effect that education can have when schools employ an ethos of care.

In Chapter 3 Alan Smith explores the relationship between education and reconciliation in his native Northern Ireland. More than a decade has passed since the signing of the Belfast (Good Friday) Agreement in 1998, therefore few children, and indeed few new teachers, have direct memories of the conflict in Northern Ireland. However, only now is education explicitly entering the reconciliation agenda, which has been consistently funded by the European Union (EU) since 1995. Smith shows that while the social dimensions of reconciliation, like education, have been slow to enter the EU agenda and the 'peace economy' it has fostered, they have long been important to Northern Irish communities. Parents and community groups were active during the conflict in encouraging inter-group contact and in lobbying for and creating Northern Ireland's first integrated schools. Smith's work usefully explores education and reconciliation in Northern Ireland with a wide lens, highlighting the priorities, approaches, accomplishments and challenges of various actors whose stakes in the processes of education and reconciliation vary from external observer to intimate participant.

In Chapter 4 Briony Jones revisits several days of protest by secondary students in Brčko, Bosnia-Herzegovina as their schools were ethno-nationally integrated according to an international agenda for reconciliation and peaceful coexistence. These protests were read as the manipulation of young people by ethno-national political forces by the Brčko District officials and by the international community and were therefore largely ignored. Jones demonstrates how they in fact represented politically astute and agential responses of young people whose concerns were not taken into account by the reformers who envisioned their reconciliation. Jones explains how the young protesters were not necessarily protesting against the integration of Bosniak and Bosnian-Serb students and school systems per se. Instead, they were concerned with the pace of integration and the attendant security and economic risks it imposed upon their lives. Given that the integration of schools in Brčko District is much-heralded within BiH and beyond, Jones' revisiting of the circumstances of integration and her disclosure of the experience from the perspective of those young people who were critical to it, yet whose view points were left out of official accounts, offers a nuanced and necessary portrait of the complexities of reconciliation in practice.

Like Alan Smith did in Chapter 3, David Johnson in Chapter 5 reflects on education and reconciliation since a momentous event in his native country, in this case the TRC in South Africa. Here Johnson looks in particular at the transformation (or lack thereof) of higher education in South Africa since the end of apartheid. While policies have changed drastically and universities are no longer formally segregated, Johnson's case study of one university's attempts to deepen its possibilities for integration by offering simultaneous interpretation services to students again pulls up nuances and complexities of reconciliation in practice. Conducted at a time when special task teams were ordered by the Ministry of Education to investigate a series of racially motivated incidents on university campuses, including the one that Johnson's research focuses on, the case study shows both the lengths to which South Africa has gone to try to address the legacies of apartheid, as well as the still firm presence of those legacies in higher education. Johnson's study soundly demonstrates that the removal of official barriers and the transformation of policy alone cannot succeed in creating unity, much less reconciliation.

In Chapter 6 Julia Paulson traces the impact of the recommendations for educational reform made by Peru's TRC. The TRC called for a large-scale reform of education, which it deemed essential to promoting reconciliation in the country and to ensuring that violent conflict did not recur. While research respondents were unanimous in their agreement that this reform had not happened, Paulson shows how the TRC nonetheless had particular impacts in Peru's educational sector. These impacts were politically motivated and lent momentum to certain policy initiatives and contributed to the inertia of others. Paulson demonstrates that these moments of momentum and inertia employed various discourses and at times relied on assumptions and envisioned outcomes that were contrary to the vision of reconciliation put forward by the TRC, a vision that prioritized the transformation of inequalities and the acknowledgement of conflict-related injustices. Again, the difficulties of educational transformation are demonstrated in the chapter, as are the limited possibilities for reconciliation through education without such transformation.

Finally, in Chapter 7 James Kearney takes readers inside Rwanda's flagship *Ingando* Peace and Solidarity Camp. Here young Rwandans bound for university spend weeks relearning Rwandan history and undergoing military training as part of a vast government scheme to foster unity post-genocide. Kearney describes a revised version of history instilled at *Ingando* that erases ethnic identity in the country in favour of a unified Rwanda. Kearney's ethnographic research within *Ingando* explores the ways in which young people respond to the imposition of a new history and hours of military training in the name of peace and unity. Kearney offers a fascinating account of reconciliation as crafted and imposed by Rwanda's post-genocide government and as interpreted by a generation whose families and communities experienced a past in which ethnicity existed ultimately. *Ingando* is unique in its explicit and clear mobilization of education towards an equally explicit vision of reconciliation through national unity – as Kearney shows, the effects of this unique strategy are less clear and straightforward.

The conclusion to the volume considers the chapters together as a whole. From the chapters emerge clear insights around the following themes: context, children and young people, historical narratives, contact and integration, changing attitudes and values and universal frameworks. These insights together provide material, based on the empirical evidence offered within the chapters, for better understanding the nature of reconciliation itself and education's role within it. As described in the conclusion, these chapters suggest that education for reconciliation ought to centre upon an ethos that enables those participating in it to define and enact their own reconciliatory processes. And, importantly, this enabling ethos must be one part of a broader project to challenge and transform the injustices and inequalities that were features of violent conflict.

Reference list

Allport, G. W. (1954), *The Nature of Prejudice*. Reading: Addison-Wesley.

Barakat, B., Z. Karpinska, and J. Paulson (2008), *Desk Study: Education and Fragility*. INEE, http://ineesite.org/uploads/documents/store/doc_1_FINAL-Desk_Study_Education_and_Fragility_CERG2008.pdf (accessed 17 August 2008).

Donnelly, C., and J. Hughes (2009), 'Contact and culture: Mechanisms of reconciliation in schools in Northern Ireland and Israel', in J. R. Quinn (ed), *Reconciliation(s): Transitional Justice in Postconflict Societies*, Montreal and Kingston, Canada: McGill-Queen's University Press, 147–74.

Hamber, B., and G. Kelly (2009), 'Beyond Coexistence: Towards a working definition or reconciliation', in J. R. Quinn (ed), *Reconciliation(s): Transitional Justice in Postconflict Societies*, Montreal and Kingston, Canada: McGill-Queen's University Press, 286–310.

Kelsall, T. (2005), 'Truth, lies, and ritual: Preliminary reflections on the Truth and Reconciliation Commission in Sierra Leone', *Human Rights Quarterly*, 27, 2, 361–91.

Laplante, L. J. (2008), 'Transitional justice and peace building: Diagnosing and addressing the socioeconomic roots of violence through a human rights framework', *International Journal of Transitional Justice*, 2, 3, 331–55.

Minow, M. (1998), *Between Vengeance and Forgiveness: Facing History after Genocide and Mass Violence*. Boston: Beacon Press.

Parmar, S., M. J. Roseman, S. Siegrist, and T. Sowa (eds) (2010), *Children and Transitional Justice: Truth-Telling, Accountability, and Reconciliation*. Cambridge, MA: Harvard University Press.

Quinn, J. R. (ed) (2009), *Reconciliation(s): Transitional Justice in Postconflict Societies*. Kingston and Montreal, Canada: McGill-Queen's University Press.

Sampson, S. (2003), 'From reconciliation to coexistence', *Public Culture*, 15, 1, 181–86.

Sinclair, M. (2004), *Learning to Live Together: Building Skills, Values and Attitudes for the 21ˢᵗ Century*. Paris: UNESCO.

Smith, A., and T. Vaux (2003), *Education, Conflict and International Development*. London: DfID.

Steiner-Khamsi, G. (2003), 'Transferring education, displacing reforms', in J. Schriewer (ed), *Discourse Formation in Comparative Education* (2nd edn). Frankfurt: Peter Lang.

Tully, J. (2004), 'Reconciliation and dialogue: The emergence of a new field', *Critical Review of International Social and Political Philosophy*, 7, 3, 84–106.

Tutu, D. (1999), *No Future without Forgiveness*. New York: Doubleday.

UNICEF Innocenti Research Centre (2009), 'Draft Children and Transitional Justice Key Principles Document: For the Involvement of Children and the Consideration of Children's Rights in Truth, Justice and Reconciliation Processes', (accessed 10 June 2009).

United Nations General Assembly (2010), 'The right to education in emergency situations, A/64/L.58', www.ineesite.org/uploads/documents/store/UN_Resolution_Education_in_Emergencies.pdf (accessed 22 July 2010).

Wilson, R. A. (2001), *The Politics of Truth and Reconciliation in South Africa: Legitimizing the Post-Apartheid State*. New York: Cambridge University Press.

1

Young People and Conflict: The Implications for Education

Jason Hart

There is a discernible trajectory common to programming offered by international organizations assisting young people living in the midst of armed conflict. Whenever a new need is identified the tendency has been to import, fairly wholesale, the approach to address that need as used in developed and non-conflict affected countries. Then, as problems arise in implementation, modifications are made in order to adapt the approach to local circumstances. Nevertheless, some continue to pursue the original approach, often on the grounds of 'scientific objectivity', rejecting the argument that local culture and conditions should determine the nature and content of interventions. This has been seen perhaps most obviously in relation to the rapid development of mental health programming for children and others living in war zones. Early approaches principally employed diagnostic tools created in US and European universities and centred particularly around the treatment of trauma understood in terms of post-traumatic stress disorder. However, recent years have witnessed increasing interest in more culturally sensitive and locally relevant approaches spurred by the experience of practitioners whose early efforts failed to achieve their stated aims (e.g. Miller et. al., 2006; Wessells and Monteiro, 2004). This process of trial and error may well come with a cost in terms of mistrust from the people who, often with some justification, resent being treated as guinea pigs for the latest programming fad of outsiders.

This chapter is written in the hope that the emerging interest among international organizations to pursue reconciliation through educational programming should, as far as possible, avoid this troubling trajectory. The signs so far give cause for some concern: scholars and practitioners seem active in the production of various tools and models which seem to be informed by norms, values and technical considerations rather more than by detailed understanding of the lives of the intended beneficiaries. Like much of the early mental health programming, peace education materials often appear to be precooked. In the course of my own work, particularly in the Occupied Palestinian Territories and, to a lesser extent in Sri Lanka, the inappropriateness of some of the advocated approaches has produced bewilderment and even antagonism among young participants.

The starting point for my own research as an anthropologist has always been with children rather than the institutions of education. Put broadly, my concern has been to understand children's lives in the midst of political violence and marginalization, and the contribution that schooling makes to their processes of learning and to their material conditions. As a consequence of engaging with young people themselves, I approach assumptions that formal education necessarily plays a particular or significant role in children's lives with a questioning frame of mind. In settings of political violence it has struck me that the role of Western-style schools as legitimate sources of learning may be especially open to question. Therefore, while I may be poorly placed to discuss issues around the technical and institutional aspects of education-for-reconciliation initiatives, I believe that I can contribute to reflection about the conceptual and methodological framework within which such interventions are implemented.

It strikes me that a considerable disparity exists between the claims made for school-based education as a means of building peace and the evidence regarding the outcomes of specific activities. Not only have the rigorous evaluations of 'peace education' projects been few in number, but the findings generally do not provide clear endorsement for the assertions of the numerous advocates of such projects within academia and in agencies such as UNESCO (e.g. Colenso, 2005;

Johnson and Johnson, 2005; Davies, 2004). Findings from the two conflict-affected settings where research into the outcomes of peace education has been pursued most thoroughly – Israel–Palestine (Salomon, 2006; Kuppermintz and Salomon, 2005) and Northern Ireland (Nolan, 2007; Niens and Cairns, 2005) – reveal a range of immense challenges involved in achieving measurable, let alone sustained, change.

The limited impact of educational initiatives that the evaluative literature identifies relates, I would contend, to the insufficiency of efforts to address the lived experience of young people within specific social, political and economic conditions. In this chapter, therefore, I seek to offer a contribution to debates concerning education and reconciliation by exploring dimensions of experience that appear to have particular bearing upon the design and implementation of initiatives. The text is organized around consideration of two sets of relationships: first, that of young people to political violence and, more briefly, that of young people to formal schooling. My aim is to open up questions regarding the frame of reference within which reconciliation through educational activity is pursued. In the process of pursuing this aim, I hope to illustrate some of the key structural factors beyond the immediate realm of the classroom that impact the possibilities for reconciliation. In the following discussion I shall use the terms 'children' and 'young people' interchangeably. The section of the population that I have in mind, however, is roughly those in the age range 10 to 18.

Young people and political violence

The dominant discourse on 'children and armed conflict'

In recent years we have witnessed the emergence of a popular discourse around young people living in situations of armed conflict and forced migration, sometimes referred to in practitioner circles as the field of Children and Armed Conflict (CAC). Since this discourse has significantly informed educational intervention, including for purposes of peace building and reconciliation, it is worth taking a little time here to explain its conceptual and methodological underpinnings. Scholars and practitioners within three distinct fields have contributed most particularly to the shaping of this discourse: mental health, human rights (e.g. Amnesty International, 1999; Kuper, 1997; Cohn and Goodwin-Gill, 1994), and, more latterly, international security (e.g. Brocklehurst, 2007; Reich and Achvarina, 2006; Singer, 2005). While each of these considers issues and employs methods specific to their field, they all share a common disposition towards universalism. This sets them apart from colleagues in anthropology, sociology and cognate disciplines whose focus has tended more towards the local and whose research, employing largely qualitative methods, has resulted in ethnographic studies of children in particular settings of political violence.

The reverence commonly accorded to statistical data coupled with the authority vested in those who speak with apparent global expertise have secured for scholars in the fields of mental health, human rights and international security an influential role in the development of popular understanding of the situation, needs and struggles of young people living amidst armed conflict. Universal categories of experience – such as 'child recruitment', 'trauma/ resilience', 'separated children' – have emerged as key elements of the CAC discourse. These categories allow for policy making at a cross-national level, since the same apparent problem is to be addressed in diverse contexts. However, the important specificities of context – cultural, political, social and economic – are often obscured or rendered as a mere add-on; the relevance of the categories themselves is rarely questioned. We may wonder about the benefits of such a macro-level approach for the main stakeholders, such as young people, policy makers and the various experts within academia and practitioner circles. My own suspicion is that the sidelining of context for the sake of macro-level policy making often fails to serve the interests of children.

The scholarly and practitioner literature on education and peace building/ reconciliation in settings of armed conflict reveals a similarly global outlook. The formulation by educationalists of various methods and approaches of assumed universal applicability (give or take a little adaptation) is predicated on the assumption of a common experience among young people in the world's conflict zones and displacement camps. The following quote from a World Bank publication is illustrative of this assumption and of the thinking around the virtues of a school-based response:

> War transforms the roles of children and youth in ways that become extremely difficult to reverse. In a context where families and communities are often divided or dispersed by the upheaval of conflict, schools are seen as key institutions that will play the major role in rebuilding core values, in instilling new democratic principles, and in helping children recover lost childhood. (Buckland, 2005, 16)

In assuming that the experience of life across diverse settings of political violence and displacement is more or less the same, the need to engage with young people in order to learn about their own perspectives is generally rendered as less than critical. This view is reinforced particularly by much of the literature written by mental health scholars who, as already noted, have played a highly influential role in shaping popular understanding of children's lives amidst political violence. The approach of most psychologists and psychiatrists working in the world's war zones has been to treat children in individualistic terms, focusing on the causation, symptoms and solution to their trauma. More recently this has broadened in terms of, first, greater consideration of a child's social and cultural context and, second, the promotion of resilience as well as, or instead of, the treatment of trauma. Nevertheless, the view of young people in situations of political violence that emerges from the majority of the mental health literature remains very limited, with a marked tendency to consider young people as either trauma victims or resilient survivors. Little is generally learned from this literature about the daily lives of the young: their motivations, social and economic roles and responsibilities and political engagements rarely appear.

The conceptual framework within which educationalists develop ideas about peace building/reconciliation appears to draw heavily on the view of young people in settings of political violence constructed through the work of mental health scholars. Notions of political violence solely as a source of damage to the young leading to 'lost childhood' – as stated by Buckland in the quote above – owe their provenance principally to the work of psychologists and psychiatrists. In addition, human rights advocates have played an important role here given their focus on extreme violations. The worst cases of harm and exploitation – particularly in relation to the military recruitment of children – are understandably central to rights advocacy. However, this can serve to promote a generalised and superficial understanding of children's daily life experience and their often complex engagement with political violence: intellectually and emotionally, as well as in terms of physical action. Recognition that empirical investigation is needed for the development of educational interventions that are meaningful and relevant would seem to require an understanding that children living amidst armed conflict are not only, or even necessarily, damaged victims.

The experience of political violence

The ways in which political violence affects and shapes the lives of young people are too numerous and wide-ranging to be discussed comprehensively here. Instead, I shall focus on specific dimensions of experience that may have relevance for efforts to promote reconciliation through education. Since such efforts are oriented towards the promotion of attitudinal change among young people,

I consider below some of the ways in which actual experience creates challenges to realization of this aim.

Understanding of the ways that children's socialization occurs amidst political violence remains at a rudimentary stage (Boyden, 2003). Discussion of children who have lived through periods of intense armed conflict has often invoked notions of a 'lost generation' who lack the correct outlook and sentiments to contribute as members of a stable, democratic society (e.g. Aden, 2009)[1]. This view takes as a given that the young are socialized through their everyday experience into the use of violence as a legitimate means to solve problems and achieve goals.

The literature on education for peace building and reconciliation is driven by the converse conviction: that the experience of political violence is of relatively little consequence for the ideas and disposition of young people. 'Students should understand the horrendous consequences of armed conflict, so that they are not attracted to a false ideal of the nobility of modern war', writes Margaret Sinclair in *Learning to Live Together*, arguing for the importance of efforts to teach conflict-affected children about International Humanitarian Law (2004, 35).[2] Such a view sidesteps questions regarding the lessons about war that children gain from their own experience. Whatever enmity results from such experience may, it seems, be corrected through a well-designed educational intervention. While this view is obviously more optimistic than the 'lost generation' perspective, it relies on an equally unsatisfactory consideration of young people's socialisation within settings of political violence.

The conventional understanding of socialization as a one-way process in which the child receives the ideas and values of parents, teachers and other instructors has long been discredited. Increasingly it is understood that the young are active in the construction of meaning. This point has been succinctly expressed by the anthropologist Christina Toren in the following manner:

> In the course of growing up you could not help but enter into manifold relations with others and, in so doing, you made meaning (or what might also be called knowledge) out of your experience in the world. Other people had structured the conditions of your experience, indeed other people explicitly instructed you about certain aspects of the world, but it was you who made meaning out of the meanings they presented you with. (1999, 8)

If meaning/knowledge is the product of a child's ongoing negotiation with the material and ideational environment – in the form of 'manifold relations' – then we cannot predict the consequences of engagement with any discrete body of information. In a setting of political violence and marginalization the child's everyday environment is likely to be fraught with conflicting messages and with considerable divergence between norms in the form of, inter alia, laws, statements of values, discourses of rights and actual experience. Unlike their peers in countries of relative peace and stability, children living in many of the world's war zones routinely witness the failure of high-minded principles to prevent the regular violation of civilians by those in possession of military–political power. The meaning/knowledge that they construct from encounters with the abusive exercise of power will be mediated by innumerable factors and forces, of which classroom-based instruction may not be among the most important.

The violence of military occupation

Generations of Palestinian children have experienced physical, verbal and structural violence resulting from the abuse of power by the State of Israel. This has been manifest most directly by the Israeli army, police and the extremist settlers who have attacked civilians, including children, with routine impunity and denied them access to educational, health and recreational facilities. In the area of al-Tuwani in the Southern West Bank for example, children are routinely attacked by settlers on their way to and from school, requiring (often inadequate) intervention by the Israeli security forces (Beinin, 2007). Since 2000, the State of Israel has arrested and detained around 6,500 Palestinian children aged 12 to 18 in its jails, many of them without charge (DCI/PS, 2009). The meaning/knowledge that children themselves construct from such experience, combined with the information they receive from family and community, media, school and peer groups, is inevitably diverse. The historical record shows us that, at times, such meaning/knowledge has led some to involve themselves in acts of physical violence, notably during the first Intifada when the image of the stone-throwing child became emblematic of Palestinian rebellion against Israeli occupation.

Even for those who do not engage in physical violence, the enmity towards Israel is commonly strong. In the summer of 2005 I had the opportunity to talk with a large number of young Palestinians in various locations in the West Bank and East Jerusalem about the challenges they experienced in their everyday lives resulting from the Occupation and the meaning that they constructed out of this experience. One of the most articulate respondents was 14-year-old Rula – a keen student from a middle class family.[3] Although her family resided near Ramallah, Rula attended school in Jerusalem roughly 10 miles away and, in the days before the construction of roadblocks and checkpoints, no more than 20 minutes by shared taxi. At one point in our conversation I asked Rula about the commute to school:

> Jason: Tell me about your journey to school every day.
>
> Rula [laughing]: Don't speak about it! I get up at 5.30. By 6.10 I'm at Qalandia [a major checkpoint]. Later than that and it can be full and you wait half an hour. They open the cases and check. Sometimes they tell us to go back. Bother us a lot. Sometimes they take all our IDs and make us wait a long time. You're there and the wall is around you and the soldiers are shouting at you. You leave a clean house and get to the checkpoint and it's another world. It's hard. You just want to get to school, the simplest thing. Especially in winter, it's harder. They make us wait longer. Sometimes there have been problems. The soldiers close the checkpoint. During the time of examinations. We use Atarot sometimes and sometimes Hizma [checkpoints that can be driven through]. If someone on the bus has daffeh [West Bank] ID they send the bus back. Sometimes in Jerusalem there are soldiers who stop us in the street.
>
> Jason: What did you learn from this experience?
>
> Rula: Sabr! [patience, forbearance]. They talk about child rights. They don't see our situation. Our parents send us out early in the morning and don't know if we will return. There are girls who gave up school because of the trouble on the way and the cost of the journey. Education is the biggest weapon for us. They want to stop us. I don't speak only of myself, I speak of hundreds of children. Israel is at first and last aggressive. It took the land. It will also do everything possible to steal the education from the children, to make them ignorant. Education is the simplest right that should be given to children. I also learned isra' (determination). I must get there, persevere. I must have my land, my country.

In recent years various Israeli scholars, advocacy groups and politicians have argued that the Palestinian authorities and media have actively sought to indoctrinate and incite children to hate Israel and its Jewish citizenry.[4] Little or nothing is said by such commentators about the occupation-related experience of Palestinian children, such as Rula, and about the ways that this experience may inform their attitudes. In spite of her ironic humour, as she spoke, Rula's anger and bitterness were palpable: it was clear that her strongly antagonistic feelings were born of everyday encounters with the occupation. Israeli commentators persist in suggesting that the remedy for such feelings lies in classroom-based programmes:

> The only tenable conclusion is that, to reach a viable peace treaty, rework-
> ing of the textbook teachings should be mandated as a condition of any
> upcoming peace process. The reversal of the nationalist message by pro-
> longed in-depth re-education to peace and reconciliation with the state
> of Israel would be easier than reversal of the religious exhortations to
> martyrdom to destroy the state of Israel, but nevertheless these too would
> have to be intensively pursued. (Burdman, 2003, 110–11)

While Rula showed no interest in or inclination towards acts of physical violence against Israelis – military or civilian – it is doubtful that her feelings would
be assuaged by fine-sounding messages delivered in the classroom, no matter
how expertly designed and delivered, while her daily experiences of occupation
remain unchanged. Yet, I would contend that the arguments put forward by
Burdman and others within Israel retain credibility precisely because of the
widespread belief that antagonistic attitudes can be shaped through educational
messages alone and, conversely, that a child's engagement in reconciliation can
be promoted through alternative messages. The underlying assumption is that
the disposition of young people is informed to a decisive extent by curriculum
and through classroom praxis (e.g. Davies, 2004, 2008; Sinclair, 2004). In this
way, highly partisan arguments from authors such as Burdman about the indoctrination of children by the 'enemy' draw upon and are legitimated by the discourse of peace education itself, developed largely on the basis of normative
assumptions, rather than empirical evidence.

Psycho-emotional consequences of conflict

Inevitably for children, as for adults, everyday exposure to the direct and indirect
effects of armed conflict may produce a range of psycho-emotional responses.
However, for the most part, the focus of mental health scholars, human rights
advocates and humanitarian practitioners has been upon the psycho-emotional
states associated with trauma. Thus depression, anxiety, hyperactivity, night-
mares and shortening of attention span are among the conditions identified for
treatment. Emotions associated with political engagement – such as anger and
frustration – figure in occasionally and are similarly framed in terms of trauma.
The required response should be some form of psychosocial intervention.

> A special emphasis should be placed on activities that allow children to
> express themselves, resolve psychological/social/behavioral problems and
> encourage their desire to become positive and supportive members of
> their community. (Arafat with Boothby, 2003, 46)

An approach such as this seeks to manage children's reactions to the daily experience of grossly asymmetrical relations of power – as exercised in this case by Israeli authorities over Palestinians – and the politicisation that is likely to result. The classroom is rendered as a place of therapy. Such an approach is part of a process by which emotions of anger and frustration are conceptualized as pathological, and their potentially disruptive effects as in need of neutralizing. Vanessa Pupavac (2004) has described this process as 'therapeutic governance' derived from social psychology and increasingly pursued as part of a security paradigm that seeks to transform political subjects into humanitarian objects in need of healing.[5]

Yet it is highly questionable that a 'classroom as therapy' approach would prove effective. First, the negative experiences that give rise to emotions such as anger and frustration are ongoing. For Palestinian children, negotiation of checkpoints and the abuse of Israeli soldiers remains part of the journey to and from the classroom: the constraints and risks for many growing greater year after year as policies of closure and control become increasingly punitive. When 'crisis' becomes the context for daily life rather than a specific, time-bound event, can therapy and educational efforts intended to foster a reconciliatory disposition hope to neutralize the inevitable resentments engendered? (Vigh, 2008, 4).

Second, we cannot assume that therapeutic and peace education approaches are equal to the task of diffusing the powerful emotions experienced by the young. Recent research by Rita Giacaman and colleagues at Birzeit University (2007) explored the effects of living under occupation in terms of Palestinian children's feelings of humiliation. The strength and pervasiveness of such feelings noted by these researchers were considerable, impacting negatively on the physical and emotional health of children to a significant extent. The remedy for humiliation must surely lie in the restoration of dignity, which in turn requires the recognition of one's humanity and removal of non-legitimate control over one's life (Margalit, 1996, 115–19). Yet classroom-based therapy and peace education initiatives, even if they focus upon the promotion of self-respect, seem unlikely to overcome the 'chronic and ongoing' experience of humiliation due to the actions of the occupation forces (Giacaman et al., 2007, 570).

Third, there is a potentially disabling inconsistency between the language and orientation of peace education on one hand, and the moral/ideological framework within which children's resilience is constructed by and for them, on the other. Much of the discourse around educational initiatives intended to promote reconciliation employs a universalistic human rights focus seeking, consciously or otherwise, to replace more localized moral frameworks, including those rooted in faith. Lynn Davies, for example, in a recent book *Educating Against Extremism* (2008) has argued for the replacement of faith – with its potential for divisiveness, lack of choice and inequity – with the 'ecumenical and universal' values of human rights as the moral base for schooling (159–63).

I shall leave aside the complex issues around the localization of the rights discourse that, in practice, may blur the assumed distinction between (secular) human rights and particularistic faith.[6] Of greater matter for this discussion is the observable fact that in many situations of extreme adversity, including the Occupied Palestinian Territories, children make sense of their suffering and find solace and strength through prayer and religious ritual. Numerous researchers who have explored the factors contributing to the resilience of children growing up in war zones and other settings of extreme adversity attest to the importance of faith (eg. McAdam-Crisp, 2006; Boyden and Mann, 2005; Garbarino, 1999). This should encourage us to question the potential relevance and consequences of an approach to reconciliation that draws upon a value system that runs counter to that which is familiar and from which children draw comfort. When therapeutic approaches encourage children's spiritual engagement as a way to find meaning amidst widespread suffering, we may wonder if an approach to reconciliation through education that promotes a determinedly secular, human rights framework carries the risk of either undermining the former or rendering itself, at best, irrelevant and, at worst, alienating.

The political economy of conflict

Within the literature on child military recruitment there has been a strong tendency to consider the involvement of young people in armed conflict primarily in terms of attitudes and dispositions. For the most part, the focus has been on the mindset of those groups that routinely recruit children, with some consideration also given to the thinking of children themselves: largely concerning their lack of intellectual or moral competence to make an informed decision about warfare. Consideration of the material factors that promote children's involvement in military action – either as children or in their future lives as young adults – has emerged. Yet the focus has been limited principally to immediate circumstances. That is to say, some authors have considered the lure of military groups that offer food and other commodities to children whose basic needs may otherwise not be met while the subject of children's longer-term socioeconomic trajectories has been considered far less.

The effect of growing up in a militarized society and economy is an issue of relative neglect within the efforts to promote reconciliation through education. It is evidently the case that in many countries around the world engagement in military activity is not only valorized but, more importantly, represents a means to socioeconomic advancement. However skillfully the messages conveyed through peace education initiatives, if the only or principal path for a child to secure his or her economic future lies in military activity, then we should anticipate that the impact of such initiatives may be greatly mitigated.

Fieldwork undertaken by Jesse Newman in Sri Lanka in 2005 revealed a pronounced contradiction between school-based initiatives and the economic prospects of the students. The settings for this research were three Sinhala villages in an impoverished rural area of the Vavuniya District. This is an area of the country where fighting between the Sri Lankan Army and the Liberation Tigers of Tamil Eelam (LTTE) had occurred sporadically over many years. Despite 4 years of relative calm following the 2001 ceasefire between the warring parties, the local economy had not managed to develop. Employment opportunities were extremely scarce and lack of land combined with the poor state of local infrastructure had compounded the poverty of many families. In such a setting, enrolment with the army or home-guard represented the most obvious means to a reasonable livelihood. Indeed, while teachers earned around 8,000 Sri Lankan Rupees per month, home-guards earned 12,000 and members of the army 15,000. The presence of many well-dressed, relatively wealthy soldiers stationed nearby reinforced the message given to village boys that the military would be a respected and attractive career choice; moreover, employment in the army required schooling only until grade 8. It is little wonder then, that so many chose to enlist, ultimately fighting an enemy about whom they may have otherwise cared relatively little. In this way, such boys rejected the messages conveyed about peace through the classroom and, in many cases, rejected even the school in which this education was pursued in favour of a combat role.

In countries that retain a system of compulsory military service, the effect of economic factors may be less pronounced yet still remain deeply significant for particular sections of the population. Israel is one such country. Here, acceptance as a full member of society may now depend less on military service than it did in the early decades of the state. However, the relationship between the nature of one's service and subsequent socioeconomic status remains strong. Engagement in one of the elite commando units is an important means to acquire social capital and, in a highly militarized society, can open doors for employment and social opportunities following completion of service. Small wonder, then, that those young people from outside the Ashkenazi elites strive to gain entry to such units, seeing this as a means to achieve 'mobility', 'civil rights' and 'social remuneration' (Levy et al., 2007, 143–45). This strategy might also be applicable to women, at least in the reported view of the current Israeli Minister for Education, Gideon Sa'ar.[7]

The militaristic orientation of the Israeli education system is profound, reflecting the fact, as noted by Barak and Sheffer (2007), that 'military values penetrate and influence most civilian spheres' (11). Indeed, as Haggith Gor (2003) has argued, the militarization of children begins in kindergarten. A powerful illustration of the orientation of the Israeli education system appeared in a recent article in the national newspaper *Ha'aretz* which reported on a secondary school where the parents' committee had allegedly blocked the efforts of one of the teachers to organize a presentation by a joint Israeli–Palestinian dialogue group of bereaved families (Kashti, 2010). According to a local municipal official interviewed, this particular school enjoys 'high ranking, seventh in the country, in the numbers for completing an officers course, a pilots course, and in the numbers for serving in quality positions in the IDF [Israel Defense Forces]' (ibid.). This statement lent credence to claims by teachers and students that the principal and parents' committee did not wish to jeopardize the school's success in recruiting for elite units – a key goal of the current Government of Israel[8] – by giving this dialogue group a platform.

In such a setting of militarized education, the challenge for peace education might entail more than simply a change to the culture of the classroom in order to reflect the values of reconciliation and coexistence. Rather the sustained impact of such an initiative would seem to require efforts to address the ways in which the education system and the wider society and economy encourage and reward young people who take on a warrior role. I would argue that this suggests the vital importance of locating reconciliation efforts within both a broad political–economic and a cultural context, eschewing the assumption that it is principally attitudes towards the 'other' that need to change for peaceful coexistence to become possible.

Schooling in conflict-affected settings

A basic prerequisite for peace education and reconciliation efforts is the attendance and active engagement of children. However, for many different reasons children living amidst conflict are often absent from the settings where such initiatives take place. Even when physically present their interaction with the initiative may be constrained by well-established patterns of pedagogic practice that discourage engagement with new ideas or by content that fails to speak to their own experience and understanding.

An institution-centred approach to peace education that focuses on issues such as methodology, content and teacher training can leave unknown the reasons for children's non-attendance and non-engagement. Yet, this approach has hitherto dominated the development of peace education, reifying assumptions about the central stakeholders – young people themselves – as an homogenous group, engaging in mechanistic fashion with the material and activities put before them. A more children-focused, ethnographic approach seems vitally needed to complement and inform the institutional bias that currently prevails.

Non-attendance

There are many reasons why children living in settings of armed conflict or immediate post-conflict may attend school irregularly or not at all. The conventional factors leading to non-enrolment and attrition such as household poverty, opposition to girls' schooling, poor infrastructure, lack of birth certificate, violence at school, and so on, are not only likely to apply in many war zones but are often exacerbated by conflict itself. For example, even in places where children might ordinarily be expected to contribute to the household budget or to undertake various domestic responsibilities, armed conflict often greatly increases their duties. Death, injury or dispersal of primary caregivers may compel the young to take on social and economic roles that confound common understandings of childhood and children's capacities. In many war zones, child-headed households are a common phenomenon, while an increase in the number of children living on the street has been reported in various locations (e.g. Veale and Doná, 2002; Duke, 1995). For such children, attendance at school may be a distant dream.

In addition to the obstacles to attendance experienced directly by children, the school itself can become a place of risk. In some conflict zones, the school building is a particular target for military forces. In many impoverished rural communities this may be one of the few relatively solid buildings and, as such, is deliberately targeted with a view to demoralizing or dispersing a population. It may also represent the authority of the state, and thus be a particular target of insurgents, as has been witnessed in Nepal (Shields and Rappleye, 2008, 95).

In other locations the school is a key recruiting ground where mobilization campaigns and even forcible conscription occur. The LTTE in Sri Lanka, for example, were notorious in this regard to the extent that, in one case at least, parents themselves burned down the school building to prevent efforts to enlist their children (Bush, 2000). Or, it may be that children are especially vulnerable to forcible recruitment on the journey to and from school, thus leading their parents to keep them at home.

Political–military forces sometimes act systematically to deny children access to school. This is a claim made commonly against the Bhutanese government, for example, in respect of children from the Nepali-speaking minority in the south of the country (Human Rights Watch, 2007). It has been widely claimed that in blocking access to education the aim was to encourage the emigration of large numbers of a population who place great value on formal education. In the occupied Palestinian territories, as we have seen in the account of Rula, the Israeli authorities systematically hinder children's movement to and from school through the use of checkpoints, curfews and closures (DCI-Pal, 2000). Many Palestinians would concur with Rula that this is part of a deliberate policy to prevent their social and educational advancement as a people. Meanwhile, the closure of schools as part of general strikes by the Palestinians to protest the occupation adds a further obstacle (World Bank, 2002).

Non-engagement

The notion that school is a primary site in which values are produced and reproduced seems central to the effort to promote reconciliation through educational initiatives. Yet, here again I would question whether normative assumptions may not, in some cases, be at odds with the evidence. For the poor and marginalized it would seem especially likely that schooling is primarily a means to socio-economic advancement rather than an inherent good in itself. The aim is to acquire the qualifications that, it is hoped, will enable such advancement (Jeffrey, Jeffery and Jeffery, 2005). The straightforward memorization of tracts of high status information relating to core school subjects is often the key to academic success; many education systems around the world prioritize standard exam content and place scant emphasis on the development of creative and analytical thought. The standing of the school itself and of individual teachers may depend on the success of students in examinations above all else. This has at least two potentially negative implications for peace education initiatives. First, as a non-examined element of the curriculum there may be no incentive to engage with the material presented since success here is not measurable in instrumental terms. Secondly, where rote learning is the norm, the expectation that children will engage imaginatively and critically with reconciliation-related material may be unrealistic.

When schooling is seen primarily as a means to socioeconomic advancement, other institutions are given full scope to vie with each other in shaping children's evolving attitudes. Religious organizations, the household, neighbourhood, youth club, peer group, media and the internet, among others, are likely to be important venues within which ideas about self and others are formed. Settings affected by armed conflict are often replete with explicit and contentious messages that are directly intended to influence children's attitudes. In my own doctoral fieldwork in a Palestinian refugee camp in Jordan, children fashioned a conceptual relationship to 'Palestine' by drawing on sources that included, at one extreme, the Islamists running the youth club and centres of Quranic learning who presented 'Palestine' as a Muslim land currently violated by Jews from whose control it should be rescued. At the other extreme, some children were exposed to Israeli satellite TV channels that presented the same physical space as a modern land of opportunity for fun, sophisticated consumerism and sexual adventure. Unsurprisingly, therefore, the adolescent boys who engaged in my research expressed views about Israel that ranged from principled antagonism and the readiness for armed invasion to the strong desire to visit and experience its pleasures as a tourist or guest worker (Hart, 2004).

Conclusion

The quest to promote reconciliation in settings where lives have been severely affected by years or even generations of armed conflict is unquestionably an admirable one. Educational initiatives are an obvious element of such an endeavour. In this chapter, I have drawn upon my own work and that of colleagues to suggest some of the reasons that the positive impact of such initiatives may be limited. The common denominator is a lack of fit with the lived experience and conditions of the children who are intended to enter into processes of reconciliation in their classrooms.

The means to render efforts more relevant and thus more effective begins, I would suggest, with the willingness to forego pre-cooked curricula, models and techniques in favour of a more dialogic and open-ended approach. Within the classroom this may entail working from the knowledge and perspectives that children have acquired in the specific setting of armed conflict where they have grown up, rather than laying out prescribed knowledge. The most important quality of teachers may be the humility to listen without passing judgement and the patience to work at a pace that suits each group rather than that dictated by a handbook.

I have also alluded to some of the factors that underpin conflict and ensure the involvement of successive cohorts of the young. The systematic abuse of power and the workings of a war economy are two obvious elements of an environment that is liable to encourage children to engage in political violence to an extent that educational initiatives alone are insufficient to counter. Moreover, as highlighted by other contributors to this book, the failure of formal education to deliver on the oft-stated promise of enabling social mobility, even to the extent of exacerbating inequality, may mean that in some settings school contributes more to the perpetuation of conflict than it does to its amelioration.

Guiding questions

Why are similar programmes consistently pursued in very different situations affected by conflict around the world?

How might children's lived experiences of conflict inform programme design in situations affected by conflict?

What are the important roles for and questions to be asked by educational researchers in conflict-affected situations given the insights raised in this chapter?

Notes

1 For a critique of this view in relation to the young people who lived through the years of anti-Apartheid struggle in South Africa, see Dawes, 2008.

2 Elsewhere, I have written an account of a group of Palestinian refugee children's rejection of efforts to teach them about IHL, due to the fact that these ideals did not relate to their own experience. See Hart, 2007, 10.

3 Name changed to preserve anonymity.

4 See, for example, Burdman, 2003. Also, Teach Kids Peace: www.teachkidspeace.org/docTemplate.php?id=22 and Palestinian Media Watch: www.palwatch.org/ (both accessed 01 December 2010)

5 Tellingly, Daphne Burdman – in her account of the indoctrination of children by the Palestinian authorities – offers strong endorsement of such an approach as part of the process of rendering young Palestinians amenable to the political status quo (2003, 115).

6   For example, Firer and Barhoum (2006) report on Palestinian school textbooks that speak of a child's right 'To be raised to believe in God and observe the Prophet Mohammed as a model' (219).

7   'Sa'ar said that he finds it particularly important to encourage girls to enlist in combat service, being the former chairman of the Knesset Committee for the Advancement of Women' (Zelikovich, 2009).

8   According to current Minister for Education, Gideon Sa'ar '[t]he Education Ministry regards with great significance the issue of encouraging IDF service, increasing recruits' rate and combat recruits' rate' (Zelikovich, 2009).

Acknowledgement

I am grateful to Julia Paulson and Mitsuko Matsumoto for their efforts in organizing the seminar series that gave rise to this volume and, most particularly, to Julia for her editorial input to the production of this chapter.

Reference list

Aden, S. (2009), 'Let's redeem Somalia's lost generation', *Africa News Online*, 10 April, http://africanewsonline.blogspot.com/2009/04/lets-redeem-somalias-lost-generation.html (accessed 4 January 2010).

Amnesty International (1999), *In the Firing Line: War and Children's Rights*. London: Amnesty International.

Arafat, C., and N. Boothby (2003), *A Psychosocial Assessment of Palestinian Children*. Washington D.C.: Save the Children.

Barak, O., and G. Sheffer (2007), 'The study of civil–military relations in Israel: A new perspective', *Israel Studies*, 12, 1, 1–28.

Beinin, J. (2007), 'Letter from Al-Tuwani', *Middle East Report 244* online, www.merip.org/mer/mer244/beinin_tuwani.html (accessed 20 January 2010).

Boyden, J. (2003), 'The moral development of child soldiers: What do adults have to fear?' *Peace and Conflict: Journal of Peace Psychology*, 9, 4, 343–62.

Boyden, J., and G. Mann (2005), 'Children's risk, resilience and coping in extreme situations', in M. Ungar (ed), *Pathways to Resilience*. Thousand Oaks, CA: Sage, 3–25.

Brocklehurst, H. (2007), 'Children and war', in A. Collins (ed), *Contemporary Security Studies*. Oxford: Oxford University Press.

Buckland, P. (2005), *Reshaping the Future: Education and Postconflict Reconstruction*. Washington D.C.: The World Bank.

Burdman, D. (2003), 'Education, indoctrination, and incitement: Palestinian children on their way to martyrdom', *Terrorism and Political Violence*, 15, 1, 96–123.

Bush, K. (2000), *Stolen childhood: The impact of militarized violence on children in Sri Lanka*. Ottawa, Canada: CIDA/SAP.

Cohn, I., and G. Goodwin-Gill (1994), *Child Soldiers: The Role of Children in Armed Conflict*. Oxford: Oxford University Press.

Colenso, P. (2005), 'Education and social cohesion: developing a framework for education sector reform in Sri Lanka', *Compare: A Journal of Comparative and International Education*, 35, 4, 411–428.

Davies, L. (2004), *Education and Conflict: Complexity and Chaos*. London, UK: Routledge.

— (2008), *Educating Against Extremism*. Stoke-on-Trent, Straffordshire: Trentham Books.

Dawes, A. (2008), 'Political transition and youth violence in post-apartheid South Africa: In search of understanding', in J. Hart (ed), *Years of Conflict: Adolescence, Political Violence and Displacement*. Oxford: Berghahn Books.

DCI-Pal (2000), *A Generation Denied: Israeli Violations of Palestinian Children's Rights*. Ramallah: Defence for Children International – Palestine Section.

DCI/PS (2009), 'Palestinian Child Prisoners: The systematic and institutionalised ill-treatment and torture of Palestinian children by Israeli authorities', Ramallah, June.

Duke, L. (1995), 'For Angola's street children, the war isn't over', *Washington Post*, 10–16 July.

Firer, R., and M.I. Barhoum (2006), 'Children's rights in Israeli and Palestinian textbooks', in C. W. Greenbaum, P. Veerman, and N. Bacon-Shnoor (eds), *Protection of Children During Armed Conflict: A Multidisciplinary Perspective*. Antwerp: Intersentia.

Garbarino, J. (1999), 'What children can tell us about the trauma of forced migration', Seminar presented at the Refugee Studies Programme, University of Oxford, Oxford, UK.

Giacaman, R., N. Abu-Rmeileh, A. Husseini, H. Saab, and W. Boyce (2007), 'Humiliation: the invisible trauma of war for Palestinian youth', *Public Health*, 121, 563–71.

Gor, H. (2003), 'Education for war in Israel: Preparing children to accept war as a natural factor of life', in K. Saltman and D. Gabbard (eds), *Education as Enforcement: The Militarization and Corporatization of Schools*. London: Routledge/Falmer.

Hart, J. (2004), 'Beyond struggle and aid: Children's identities in a Palestinian refugee camp in Jordan', in J. Boyden and J. de Berry (eds), *Children and Youth on the Frontline: Ethnography, Armed Conflict and displacement*. Oxford: Berghahn Books.

— (2007), 'Empowerment or frustration? Participatory programming with young Palestinians', *Children, Youth and Environments*, 17, 3, 1–23.

Human Rights Watch (2007), *Discrimination against Ethnic Nepali Children in Bhutan: Submission from Human Rights Watch to the Committee on the Rights of the Child*. Human Rights Watch Online www.hrw.org/legacy/backgrounder/crd/2007/bhutan1007/ (accessed 7 February 2010).

Jeffrey C., P. Jeffery, and R. Jeffery, (2005), 'Reproducing difference? Schooling, jobs, and empowerment in Uttar Pradesh, India', *World Development*, 33, 12, 2085–101.

Johnson, D., and Johnson, R. (2005), 'Essential components of peace education', *Theory into Practice*, 44, 4, 280–92.

Kashti, O. (2010), 'High school bans Israeli–Palestinian dialogue group due to parents' pressure', *Ha'aretz*, www.haaretz.com/print-edition/news/high-school-bans-israeli-palestinian-dialogue-group-due-to-parents-pressure-1.290741 (accessed 18 May 2010).

Kuper, J. (1997), *International Law Concerning Child Civilians in Armed Conflict*. Oxford: Oxford University Press.

Kupermintz, H., and G. Salomon (2005), 'Lessons to be learned from research on peace education in the context of intractable conflict', *Theory into Practice*, 44, 4, 293–302.

Levy, Y., E. Lomsky-Feder, and N. Harel (2007), 'From "obligatory militarism" to "contractual militarism": Competing models of citizenship'. *Israel Studies*, 12, 1, 127–48.

Margalit, A. (1996), *The Decent Society*. Cambridge, MA: Harvard University Press.

McAdam-Crisp, J. (2006), 'Factors that can enhance and limit resilience for children of war', *Childhood*, 13, 4, 459–77.

Miller, K., M. Kulkarni, and H. Kushner (2006), 'Beyond trauma-focused psychiatric epidemiology: Bridging research and practice with war-affected populations', *American Journal of Orthopsychiatry*, 76, 4, 423–33.

Newman, J. (2005), 'Schooling in a rural Singhalese community in Sri Lanka', unpublished fieldnotes. University of Oxford: Refugee Studies Centre.

Niens, U., and E. Cairns (2005), 'Conflict, contact, and education', *Theory into Practice*, 44, 4, 337–44.

Nolan, P. (2007), 'Difference, diversity and difficulty: Problems in adult peace education in Northern Ireland', *International Journal of Educational Development*, 27, 2, 282–91.

Pupavac, V. (2004), 'War on the couch: The emotionology of the new international security paradigm', *European Journal of Social Theory*, 7, 2, 149–70.

Reich, S., and V. Achvarina (2006), 'No place to hide: Refugees, displaced persons and the recruitment of child soldiers', *International Security*, 31, 1, 127–64.

Salomon, G. (2006), 'Does peace education *really* make a difference?' *Peace and Conflict*, 12, 1, 37–48.

Shields, R., and J. Rappleye (2008), 'Differentiation, development, (dis)integration: Education in Nepal's "People's War"', *Research in Comparative and International Education*, 3, 1, 91–102.

Sinclair, M. (2004), *Learning to Live Together: Building Skills, Values and Attitudes for the Twenty-First Century*. Paris: UNESCO.

Singer, P. (2005), *Children at War*. New York: Pantheon Books.

Toren, C. (1999), *Mind, Materiality and History: Explorations in Fijian Ethnography*. London: Routledge.

Veale, A., and G. Doná (2003), 'Street children and political violence: A socio-demographic analysis of street children in Rwanda', *Child Abuse and Neglect*, 27, 3, 253–69.

Vigh, H. (2008), 'Crisis and chronicity: Anthropological perspectives on continuous conflict and decline', *Ethnos*, 73, 1, 5–24.

Wessells M., and C. Monteiro (2004), 'Healing the wounds following protracted conflict in Angola: A community-based approach to assisting war-affected children', in U. P. Gielen,

J. Fish and J. G. Draguns (eds), *Handbook of culture, therapy, and healing.* Mahwah, NJ: Erlbaum, 321–41.

World Bank (2002), *Fifteen Months: Intifada, Closures and the Palestinian Economic Crisis: An Assessment.* Jerusalem: World Bank.

Zelikovich, Y. M. (2009), 'Education minister: More combat soldiers needed', *Ynet News*, 8 May. Online: www.ynet.co.il/english/articles/0,7340,L-3757512.00.html (accessed 3 June 2010).

2

Reconciliation Through Relationships Among Teachers and Sub-Saharan African Families in the USA

Sarah Dryden-Peterson

Chapter Outline

In 2007, 1.4 million of the 38.1 million foreign-born residents of the United States were born in Africa (Terrazas, 2009). While they make up only 3.7 per cent of the foreign-born population, the number of African migrants[1] more than tripled between 1990 and 2000, and Africans are the fastest growing migrant population in the United States (Dixon, 2006). The African population in the United States is diverse in terms of countries of origin, reasons for migration, education levels, and economic and social conditions (Hume, 2008; Arthur, 2000). Yet three broadly generalizable characteristics of this population make it particularly interesting in an examination of processes of reconciliation.

First, many Africans who arrive in the United States – and all of those included in this study – have experienced conflict in their home countries, be it widespread armed conflict or individualized persecution. In building new lives in the United States, they are attempting to reconcile themselves with past experiences. Second, in the process of migration, African migrants have experienced dislocation. In building new lives in the United States, they are seeking to reconcile relationships with others in rebuilding networks of social relationships. Third, in settling in the United States, African migrants are inserted into a context of structural violence in which discrimination disproportionately impacts blacks. In building new lives in the United States, they are seeking spaces of social equality and possibilities for social transformation through a process that can be described as reconciliation.

This chapter sets forth an argument for reconciliation as a process of building a new life and illuminates the school as a site of this reconciliation. The approach towards reconciliation presented is unique in centring on the individual and community rather than on groups in direct conflict. Indeed, what emerges from this research is a conceptual approach to understanding reconciliation as it connects to vision of self, relationships with others, and experience in society. These three aspects of reconciliation are illustrated through an ethnographic case study that explores the experiences of African migrant parents in their interactions with an elementary school in the northeastern United States. The empirical case provides much needed evidence of what reconciliation consists of and looks like in practice. The chapter concludes with a discussion of how the experiences of African migrants in the United States contribute to theoretical understandings of processes of reconciliation and outlines practices that schools might productively adopt in seeking to promote these processes.

Reconciliation as building a new life

A focus on reconciliation has been adopted at international, national and local levels as a central component of rebuilding conflicted and divided societies. Truth and Reconciliation Commissions in South Africa, Sierra Leone, Peru and Timor Leste, among others, have espoused the idea that in order for healing to take place in society, its members must come to terms with the past and forge a common outlook in building the future (Paulson, in Chapter 6 of this volume; TRC Commissioner Sierra Leone, 2004). With little clarity about what reconciliation is or how it might be pursued in practice, it is unsurprising that there is even less certainty about exactly how it can be fostered via education. The processes and outcomes of reconciliation, however, remain little understood.

In particular, while many national attempts at reconciliation assume a principle role for schools (Soudien, 2002), the conceptual links between education and reconciliation are under-explored both conceptually and empirically.

Theoretical work on reconciliation, much of which grows out of the peace education and conflict resolution literatures, emphasizes necessary change in 'the motivations, goals, beliefs, attitudes, and emotions that prevail among the great majority of the society – regarding the conflict, the nature of the relationship between the parties, and the nature of the parties themselves' (Bar-Tal and Rosen, 2009, 558). The literature is centred in the experiences of societies that have undergone violent conflicts on a macro level and relates primarily to reconciliation of a group with a particular 'other'. But, at core, reconciliation is about individuals, families and communities building new lives and learning to live together (Kelman, 2004, 113). My research demonstrates that these processes also occur outside of situations of armed conflict and extend beyond inter-group reconciliation. Examination of the experiences of African migrants in the United States sheds light on reconciliation as processes of change that enable people who have experienced dislocation to learn to live together across social divides, and on the particular role of schools in those processes. In this chapter, I examine these processes of change at three levels: in relation to the self, to others and to society.

Reconciliation within the self

Reconciliation involves rebuilding one's life on two sides of a dislocating event or series of events (Obura, 2003; Lederach, 1998). While the literature often assumes that dislocations preceding reconciliation involve inter-group conflict, I argue here that the rebuilding processes of reconciliation can follow from multiple types of dislocation, and their interactions. Such is true for African migrants in the United States, who have experienced geographic, economic, social and psychological dislocations of cross-border migration, often subsequent to initial dislocations due to armed conflict and/or persecution. The process of building a life after migration has been well-explored both theoretically and empirically, and there is a vast amount of literature on this process, though it is not conceived of as reconciliation but as integration (or assimilation). These literatures centre on an individual's experience of building a new life and, in this way, inform the individual aspect of self-reconciliation.

Self-reconciliation for migrant families involves building a new life that includes individual achievement or change. There are several agreed upon indicators of this type of 'success' in integration in the United States, including socioeconomic advancement, residential desegregation, English fluency and intermarriage (Alba and Nee, 2003; Bean and Stevens, 2003; Gordon, 1964). An additional indicator critical to the experiences of refugees is overcoming trauma and achieving mental stability (Lindert et al., 2009; Porter and Haslam, 2005). The integration literature describes how individuals imagine a better life in these ways and set about constructing that life within the parameters of their own sphere of action. The experiences of conflict-affected African migrants explored in this chapter, however, demonstrate how theories of integration that centre the process of building a new life in the self and individual betterment are important, but also limited. Their processes of integration involve other aspects of reconciliation, specifically as centred in relationships.

Reconciliation as centred in relationships

Synthesizing theories of integration with theories of reconciliation highlights the interactive processes inherent in building a new life. Reconciliation is centred in the transformation of relationships (Kelman, 2004). Much of the reconciliation literature focuses on this transformation of relationships between groups of people engaged in or previously engaged in conflict. Yet the individual-level dislocation of conflict or migration, or a combination of the two, also necessarily disrupts social relationships. Migrants leave behind in their home countries relationships with family members (and extended kin-like ties), friends, work colleagues, teachers, pastoral leaders and more. I argue here that building relationships and ties of interconnectedness not with a pre-determined and conflicting 'other', but with others generally and with the broader community is a primary goal of African migrants in the United States. The relationships themselves and the experience of building and sustaining them have intrinsic value. This role of relationships is central to the processes of building a new life for African migrants and opens new possibilities for understanding the concept of reconciliation.

Critical to this endeavour is the African worldview[2] of *ubuntu*, often referred to as African humanism (Bell, 2002). This cultural worldview expresses the essence of what it means to be human, premised on the idea of interconnectedness: you cannot be human all by yourself. Instead, the individual achieves personhood through interactions with others: 'I am because we are'. (Masina, 2000; Mbiti, 1990). The idea of *ubuntu* mirrors Kelman's (2004) conception of reconciliation, based not only in a pragmatic partnership based on self-interest, but in relationships of trust, reciprocity and mutual responsiveness. How these relationships of reconciliation develop, and the role of schools in the process, is explored in depth in this chapter.

Reconciliation as a societal endeavour

The context in which African migrants build relationships of reconciliation in the United States shares important characteristics with the conflict and post-conflict settings in which reconciliation is usually examined. In particular, African migrants enter a context of structural violence, particularly related to race, which contributes to the absence of 'positive peace' (Galtung, 1969), even in this comparatively settled nation. For example, once they set foot in the United States, African migrants face the imposition of racial categorization, particularly a 'perceived low racial status' compared to whites (Waters, 2001; Arthur, 2000, 79). Dodoo and Takyi (2002) document a significant earnings differential for African migrants based on racial discrimination. They find that black Africans in the United States have wages that are 19 per cent less than white Africans, after controlling for relevant characteristics, including country of origin and education level, which is a larger difference than between native-born white and black Americans. Portes (1998) argues that this type of structural constraint based on race impacts the ways in which migrants are able to build new lives in the United States. His theory of 'segmented assimilation' suggests that black migrants are likely to integrate into situations of permanent poverty and/or isolation from white, middle-class society.

Putnam's (2007) new research suggests that conditions for reconciliation may be limited in this context. He argues that social capital – social relationships associated with resources and embedded with norms of reciprocity and trust that can facilitate mutually beneficial cooperation[3] – is harder to build in racially and ethnically heterogeneous settings,[4] where most migrants live. Depending on the pre-existing characteristics of the migrants, residential desegregation can be associated with economic and language integration, for example (Bauer et al., 2005; Edin et al., 2002; Espenshade and Fu, 1997). However, using survey data from the United States, Putnam (2007) finds that where diversity is higher, *trust* is lower. He provides evidence for what he calls 'constrict theory', that racial and ethnic diversity reduces both in-group and out-group trust (144); in other words, 'Americans distrust not merely people who do not look like them, but even people who *do*' (148).

In this context, what are the possibilities for African migrants to build new lives based in concepts of reconciliation with self, with others and with society?

In what ways might schools contribute to reconciliation along these three dimensions? These questions guide the following analysis.

The case study

Merrimack Valley and African migrants at Merrimack Valley Elementary School

The state of Massachusetts in the northeastern United States is home to 5.4 per cent of the African migrants to the US and, just as in the country as a whole, Africans are the fastest growing foreign-born population in the state, at 439.1 per cent between 1990 and 2005 (Bump et al., 2005). Merrimack Valley,[5] the site of the school examined in this chapter, is a small city with a population of 105,167 at the time of the 2000 census. Twenty-two per cent of the population of Merrimack Valley is foreign-born, more than twice the national average and almost twice the state average. Of the foreign-born population, 54 per cent is from Asia, 22 per cent from Latin America, 16 per cent from Europe and 6 per cent from Africa (Lotspeich et al., 2003). The Africa-born make up only 1.3 per cent of the city's population, however, they make up 30.9 per cent of the non-Hispanic black population (U.S. Census Bureau, 2000), one of the highest percentages in the country (Logan and Deane, 2003). The migrant population of Merrimack Valley is residentially distributed across the city; all of the census tracts are at least 10 per cent foreign-born and the largest concentration of the foreign-born in a single tract is 45 per cent (Lotspeich et al., 2003, 7).

Merrimack Valley Elementary School has the highest proportion of African students in the district, at 12.9 per cent. It is one of a few 'low incidence' schools in the district, meaning that its children come from language groups represented by low numbers of speakers in the United States. Data collected for this study revealed certain characteristics of the school population and the African migrant population in particular. Half of the students have a language other than English as their first language. Eighty-four per cent of the students are eligible for free or reduced lunch. The children are from 36 countries, and the families of 22 students have recently arrived from sub-Saharan Africa. These African students are from Cameroon, Ghana, Kenya, Liberia and Zimbabwe. All of the African families are Christian. The African parents have been in the United States on average 5.6 years, and 90 per cent self-describe as 'fluent' in English. Ninety per cent of the parents have a high school education or higher, and all are employed, although none in a management position or a job that demands a highly credentialed skill. All of the families have two parents at home.

The ethnographic case study approach

This study uses an ethnographic case study approach.[6] Typical of an embedded case study (Yin, 2003, 43–44), my data collection focuses on two related units of analysis: a school and the parents whose children attend it. Over the course of one year (August 2007 to August 2008), I used a range of strategies to collect data, including document collection, in-depth interviews (n = 24) and partici-pant observation (1 day per week for 41 weeks), through which I examined dynamic processes of integration within the school context. My analytic strategy involved the development of a coding system of *emic* codes that emerged induc-tively from the participants and *etic* codes that I assembled deductively from the literature (Strauss and Corbin, 1998). I coded all of the interviews, interview profiles, and observational fieldnotes line-by-line, using classical, free, and in vivo coding processes (Strauss and Corbin, 1998; Miles and Huberman, 1994). To interpret the findings, the various data sources were triangulated and com-pared to the literature.

Merrimack Valley Elementary School: An ethnographic case study

I drive almost to the centre of Merrimack Valley and then take a sharp turn up a hill. The street is lined with clapboard houses that sit right on the street; there are no trees, no lawns. And there are no people. The street is deserted. From the outside, the school looks deserted, too. It is an old, brick building (the oldest school building in the city, built in 1852) that looks as if it would have been splendid in its day. It is now sunken about six feet below street level and surrounded by a big concrete slab. Here, too, it seems the only green is the weeds that dare to poke up through the cracks in the concrete. I descend into the concrete pit still without seeing any signs of life. Then, on the concrete, I see markers of children: happy hop-scotch boards drawn in florescent colours, an old playground surrounded by new mulch, and a series of benches around the one tree that look like perfect places to sit and tell secrets.

The air of welcome hits me when I enter the (unlocked) door. The walls are painted in rainbow colours, and I see welcome signs all around me, in English and in Spanish. There is carpet on the floor, and I hear the gentle voices of teachers and students engaged in conversations. I walk up the steps and introduce myself to the secretary. Her office is across the hall from the Principal, but she can see the Principal from her chair, through both of their open doors. I can hear the Principal on the phone with a parent, describing a fight that took place earlier that morning. While I sit in the hall waiting for my meeting with her, several teachers walk by. They all greet me warmly and ask how I am; they know I am a stranger in their school, but they don't treat me like one. And I don't feel like one. (From fieldnotes, 2007)

From the outside, Merrimack Valley Elementary School resembles what African parents in the United States have come to see as common among institutions that they once believed might hold potential as spaces of reconciliation, of building new lives. The school is deserted, run-down, and one has to look hard to see signs of life. Once entering the school, however, all of the African parents at Merrimack Valley describe the same feeling I had: an overwhelming sense of welcome. 'Inside', says Umwami, from Kenya, 'we met the contrast of the outside'. With a warmth familiar to him from his Kenyan home, Umwami describes how whenever he arrives at the school it 'is like they are expecting you'. At this school, Imelda, also from Kenya, says, 'you feel free'. Melody, from Zimbabwe, describes how 'I feel like I am part of it . . . they treat you like one of [them]'. The school is a critical space of reconciliation in the lives of these parents.

There are three particular ways in which Merrimack Valley Elementary School fosters reconciliation among its African parents. The first focuses on reconciliation of the self, fostering conditions under which parents can care for their families, including promoting academic success for their children. The second focuses on reconciliation with others, through cultivating relationships between parents and teachers that are based in reciprocal care and shared responsibility for children. And the third focuses on reconciliation with a new society, providing a model of how American society might be transformed through these forms of reconciliation of self and with others. Each of these themes is discussed below.

Building a new life for one's self

The African families at Merrimack Valley Elementary left their home countries amid widespread armed conflict in Liberia or facing political, linguistic and ethnic persecution in Zimbabwe, Cameroon, and Ghana and Kenya, respectively. In hushed tones so that their children do not overhear, parents discuss how building a new life in the United States is a process of reconciling their experiences of conflict and persecution. They recount the years they spent living in refugee camps or in hiding, the family members who have been killed or are missing, the threats on their own lives, and their on-going worries about what the future holds in their home countries in terms of reconstruction, the cessation of conflict, or the establishment of human rights. They are also in the process of reconciling their migration experiences. All parents are clear that, given the choice, they would have preferred to stay in their home countries.

African parents at Merrimack Valley describe the school as playing a central role in assisting them in coming to terms with the dislocation of conflict and migration and creating new lives in the United States. Merrimack Valley Elementary fosters this reconciliation in two ways: through developing in children academic skills that will help them progress to higher education and be successful in the job market, and through facilitating the acquisition of information, knowledge and skills that allow African parents to care for their children in a new country.

African migrant parents at Merrimack Valley are optimistic about building new lives in the United States for one central and shared reason. 'We came to this country . . . with only one desire: to educate our children', explains Umwami. In this way, the reconciliation of self for African parents is inextricably linked to the educational experiences of their children. African parents compare their experiences at other schools and at Merrimack Valley in explaining how this school is effective in helping African migrant families to build new lives in the United States. Annette, from Kenya, describes the different experiences of learning that her daughter, Rina, had at a previous school and at Merrimack Valley:

> She was not performing good. We took a long time [to go talk to them] because when we took her to the private school, we were thinking that private school, it can be more better than a public school . . . [Finally], I went to the school. I told her [teacher], this kid is not doing good and she's lonely. Would you mind finding her a friend? . . . The teacher is not helping her . . . So I have to tell the principal I need to change her [school] because she's not doing good and she's feeling so many complainings in home . . . I was thinking she could be very happy when she came here [to the United States] so you can imagine her telling me 'Mommy, I want to go back home to Kenya.' . . . She don't want to learn. You can tell her, 'Can I help you to learn today'? [She will say], 'I'm having a headache.' I cannot force her. . . . So then I took her to the public school [Merrimack Valley] and I told the teacher . . . her problem about [how] her learning is down and asked them how they can able to help me to improve on her learning. They were telling me that she has a problem in understanding, or disability. But I told her no, this kid is bright. She need put more effort and help from

the parent and the teacher. She is good. She know how to learn. But it's like the laziness and the frustration and all those kind. So after [that conversation], the teachers were so good in [Merrimack Valley] School. They help me a lot. And she was given a program where she will be going after class program and the class teacher, she was so good and understanding about her problem because we came together and then we came to discuss what's her problem and how you are able to improve . . . So we put more effort, me and my husband, so we can further study her weakness and everything and the teacher, too. And they are good to her and then they have been helping her and she has really changed. A difference of one year, she have really done a good job.

This focus on learning, and helping struggling children to succeed, permeates Merrimack Valley School. Twice a day, for forty minutes, all of the children and all of the adults in the school work in small groups of eight on literacy and numeracy activities. Every corner of the school is used – the classrooms, hallways, teachers' offices, computer lab and cafeteria – to enable a focus on the particular academic needs of individual children within these small group interactions between adults and children. African parents are pleased with the kind of instruction their children receive at the school and how they believe it will prepare their children for the academic success they see as integral to building a new life in the United States. While the school as a whole struggles to demonstrate on standardized tests the kind of learning that takes place daily in classrooms, there is evidence that the African students, in particular, are fulfilling the goal with which their parents came to the United States and, in doing so, are helping to reconcile their parents' ambivalence about life in this new country.

For African parents, Merrimack Valley also provides tangible benefits in terms of information, knowledge and skills that allow them to take care of their families in the United States. Catherine, from Kenya, says, 'there are a lot of things that are new for me, and it is not the way we do it in our country, so I need someone to tell me how to do it'. The school provides access to a limited number of services, such as free clothing and social workers. While service provision of this kind can feel like charity or can appear judgmental, African parents at Merrimack Valley appreciate the thoughtfulness and genuine care with which it is offered. Through the relationships with teachers that will be examined in the next section, they also have access to information about the school curriculum and student assessment as well as resources about a range of discipline strategies to evaluate and try. African parents say that this type of information helps them to understand the American education system and augments the ways in which they can support their children in this new environment, again contributing to their self-reconciliation with life in the United States.

Building a new life with others

Students' academic success, as outlined in the previous section, contributes to African parents building new lives for themselves; it is also central to the core mission of schools. Yet this reconciliation with the self is but one way in which Merrimack Valley Elementary School is involved with reconciliation processes. In particular, the relationships that African parents develop with teachers at the school are instrumental in shaping the ways in which African parents come to see themselves as part of a community, in which they learn to 'live together' in a new society.

While the reconciliation literature often concentrates on groups who are or were in conflict learning to live together, this study demonstrates that building relationships between individuals and groups with no history of explicit conflict can be important as well. Relationships connecting people to one another in a community are central to reconciliation for African migrant parents at Merrimack Valley for two reasons. First, they are a form of interaction familiar to them from their home countries. For example, Clémence, from Liberia, explains the way that neighbours in her country interact around the raising of children:

> If you were a neighbour and you stopped by, you will say to [my son], 'You better go home because I will tell your parents'. He will go home because he knows I will discipline him right away if you call. I won't go to you and say, 'Why did you call me about my child?' We don't do that at home. . . . If I can train my child, I am able to train my neighbour's child. That's the way we have been brought up.

Second, African parents are, universally, astonished to see the lack of this kind of interaction in the United States. Oliver, from Cameroon, explains that, from his perspective, 'the American culture is that people don't mix very much in the community. People live by themselves'. The building of relationships within the school involves a reconciliation of these experiences.

At Merrimack Valley Elementary all of the school staff know each child, and most parents, by name. At the last school-wide assembly of the year, the Principal presents each student with a medal and a book for summer reading.

She does not read the names of the children from a list, but simply calls their names as they approach her, in any order. When parents arrive to pick their children up at school, teachers wave hello and greet them by name. And, from inside her office, the Principal notices that Catherine, Silas' mother, is in the playground. She dashes outside for an instant to greet her, to tell her that Silas, who struggles with his behaviour, has had a great day.

Within this welcoming environment, parents and teachers develop partnerships that are based in their shared interests of student success, but that evolve to include mutual responsiveness and reciprocity. Sylvia, from Kenya, compares her son's old school to Merrimack Valley, demonstrating how these central aspects of reconciliation are fostered at this school:

> When we were in [another local] school, I used to fight with the teachers, I was very defensive of [my son] Oluka, even though I knew at a point he was wrong. But I was not feeling confident. I was not feeling like they are really handling Oluka the way he's supposed [to be handled] . . . So, I didn't feel the trust, but now whatever they say in [Merrimack Valley] school, I'm willing to work with them, because I trust them. I trust what they say because I they [are] already meeting us half way to work with Oluka . . . You can see the concern and the care, and you trust somebody who is taking care of your kid.

Sylvia identifies trust as the central aspect of her relationship with Oluka's teachers. The way the teachers talk to her, the care they exhibit and the good feelings they inspire in her make her trust what they say and recommend in terms of helping Oluka to be successful in school. Sylvia also has repeated experience with the teachers through which she can observe their patience with Oluka and their determination to ensure he meets his goals. Instead of feeling, as she did at Oluka's previous school, that she needs to be a guardian against the misunderstanding and mistreatment of her son, she has discovered a school that fosters relationships that enable teachers and families to live together.

The negotiations and compromises involved in building these relationships are central to processes of reconciliation. 'Meeting us halfway', as Sylvia describes it, is a kind of mutual accommodation that parents and teachers afford to each other. The mostly white and long-time resident staff and the African newcomer parents have found pathways to this accommodation, across cultural differences and social divisions, through one central mechanism: explicit acknowledgement of their common ground based in the caring of children. African parents see that for all the teachers might not know about their cultures, they know their children deeply. Sylvia describes how Tara, Oluka's teacher, knows him:

> I felt like she even take time to learn to know Oluka, what he want, and she made me aware more. Like Oluka wanted to be the boss in class, and I was like, well, that's what Oluka does at home with me. When Daddy is not here, he want to be the boss. . . . . I didn't even realize that until Ms. Tara brought it up, and so I felt like she knows him – she's studied Oluka enough to know that he want to be the boss.

At the same time teachers help parents to understand their children, parents help teachers as well. Umwami describes how his son's teacher approached him with a concern that Jacob was repeating the teacher's words after she gave directions or asking her to repeat the questions. Umwami had not noticed this pattern, but he shared the teacher's concern for Jacob's learning. Jacob's father told the teacher that she could 'involve any specialist because at the end of the day, we want the child to get the best'. However, instead, they together decided on a simple strategy to test whether the issue was speech-related or language-related, realizing that, as Jacob's father proposed, 'if it is a speech problem, for example, it would be common to other languages'. Over the course of a few weeks, his father thus listened carefully to Jacob's speech in his three languages – Luyia, Kiswahili and English – and determined that Jacob repeated words only in English, not in his native Luyia or more fluent Kiswahili. The teacher quickly arranged for more English as a Second Language (ESL) support.

It is this mutual accommodation, based in shared care for children, which allows both parents and teachers to trust each other, a trust that becomes the basis for the ongoing, peaceful living together that is central to reconciliation for African migrants in the United States.

Building a new life in society

The kinds of relationships parents develop inside the school contribute to their reconciliation with self, through realization of goals for their children's academic success; they also foster reconciliation with others, through the development of mutually-interested partnerships with teachers. The experience of these forms of reconciliation further expands the hopes of African parents for broader reconciliation with a new society. The reconciliation that African parents experience at Merrimack Valley Elementary School begins to transform, in small ways, how they see themselves in relation to the context of structural violence in the United States.

In particular, at times, the kinds of relationships that African parents build with teachers at Merrimack Valley are also evident in interactions outside of the school. Many parents attribute the success of these outside-of-school interactions to the practice at developing relationships they have had inside the school. For example, on a sunny spring day, Kalaitu and I are eating Greek sandwiches at the Quick Picks Deli in downtown Merrimack Valley. Kalaitu, from Sierra Leone, is a former Merrimack Valley parent and now the African parent liaison for the Merrimack Valley District High School. It is a lively lunch hour and the restaurant is filled with customers, mostly men in work clothes and a few older couples who look as if they have decided to slip out of work and meet for lunch. Everyone, besides Kalaitu, is white.

In the middle of our conversation, a man who had been sitting at the table next to us comes over. He is white and older, with white hair and a slightly reddened face. He wears dark blue casual pants and a blue- and white-striped golf shirt. The following conversation ensues:

> He says, 'Excuse me, are you from Africa?'
> Kalaitu looks up at him and, with a smile, says, 'yes'.
> 'Which country?' he asks.
> 'Sierra Leone', she replies.
> 'Oh, do you speak Swahili?' he asks.
> She says, 'No, that's East Africa'.
> 'Oh yes', he says without skipping a beat, 'Tanzania. I have been to Tanzania.
> And I've been to Burkina Faso, too.'
> 'Burkina Faso is West Africa', Kalaitu says excitedly (Sierra Leone is also West Africa).

He tells her that his son, a graduate of the Merrimack Valley Public Schools, is in the Peace Corps in Burkina Faso. When the man leaves, Kalaitu makes a motion of her eyes toward him. I cannot tell if she is making this motion to say, 'Gosh, can you believe these people?' or to say, 'Here is what I have been talking about.' It is the latter.

'That's Merrimack Valley', she says. 'People genuinely want to learn about other places.' She does not interpret the man's questioning and mistakes as ignorance but as curiosity. She has experienced this kind of curiosity and genuine interest in her background often in the context of the Merrimack Valley schools. It makes her feel good.

This kind of openness to having conversations and building relationships that contribute to the project of reconciliation – of learning to live together – does occur in Merrimack Valley outside of Merrimack Valley Elementary. However, it is not the norm. African parents are embedded in a society rife with structural barriers that result in inequalities that shape relations between people and impede larger, societal reconciliation. For example, despite on-going searches for employment that matches their skills and interests, all of the African parents at Merrimack Valley work in low-paying jobs for which they are overqualified. All but one of the parents have at least a high school education and speak fluent English. Yet seven of the parents work as Certified Nursing Assistants, companions to elderly and developmentally challenged residents of nursing and group homes. The other three work in similarly low-level jobs, as a security guard, a Home Depot salesperson and an assembly-line worker, which they describe as 'unfulfilling'. The parents explain that they feel trapped in a system that does not recognize their credentials, or their potential.

Further, Africans are not able to access political power in Merrimack Valley. They take on numerous – mostly volunteer – community roles as members of police task forces; Board members of the Merrimack Valley Community Health Centre, the Youth Soccer Association Board and other local non-profits; and organizers of local access television shows and cultural events. The Director of a local community organizing and advocacy group explains, however, that 'there are no minority representatives, no minority city counsellors, no minority members of the school committees and very few minority municipal employees, and the reality is that there is very little political sway by a huge portion of the population of [the city]'. African voices are missing from political negotiations about how people will live together in the city of Merrimack Valley.

Even the reconciliation of self and others that occurs within Merrimack Valley Elementary among teachers and parents may be limited in its transferability to other contexts outside of the school. For example, as mentioned earlier, although classroom observations show intense learning among African students at Merrimack Valley, and teachers point to evidence that African students are among the most successful in the school, the school in general struggles to help children achieve academically. Doku, from Ghana and the African tutor at the middle school to which Merrimack Valley students move in fifth grade, has been shocked by the low level of academic skills of the African students. 'These students are really not as good [as] my village students back in Ghana', he reflects. Optimism for their success beyond Merrimack Valley Elementary is further tempered by school-wide scores on standardized tests, which, while certainly an imperfect measure, place the school in the bottom 10 per cent in the state of Massachusetts (Boston Globe, 2008). This persistent achievement gap serves as an important reminder of continued barriers to societal reconciliation even in a place where immense progress has been made in reconciliation within one school community.

Reconciliation, relationships and building a new life

African migrant parents at Merrimack Valley Elementary School come to terms with the dislocation experiences of conflict and migration by focusing on building new lives for themselves and their families, with the principal goal of creating conditions for their children's success in the new country. The school plays an important role in this process of self-reconciliation by promoting academic learning for children and enabling parents with information, knowledge and skills to care for their families in an unfamiliar environment. The school also plays a critical role in reconciliation that is centred in relationships with others, a pattern of communal living familiar to parents from their home countries and missing in most aspects of their American lives. Through collective work on students' learning and discipline, teachers and parents build respectful partnerships based in reciprocity and trust. The development of these relationships assists teachers and parents alike in understanding the potential for success in common goals based on mutual accommodation. While these relationships are critical to the processes of teachers and families learning to live together across social divides, structural violence within the larger society inhibits reconciliation on a broader scale.

Parents at Merrimack Valley make explicit in their comparisons of schools what the literature also demonstrates: Merrimack Valley Elementary School is exceptional. The literature suggests that, along a spectrum, relationships between migrant families and schools are more likely to be filled with cultural misunderstandings and struggles for authority than with the care, respect and trust, all fostered through strong leadership from the Principal, evidenced at Merrimack Valley (e.g. Olivos, 2006; Delgado-Gaitan and Trueba, 1991). In the case of Merrimack Valley, we indeed see the potential role for schools in reconciliation. A re-evaluation of the framework for reconciliation outlined at the beginning of this chapter in light of the empirical data from Merrimack Valley Elementary School illuminates ways in which education and reconciliation are related and points to ways in which schools might effectively work with families from conflict-affected settings to promote reconciliation.

First, reconciliation of self depends on the establishment of conditions in the post-conflict and/or post-dislocation setting in which each individual can achieve his or her personal goals. In this case, African parents are clear that their goals centre on success for their children, and there is evidence to support this value of investment in children as common in many situations, especially after conflict and/or migration (Buckland, 2005; Burde, 2005; Davies and Talbot, 2008). As a result, schools can play a central role in fostering self-reconciliation. The case of Merrimack Valley demonstrates that this role can include targeted support for the aspects of rebuilding lives that are most central to families, including their children's success in school and tangible assistance in terms of information and knowledge about how to navigate new environments. Access to these tangible benefits through schools is well-documented in the literature on social capital (Warren et al., 2001; Briggs, 1998) and the potential for schools to play this role is widely accepted (Dryfoos and Maguire, 2002; Driscoll, 2001). While this role for schools is not widely adopted in practice (Warren et al., 2009), the evidence from this case suggests it as a promising practice for schools wishing to promote self-reconciliation.

Second, teachers at Merrimack Valley Elementary seeking to promote student success cultivate relationships with African parents. While this strategy on the part of teachers may be motivated by desires to achieve the school's mission of student learning, these relationships play a broader role for teachers and African parents alike. These relationships are reciprocal, simultaneously supporting African parents' goals of student success, a kind of mutual accommodation central to reconciliation (Kelman, 2004, 122). They are also a form of reconciliation as they serve to transform interactions between people who are often separated by social divides of race, class and power. Lindner (2009) argues that this transformation of relationships away from 'humiliation' and toward reciprocity across inequities is essential for reconciliation, which can only be achieved when 'equal rights and dignity for everybody are respected' (159). There is evidence from the field of social identity research that this reciprocity is far-reaching in its consequences for reconciliation among individuals (Kramer, 2006, 31). In particular, reciprocity allows for a renegotiation of identity: 'It transforms individuals from self-seeking and egocentric agents with little sense of obligation to others into members of a community with shared interests, a common identity, and a commitment to the common good' (Alder and Kwon, 2002, 25). This notion harkens back to the earlier discussion of the African worldview of *ubuntu*, 'I am because you are,' and highlights the value of this worldview to the relationship-building central to reconciliation (Murithi, 2009). While there is now abundant evidence of the impact of relationships between teachers and parents in promoting student achievement (Lee and Bowen, 2006; Jeynes, 2003; Henderson and Mapp, 2002; Fan and Chen, 2001), the case of Merrimack Valley Elementary School demonstrates that the benefits of these relationships on reconciliation may be equally important.

Third, the reconciliation of self and with others evident at Merrimack Valley Elementary provides a space of 'positive peace' (Galtung, 1969) in the midst of the structural violence that permeates US society. As such, it provides several lessons for reconciliation as a societal endeavour. Central to experiences at Merrimack Valley is the practice of building relationships: the practice of mutual accommodation, the practice of reciprocity, the practice of negotiation and compromise, and the practice of trust. Small spaces, such as a school like Merrimack Valley, provide situations of contact where relationships can be built (Pettigrew and Tropp, 2006; Schofield, 1995; Allport, 1979 [1954]). Additionally, as suggested by equal status contact theory (Brewer and Miller, 1988; Brehm and Kassin, 1996), schools have an inherent, and often overlooked, benefit as sites of shared interests, which is a critical foundation for reconciliation. Parent engagement with schools can be difficult to encourage (Olivos, 2006; Delgado-Gaitan and Trueba, 1991), yet the shared interest in children, which transcends culture and previous experiences, can be powerful when facilitated as at Merrimack Valley. This case indeed points to the importance of the school as a site of reconciliation for migrants from conflict-affected settings, not only with a particular 'other', but with one's self, others generally, and the larger society. The relationships between parents and teachers at Merrimack Valley are exemplary and provide models of how to move away from the broad absence of trust exhibited by the 'constrict theory' Putnam describes (2007) toward a society in which living together across social divides is practised and reconciliation thus achieved.

Guiding questions

In what ways does the reconciliation described by Sarah Dryden-Peterson in this chapter differ from more conventional definitions?

How can processes like those identified in this chapter be fostered and supported in other educational settings beyond Merrimack Valley Elementary School?

Are there ways in which education might address challenges to reconciliation such as structural violence?

Notes

1   I use the term *migrant* to describe a person who has undertaken either voluntary or forced migration to the United States. Readers may be more familiar with the terms *immigrant* (for voluntary migrants) and *refugee* (for involuntary migrants). Since the population of African migrants in the United States includes both immigrants and refugees, I have opted for the more inclusive *migrant*.

2   Pan-Africanism is obviously a historico-political construct, and applying one concept to reflect a worldview of Africans broadly risks generalizing and even romanticizing what is a diverse and sometimes divided group of cultures and countries on a vast continent. Nevertheless, many Africans see *ubuntu* as essential to how they live their lives and, I argue, to how they build their lives in the United States.

3   This definition draws on Bourdieu (1986), Coleman (1988) and Putnam (2000).

4   This basic conclusion has been reached in other studies as well (see, for example, Costa and Kahn, 2003; Keller, 2001; Webber and Donahue, 2001; Alesina and La Ferrara, 2000) and is supported by the 'conflict theory' (see, for example, Bobo, 1999; Brewer and Brown, 1998; Blumer, 1958).

5   The names of the city, school, and all participants have been changed.

6   It is part of a larger study involving four comparative case studies of multiethnic institutions (Dryden-Peterson, 2009).

Acknowledgement

This work is part of a larger comparative study that examines the role of institutions in integration of African migrants in new and old immigration destinations in the United States. A version of the paper was presented at the conference of the Canadian Society for Studies in Education in Montreal, May 2010. The author was supported by generous grants from the Harvard Graduate School of Education and the Center for American Political Studies at Harvard University. For invaluable feedback on this work, I thank Mark R. Warren, Sara Lawrence-Lightfoot, John B. Willett, Robert D. Putnam, Radhika Rao and Julia Paulson. I am most indebted to the children, families, teachers, principals, and community leaders in Merrimack Valley for sharing their experiences and ideas.

Reference list

Alba, R. D., and V. Nee (2003), *Remaking the American Mainstream: Assimilation and Contemporary Immigration*. Cambridge, MA: Harvard University Press.

Alder, P. S., and S.-W Kwon (2002), 'Social capital: Prospects for a new concept', *The Academy of Management Review,* 27, 1, 17–40.

Alesina, A., and E. La Ferrara (2000), 'Participation in heterogeneous communities', *Quarterly Journal of Economics*, 115, 847–904.

Allport, G. (1979 [1954]), *The Nature of Prejudice*. Reading, MA: Addison-Wesley Publishing Company.

Arthur, J. A. (2000), *Invisible Sojourners: African Immigrant Diaspora in the United States*. Westport, CT: Praeger.

Bar-Tal, D., and Y. Rosen (2009), 'Peace education in societies involved in intractable conflicts: Direct and indirect models', *Review of Educational Research*, 79, 2, 557–75.

Bauer, T., G. S. Epstein, and I. N. Gang (2005), 'Enclaves, language, and the location choice of migrants', *Journal of Population Economics*, 18, 4, 649–62.

Bean, F. D., and G. Stevens (2003), *America's Newcomers and the Dynamics of Diversity*. New York: Russell Sage Foundation.

Bell, R. H. (2002), *Understanding African Philosophy: A Cross-Cultural Approach to Classical and Contemporary Issues*. New York: Routledge.

Blumer, H. (1958), 'Race prejudice as a sense of group position', *Pacific Sociological Review*, 1, 3–7.

Bobo, L. D. (1999), 'Prejudice as group position: Microfoundations of a sociological approach to racism and race relations', *Journal of Social Issues*, 55, 445–72.

Bourdieu, P. (1986), 'The forms of capital', in J. G. Richardson (ed), *Handbook for the Theory and Research for the Sociology of Education*. Westport, CT: Greenwood Press, 241–58.

Brehm, S. S., and S. M. Kassin (1996), *Social Psychology* (3rd edn). Boston: Houghton Mifflin.

Brewer, M. B., and R. J. Brown (1998), 'Intergroup relations', in D. T. Gilbert, S. T. Fiske, and G. Lindzey (eds), *Handbook of Social Psychology* (4th edn), New York: Oxford University Press.

Brewer, M. B., and N. Miller (1988), 'Contact and cooperation, when do they work?' in P. Katz and D. Taylor (eds), *Eliminating Racism. Profiles in Controversy*. New York: Plenum Press, 315–26.

Briggs, X. D. S. (1998), 'Brown kids in white suburbs: Housing mobility and the many faces of social capital', *Housing Policy Debate*, 9, 1, 177–221.

Buckland, P. (2005), *Reshaping the Future: Education and Post-Conflict Reconstruction*. New York: World Bank.

Bump, M. N., B. L. Lowell, and S. Pettersen (2005), 'The growth and population characteristics of immigrants and minorities in America's new settlement states', in E. M. Gozdziak and S. F. Martin (eds), *Beyond the Gateway: Immigrants in a Changing America*. New York: Lexington Books.

Burde, D. (2005), *Education in Crisis Situations: Mapping the Field*. Washington, D.C.: Creative Associates/Basic Education Support Project, United States Agency for International Development.

Coleman, J. S. (1988), 'Social capital in the creation of human capital', *American Journal of Sociology*, 94 (Supplement), S95–S120.

Costa, D. L., and M. E. Kahn (2003), 'Civic engagement and community heterogeneity: An economist's perspective', *Perspectives on Politics*, 1, 103–11.

Davies, L., and C. Talbot (2008), 'Learning in conflict and postconflict Contexts', *Comparative Education Review*, 52, 4, 509–19.

Delgado-Gaitan, C., and H. T Trueba (1991), *Crossing Cultural Borders: Education for Immigrant Families in America*. London: Falmer.

Dixon, D. (2006), *Characteristics of the African Born in the United States*. Washington, D.C.: Migration Policy Institute.

Dodoo, F. N.-A., and B. K. Takyi (2002), 'Africans in the diaspora: Black-white earnings differences among America's Africans', *Ethnic & Racial Studies*, 25, 6, 913–41.

Driscoll, M. E. (2001), 'The sense of place and the neighborhood school: Implications for building social capital and for community development', in R. L. Crowson (ed.), *Community Development and School Reform*. Amsterdam: JAI.

Dryden-Peterson, S. (2009), 'Where is the Village? Pathways to Integration for African Migrants to the United States', unpublished doctoral dissertation, Harvard University), Cambridge, MA.

Dryfoos, J. G., and S. Maguire (2002), *Inside Full-Service Community Schools*. Thousand Oaks, CA: Corwin Press.

Edin, P. -A., P. Fredriksson, and O. Aslund (2002), *Ethnic Enclaves and the Economic Success of Immigrants--Evidence from a Natural Experiment*. Uppsala, Sweden: Uppsala University, Department of Economics.

Espenshade, T., and H. Fu (1997), 'An analysis of English-language proficiency among U.S. immigrants', *American Sociological Review*, 62, 2, 288–305.

Fan, X., and M. Chen (2001), 'Parental involvement and students' academic achievement: A meta-analysis', *Educational Psychology Review*, 1, 1–22.

Galtung, J. (1969), 'Violence, peace, and peace research', *Journal of Peace Research*, 3, 167–91.

Gordon, M. M. (1964), *Assimilation in American Life*. New York: Oxford University Press.

Henderson, A. T., and K. L. Mapp, K (2002), *A New Wave of Evidence: The Impact of School, Family, and Community Connections on Student Achievement*. Austin, TX: National Center for Family and Community Connections with Schools.

Hume, S. E. (2008), 'Ethnic and national identities of Africans in the United States', *Geographical Review*, 98, 4, 496–512.

Jeynes, W. (2003), 'A meta-analysis: The effects of parental involvement on minority children's academic achievement', *Education & Urban Society*, 35, 202–18.

Keller, R. T. (2001), 'Cross-functional project groups in research and new product development: Diversity, job stress and outcomes', *Academy of Management Journal*, 44, 547–55.

Kelman, H. C. (2004), 'Reconciliation as identity change: A social psychological perspective', in Y. Bar-Siman-Tov (ed), *From Conflict Resolution to Reconciliation*. New York: Oxford University Press, 111–24.

Kramer, R. M. (2006), 'Social identity and social capital: The collective self at work', *International Public Management Journal*, 9, 1, 25–45.

Lederach, J. P. (1998), 'Beyond violence: Building sustainable peace', in E. Weiner (ed), *The Handbook of Interethnic Coexistence*. New York: Continuum, 236–45.

Lee, J. -S., and N. K. Bowen (2006), 'Parent involvement, cultural capital, and the achievement gap among elementary school children', *American Educational Research Journal*, 43, 2, 193–218.

Lindert, J., O. S. V Ehrenstein, S. Priebe, A. Mielck, and E. Brähler (2009), 'Depression and Anxiety in Labor Migrants and Refugees, A Systematic Review and Meta-Analysis', *Social Science & Medicine*, 69, 2, 246–57.

Lindner, E. G. (2009), 'Why there can be no conflict resolution as long as people are being humiliated', *International Review of Education*, 55, 2/3, 157–81.

Logan, J. R., and G. Deane, G. (2003), *Black Diversity in Metropolitan America*. Albany, NY: Lewis Mumford Center for Comparative Urban and Regional Research, University at Albany.

Lotspeich, K., M. Fix, D. Perez-Lopez, and J. Ost (2003), *A Profile of the Foreign-Born in [Merrimack Valley], Massachusetts*. Washington, D.C.: The Urban Institute.

Masina, N. (2000), 'Xhosa practises of Ubuntu for South Africa', in I. W. Zartman (ed), *Traditional Cures for Modern Conflicts: African Conflict "Medicine"*. Boulder, CO: Lynne Rienner Publishers, 169–82.

Mbiti, J. S. (1990), *African Religions & Philosophy*. Portsmouth, NH: Heinemann.

Miles, M. B., and A. M. Huberman (1994), *Qualitative Data Analysis: An Expanded Sourcebook* (2nd edn). Thousand Oaks, CA: Sage Publications.

Murithi, T. (2009), 'An African perspective on peace education: Ubuntu lessons in reconciliation', *International Review of Education*, 55, 2/3, 221–33.

Obura, A. (2003), *Never Again: Educational Reconstruction in Rwanda*. Paris: International Institute for Educational Planning.

Olivos, E. M. (2006), *The Power of Parents: A Critical Perspective of Bicultural Parent Involvement in Public Schools*. New York: Peter Lang.

Pettigrew, T. F., and L. R. Tropp (2006), 'A meta-analytic test of intergroup contact theory', *Journal of Personality and Social Psychology*, 90, 751–83.

Porter, M., and N. Haslam (2005), 'Predisplacement and postdisplacement factors associated with mental health of refugees and internally displaced persons: A meta-analysis', *Journal of the American Medical Association*, 294, 5, 602–12.

Portes, A. (1998), 'Children of immigrants: Segmented assimilation and its determinants', in A. Portes (ed), *The Economic Sociology of Immigration*. New York: Russell Sage Foundation, 248–79.

Putnam, R. D. (2000), *Bowling Alone: The Collapse and Revival of American Community*. New York: Simon & Schuster.

— (2007), 'E pluribus unum: Diversity and community in the twenty-first century: The 2006 Johan Skytte Prize Lecture', *Scandinavian Political Studies*, 30, 2, 137–174.

Schofield, J. W. (1995), 'Promoting positive intergroup relations in school settings', in W. D. Hawley and A. W. Jackson (eds), *Toward a Common Destiny: Improving Race and Ethnic Relations in America*. San Francisco: Jossey-Bass, 257–89.

Soudien, C. (2002), 'Memory work and the remaking of the future: A critical look at the pedagogical value of the truth and reconciliation commission for peace', in G. Salomon and

B. Nevo (eds) *Peace Education: The Concept, Principles, and Practices Around the World.* Haifa, Israel: University of Haifa Press.

Strauss, A., and J. Corbin (1998), *Basics of Qualitative Research: Techniques and Procedures for Developing Grounded Theory.* Thousand Oaks, CA: Sage Publications.

Terrazas, A. (2009), *African Immigrants in the United States,* www.migrationinformation.org/USfocus/display.cfm?id=719 (accessed 11 February 2009).

TRC Commissioner Sierra Leone (2004), Truth and Reconciliation Commission Report For the Children of Sierra Leone, Child Friendly Version. Freetown, Sierra Leone: UNICEF.

U.S. Census Bureau (2000), 'Census 2000 Demographic Profile Highlights', Summary File 2 (SF 2) and Summary File 4 (SF 4). Washington D.C.: U.S. Census Bureau, http://factfinder.census.gov (accessed 27 January 2009).

Warren, M. R., S. Hong, C. H. Rubin, and P. S. Uy (2009), 'Beyond the bake sale: A community-based relational approach to parent engagement in schools', *Teachers College Record,* 111, 9: 2209–54.

Warren, M. R., J. P. Thompson, and S. Saegart (2001), 'The role of social capital in combating poverty', in S. Saegart, J. P. Thompson & M. R. Warren (eds), *Social Capital and Poor Communities.* New York: Russell Sage Foundation, 1–30.

Waters, M. C. (2001), *Black Identities: West Indian Immigrant Dreams and American Realities.* New York: Russell Sage Foundation.

Webber, S. S., and L. M. Donahue (2001), 'Impact of highly and less job-related diversity on work group cohesion and performance: A meta-analysis', *Journal of Management,* 27, 141–62.

Yin, R. K. (2003), *Case Study Research: Design and Methods* (3rd edn). Thousand Oaks, CA: Sage Publications.

3

Education and Reconciliation in Northern Ireland

Alan Smith

Introduction

This chapter identifies new challenges for reconciliation that have emerged in Northern Ireland since the signing of the Belfast (Good Friday) Agreement in 1998. It is more than a decade since the agreement, so there are few children with direct experience or memory of the conflict. Nonetheless, there is a current debate about the role that education might have in helping new generations understand what happened in the past and recognize legacies of the conflict.

A significant amount of the work on reconciliation has been funded by the European Union (EU) Programme for Peace and Reconciliation in Northern

Ireland which has provided more than €2 billion since 1995. As this chapter shows, there are some lessons to be learned from having a reliable and sustained flow of international funding, particularly in terms of being able to adapt priorities and funding mechanisms to changing circumstances. Although this approach also carries some dangers, such as the development of a peace building economy that cannot be sustained into the post-conflict phase. The current phase, PEACE III (2007–13), has adopted a working definition of reconciliation developed by Hamber and Kelly (2004) with €225 million being provided for a range of initiatives with particular emphasis on 'reconciling communities' and 'contributing to a shared society' – these imply a role for education in reconciliation in Northern Ireland. In addition, while there is no formal truth and reconciliation commission in Northern Ireland, the government established an independent Consultative Group on the Past that published a report in 2009 with 31 recommendations on acknowledging and dealing with the past.

Such initiatives, which call on education to accomplish a number of ambitious goals, pose significant challenges for educators within post-conflict societies. Education is often identified as a means toward future reconciliation, but usually with little definition about what this means conceptually or in practice. However, the case of Northern Ireland also provides examples of efforts by local actors such as parents, teachers, NGOs and community activists that emerged in the midst of conflict, that are now providing a basis for peace building in the post-conflict period. The chapter identifies some of these various initiatives and draws conclusions about the challenges still to be addressed.

The conflict in Northern Ireland

When the Republic of Ireland was established in 1921, the island was partitioned. The northern part became Northern Ireland and retained union with Britain as part of the United Kingdom. It included a majority with loyalties to Britain (mostly Protestant descendants of English and Scottish settlers from the 1600s onward), but it also contained a significant minority of mostly Catholic nationalists with political loyalties to a unified Ireland. These different political loyalties were institutionalized through governance arrangements that led to inequalities and discrimination against Catholics in voting, housing and employment, and eventually led to a violent conflict that began in the late 1960s.

Since 1969 more than 3,600 people were killed and 30,000 injured as part of 'the Troubles' in Northern Ireland. More than half of the deaths were civilians, mostly males. Fatalities were inflicted on both communities (43 per cent

Catholics, 30 per cent Protestants) and all parties to the conflict were responsible for some of the deaths - 59 per cent caused by Republican paramilitaries, 28 per cent by Loyalist paramilitaries and 11 per cent by the security forces (Fay and Morrissey et al., 1999). By the 1990s it was becoming clear that neither the use of violence nor a military response would resolve the issue and ceasefires in 1994 eventually created the opportunity for a peace process that led to a political agreement in 1998.

The education system in Northern Ireland

The education system in Northern Ireland was and continues to be characterized by separate schooling. Separation exists in terms of religion in that most children attend predominantly Protestant ('controlled') schools or Catholic ('maintained') schools. The education system is relatively small. Statutory education involves approximately 330,000 children within 849 primary, 150 secondary and 69 grammar schools (figures for 2009–10 school year). The system is administered by a central Department of Education and five local authorities (known as Education and Library Boards). There is also a Council for Catholic Maintained Schools and the government provides funds for the Northern Ireland Council for Integrated Education (NICIE) to coordinate the development of a small but, since 1981, a growing number, of integrated schools (61 schools with 6 per cent of pupil enrolments in 2009), serving students from all communities. The education system also includes 21 Irish medium schools and 12 Irish medium units within English-speaking schools (c. 2000 pupils in total) funded by government, and 9 independent Christian schools associated with the Free Presbyterian Church which do not receive government funding. In such a fragmented and identity-based education system, a key question is whether 'post-conflict' development is likely to involve struggles over assimilation, continued separate development or moves toward greater social and institutional integration.

The peace agreement

The 1998 Belfast (Good Friday) Agreement had three main elements. Firstly, it addressed the issue of sovereignty. As part of peace negotiations, the Republic of Ireland removed a territorial claim over Northern Ireland from its constitution and both governments recognized 'the birthright of all the people of Northern Ireland to identify themselves and be accepted as Irish or British, or both'. For the first time the agreement also accepted that the future constitutional status of the territory will be determined by 'the wish of the majority of the people who live there' (Northern Ireland Office, 1998). So, the agreement deferred a decision on the ultimate sovereignty of the territory and both governments promised to respect the outcome of any future decision through 'self-determination' by the people who live there. There is no detail in the agreement about the mechanism or process by which such a decision would be reached, but the implication is that it will be by some form of nonviolent political process, possibly a referendum. In this sense, the agreement managed to 'transform' the conflict, but the dispute at its core has not been 'resolved'. There has been a shift away from the use of violence towards the use of democratic politics, but the fundamental issue of Northern Ireland's sovereignty has been deferred rather than resolved. That the dispute at the core of the conflict remains unresolved has implications for the possibilities available for 'post-conflict' peace building and reconciliation in many areas, including in education as will be discussed below.

The second main element of the agreement was the establishment of new democratic institutions that share power between locally elected politicians. These replace direct rule from London. A new legislative Assembly was created of 108 local politicians, elected by proportional representation, and a 12-member executive body comprised of politicians from different parties. A First Minister and Deputy First Minister are jointly elected by members of the Assembly voting on a cross-community basis and ministers are allocated to posts according to the d'Hondt system (parties select ministerial posts in turn based on the number of seats held by each party). Decisions in the Assembly are made by a weighted majority to ensure cross-community support. Such fundamental changes to governance had significant implications for education in terms of how children and young people might learn about the new political arrangements in Northern Ireland, although this was not acknowledged explicitly at the time or identified as a transformational task for education in the Agreement.

A third element of the agreement was confidence-building measures designed to address the concerns of the conflicting parties and encourage commitment to the peace process. These included:

- *Human rights.* The establishment of a Northern Ireland Human Rights Commission and an Equality Commission with statutory responsibilities for anti-discrimination legislation related to Equal Opportunities (gender), Race Relations Act, Fair Employment (religion) and disability.

- *Decommissioning weapons.* An Independent International Commission was established to work towards the decommissioning of paramilitary weapons.
- *Demilitarization.* The British government made a commitment to demilitarization and a return to 'normal security arrangements in Northern Ireland consistent with the level of threat' (Northern Ireland Office, 1998). Practical steps have included a reduction in the number of soldiers, removal of security installations and the removal of emergency powers.
- *Policing and the Justice System.* An Independent Commission on Policing for Northern Ireland included proposals to address the under-representation of Catholics (7 per cent in 1994) through a 50:50 recruitment policy, the creation of a new Policing Board with nationalist representation and a Police Ombudsman to deal with complaints about police conduct. The name of the police service was also changed and a Criminal Justice Review Group set up, but it would take a further 12 years until there was sufficient trust between political parties to transfer powers for policing and justice to the Northern Ireland Assembly in March 2010.
- *Prisoner releases.* Those affiliated to paramilitary groups claim that their actions were politically motivated and it was clear that a political settlement would not be achieved without their inclusion. In the two years following the Agreement, 428 prisoners were released and 'a total of 1,093 prison officers were expected to leave the service by March 2000'. (BBC, 2000). This represented a reduction of 40 per cent in prison service staff mainly through voluntary redundancies following the closure of the Maze prison.
- *Support for Victims.* There were concerns that those who had been bereaved or otherwise affected by the conflict would be neglected. Recommendations led to more than £18 million to support victims of 'the Troubles'.

Referenda on the agreement were held in May 1998. In the Republic of Ireland 94per cent of voters (56 per cent turnout) approved of the proposal to amend the Irish Constitution. In Northern Ireland 71 per cent of those voting (81 per cent turnout) endorsed the Agreement.

Education for reconciliation before and since the Belfast Agreement

Although the role of education was not identified as a separate confidence-building measure, education is mentioned twice in the Agreement, once in relation to support for the development of integrated schools and once in relation to support for Irish language education. Additionally, the Agreement mentions the need to develop a 'culture of tolerance' within broader society. These references provided the basis for the Department of Education to establish two working groups. The first working group had representation from state, church, integrated and Irish language school authorities and produced a report on 'Integrating Education' (Department of Education, 1998) that affirmed government's commitment to support a 'pluralist approach to education'. Three main recommendations were that:

- a more systematic and planned approach to the development of integrated schools be adopted through, for example, the use of community audits;
- guidance and support should be provided for existing schools wishing to 'transform' to formal integrated status;
- funding and support should be provided which would help all schools meet the challenges of pluralism within society in Northern Ireland.

A second working group produced a report on 'Education for Diversity' (Department of Education, 1999) that concentrated on the role of a community relations scheme, which provides funding for schools to organize activities that bring Catholic and Protestant pupils together. The report also identified limitations within the current curriculum and highlighted opportunities for new developments such as citizenship and human rights education.

In many respects the language used by these two reports was a code for what might and might not be possible to achieve in terms of institutional transformation through education. For example, the first group was established to see what consensus could be established on policies to support 'integrated' schooling. However, it soon became clear that the representatives of the Catholic church authorities would not engage in discussion of any proposals that would threaten the continued existence of separate Catholic schools. Hence the shift in language towards 'integrating' education, meaning that cooperation and collaboration between schools might be possible, but not any changes that would involve an end to separate school structures. For the Catholic authorities the phrase 'a plural approach' was interpreted as the continuation of different types of schools, rather than any move toward common schools. This has been confirmed by more recent developments where the Catholic authorities, in response to declining pupil numbers within the overall education system, have moved to rationalize schools within their own system, rather than look to opportunities to rationalize on a cross-community basis within local communities.

Similarly, the reference to diversity in the second report reflected a shift from a focus solely on the improvement of 'community relations' between Catholics and Protestants, to 'good relations' between a wider range of groups, including ethnic minorities.

Two other points are worth noting before considering what education initiatives have emerged in Northern Ireland since the Good Friday Agreement. First, is that the agreement simply marked one important transition in a much longer process. It changed the environment in a very significant way by marking a shift away from political violence to a commitment to democratic politics. This created new opportunities for education, for example, to explore possibilities for greater contact and collaboration between schools and to address issues such as sectarianism, human rights and politics more explicitly through the curriculum. However, it is important to remember that many reconciliation initiatives had already been taking place throughout the conflict as well. The difference was a change in context and emphasis on what it was now possible to address through education. In broad terms, initiatives in the early days of the conflict emphasised maintaining contact, communication and 'mutual understanding' between divided communities. Attempts to develop shared, 'integrated' schools also emerged almost a decade before the peace agreement, but the shift in the post-conflict period raised sharper questions about the nature of citizenship, equality and human rights in a divided society.

A second important point is that the impetus for reconciliation initiatives has come from different sources. During the height of civil disturbances, particularly in urban centres such as Belfast, there was a concern about the impact of violence on children and a number of voluntary organizations emerged that provided respite for children during holiday periods. Many of these were supported by the Irish diaspora, particularly in the United States, and children often spent summer periods away from home with host families. Throughout the conflict a significant number of community-based NGOs emerged to support schools involved in cross-community contact programmes and this gave rise to an economy for such groups and a more 'professionalized' peace sector. Within schools, many of the early 'mutual understanding' programmes were initiated by individual teachers and involved extracurricular activities or the development of education materials related to the curriculum. Changes to the teaching of history in Northern Ireland is a very good example of innovation led by teachers as part of the professional development of their field. This involved teachers from Catholic and Protestant schools working together to develop joint resources to give multiple perspectives on Irish history instead of relying on single textbooks that gave a broadly British or Irish narrative.

However, in terms of institutional change, it was parents who were the instigators and prime movers for the development of shared, integrated schools with the establishment of the first school in 1981 in Belfast. Interestingly, it was independent foundations outside of Northern Ireland, such as the Nuffield and Joseph Rowntree Foundations, rather than government that provided parents with the funding for these early schools. In fact, the role of government in promoting reconciliation would merit further analysis. Suffice to say that government's role in relation to education and reconciliation is complicated by the fact that the education system in Northern Ireland became subject to direct rule by a British minister from 1972. In one respect this meant that certain policies could be introduced where previously it would not have been possible to secure consensus between local politicians. The introduction of the Education Reform (NI) Order, 1989 that included new provisions to fund integrated and Irish language schools is a good example. However, the fact that British rule was also regarded by the nationalist community to be a central part of the problem, also meant that the government had to be careful about imposing change without local support.

In general, government appears to have adopted two broad approaches to education: one was to use research to investigate how education might be involved in underpinning inequalities and adjust policies accordingly (this is reported below); the other was to encourage others such as parents and NGOs to undertake initiatives and only change policy when there seemed to be a degree of support. For example, seed funding for inter-school contact was provided many years before a formal funding scheme was introduced and only limited support was provided for integrated schools until they proved viable (i.e. a policy of voluntary integration with support from parents, rather than changing the law to bring about compulsory desegregation). It is not clear whether either of these were conscious strategies or are simply evident in hindsight, but both appear to have had some benefits in securing local ownership for these initiatives. Paradoxically, since responsibility for education has been once more devolved to local politicians in November 1998 through the Northern Ireland Assembly it has become more 'politicized' and contentious. This is partly to do with reactions to the appointment of a Sinn Féin politician with close associations to the IRA as the first Minister of Education after the peace agreement, but also because many policy issues such as support for Irish language schools, ending of academic selection and funding for preparatory schools divide politicians along sectarian lines.

As mentioned above, a range of initiatives emerged during the conflict, including some legislation and government policies, which encouraged schools to contribute towards the improvement of relations between the two main religious and cultural communities in Northern Ireland. In broad terms, these represent interventions in both the structure of education (through consideration of equity issues between existing, segregated schools and support for the creation of new, integrated schools) and the process of education (through curriculum reforms and increased contact between Catholic and Protestant pupils). They include equality issues, cross-community contact, integrated education, curriculum changes, and citizenship education based on human rights.

Equality issues

A review of fair employment legislation by the Standing Advisory Commission on Human Rights (SACHR, 1987) indicated that Catholics were twice as likely to be unemployed as Protestants. In part, this highlighted the ineffectiveness of the earlier 1976 Fair Employment Act and became the impetus for more rigorous fair employment legislation. Current legislation now requires employers to monitor the religious composition of their workforce and, where significant gaps exist, to adopt affirmative action measures including recruitment procedures which are likely to encourage applications for employment from members of the underrepresented community. The debate about the underlying explanations for unemployment differentials between the two communities also focused attention on the relationship between the labour market and the education system.

In an effort to understand whether aspects of the segregated system of schooling had contributed to higher levels of unemployment among Catholics, the Standing Advisory Commission on Human Rights (SACHR, 1989, 1990, 1991, 1992) commissioned a number of research studies that investigated various explanations. In particular it was noted that a higher proportion of Catholics left school with low or no qualifications (Cormack et al., 1992; Osborne, 1986) and that more Protestants choose scientific subjects at school and university (Cormack and Osborne, 1987). This led to research which identified underlying differentials in funding between Catholic and Protestant schools (SACHR, 1991). An unanticipated finding concerning recurrent funding revealed consistently higher levels of per capita funding in favour of Protestant pupils within primary, secondary and grammar schools (Cormack, Gallagher and Osborne, 1991). Various explanations were advanced to explain this including differences in school size and different provision of specialist teaching space (Cormack,

Gallagher and Osborne, 1992), and implications that for historical and percep-
tual reasons Catholic schools were less disposed to approach government for
funding (Murray, 1992). The research concluded that the overall impact of a
number of factors such as these had contributed to consistently lower levels
of recurrent funding for Catholic schools (Gallagher, Osborne and Cormack,
1993). The Education Reform (NI) Order, 1989 included provision for the local
management of schools whereby each school is allocated a budget that is determined by a formula largely dependent on pupil numbers.

Cross-community contact

Since the early 1970s there have been a number of 'cross-community contact'
programmes, some carried out through formal education, others through less
formal approaches, where Catholic and Protestant young people are given the
opportunity to work or socialize together in some joint endeavour. These
increased over the years, and eventually received formal Government support
from 1987 through a scheme whereby schools and youth groups have access to
a budget of some £1,000,000 per year. Research has shown that 40 per cent of
primary schools and 60 per cent of secondary schools take part in these kinds
of programmes, although only 10 per cent of all children are actually involved
(Smith and Robinson, 1996). There have been mixed reactions to these
programmes, including accusations of social engineering. However, such programmes are supported by the majority of parents from both main traditions
in Northern Ireland. In a survey (Smith and Dunn, 1990), 50 per cent of parents
felt that contact should be taking place on a weekly basis and a further 25 per
cent felt this should be happening on a daily basis. These high levels of support
seemed to reflect parents' aspirations that, unlike themselves, their own children
should have more opportunities to mix across community divisions.

Integrated education

In 1974 a group called All Children Together (ACT) was established, made up of
parents in favour of Catholic and Protestant children being educated together.
This organization opened up debate and lobbied successfully for legislation
which would allow state schools to become integrated (Education (NI) Act,
1977), but this was only invoked on one occasion. Eventually, some parents
decided to establish a new school which would exemplify their commitment to
integrated education and the first planned, integrated school, Lagan College, was
established in Belfast in 1981. This was followed by the opening of three further

integrated schools in Belfast in 1985. Over the next decade at least one new integrated school was established every year and by 1993 there were 21 integrated schools (17 primary and 4 post-primary) attended by approximately 3,500 pupils (approximately 1 per cent of the school population). By September 2009 there were 61 integrated schools in Northern Ireland. There are in total about 20,000 pupils at these schools, but this still represents only 6 per cent of all school children in Northern Ireland. The majority of school children – about one-third of a million in all – continue to attend separate schools. One of the interesting decisions from a policy perspective is whether it is better to bring about integration through compulsory legislation to 'desegregate' the education system or to encourage voluntary integration through funding and support. In Northern Ireland parents have been the main initiators of integrated schooling and the latter policy has been pursued. While some people have expressed frustration that government has not taken a more decisive lead towards desegregation, others argue that the voluntary approach leads to a deeper commitment even though fewer children are involved.

Curriculum changes

Other initiatives have involved the development of curriculum programmes that address issues related to identity and cultural diversity in Northern Ireland. Probably the best known is Education for Mutual Understanding (EMU) which emerged in the early 1970s, but it was not until 1989 that it became a mandatory, statutory feature of the curriculum for all schools in Northern Ireland. EMU had four broad objectives. These were to enable pupils to respect and value themselves and others; to appreciate the interdependence of people within society; to know about their own and other cultural traditions; and to appreciate how conflict may be handled in nonviolent ways. An early evaluation confirmed that the inclusion of EMU in the statutory curriculum had limited impact with less than a third of schools having a policy in place (Smith and Robinson, 1992). Further evaluation (Smith and Robinson, 1996) provided the stronger critique that many schools were adopting a 'minimalist' approach to EMU and this was attributed to a number of reasons, including:

- resistances within the system based around the perception that EMU had been imposed by government and suspicions that a hidden political agenda is at work;
- major difficulties with the cross-curricular model of implementation whereby EMU was supposed to permeate the curriculum, but was in danger of becoming too disparate and fragmented;

- that EMU was not addressing important social, cultural and political issues which have a bearing on community relations in Northern Ireland. Teachers still expressed reservations about addressing issues such as violence and sectarianism;
- teachers expressed reservations about their confidence and capacity to undertake community relations work which is sensitive and challenging. There was a major criticism that government had introduced EMU to the statutory curriculum without appropriate investment in the training and professional development of teachers.

The evaluation identified perceived gaps and recommended that a human rights framework might provide a firmer basis for work in EMU (ibid.).

Citizenship education based on human rights

One of the main ways of engaging young people about the future of their society is through citizenship education. A survey of 14- to 18-year-olds (Smyth and Scott, 2000) showed that young people define themselves as Irish (42 per cent), British (23 per cent) or Northern Irish (18 per cent), suggesting that identity politics are deeply ingrained. The realities of identity politics in Northern Ireland further suggest that a narrow concept of citizenship one based on national identity will be problematic in a divided society.

Therefore, one of the greatest challenges for citizenship education in Northern Ireland is whether it is possible to develop a concept of citizenship that is based on common rights and responsibilities rather than notions of national identity (Smith, 2003). Since there is no consensus on nationality in Northern Ireland, or indeed the legitimacy of the state itself, this means that the concept of citizenship when addressed in schools must be regarded as problematic and contested from the outset. Any civic or citizenship education curriculum must go beyond simple 'patriotic' models, defined solely in terms of national identity that require uncritical loyalty to the nation state.

Partly in response to this challenge and partly in response to developments elsewhere, in 2000 the education authorities initiated a pilot project in social, civic and political education in 25 post-primary schools to develop a citizenship education curriculum. The Northern Ireland programme of local and global citizenship is an inquiry-based curriculum involving the exploration of concepts in four core areas (Diversity and Inclusion; Equality and Justice; Human Rights and Social Responsibilities; and Democracy and Active Participation). Young people are required to investigate these concepts through case studies and resource materials related to local and global issues, many of them developed specially by local voluntary organizations. This involves deeply controversial and practical issues such as how to achieve a policing service that has the confidence of all sections of society or how current conflicts over cultural expression might be resolved. An overview of the curriculum requirements and evaluation of the pilot programme indicated that pupils developed more positive attitudes towards community relations, but this was accompanied by a decline in trust in political institutions (O'Connor, 2008). A similar form of citizenship education is being developed within non-formal education, through youth and community education programmes.

The European Union Programme for Peace and Reconciliation in Northern Ireland

One of the most consistent sources of funding to support the peace process in Northern Ireland has been from the European Union. The EU Special Support Programme for Peace and Reconciliation in Northern Ireland and the Border Region (PEACE I) was first introduced partly in response to ceasefires by paramilitary groups on both sides of the conflict in 1994. The first programme operated from 1995–99 and committed €667 million (€500m from the EU). The aim was:

> To reinforce progress towards a peaceful and stable society and to promote reconciliation by increasing economic development and employment, promoting urban and rural regeneration, developing cross-border co-operation and extending social inclusion. (Special EU Programmes Body, 2007, 4)

Political talks and the signing of the Belfast (Good Friday) Agreement in 1998 provided further encouragement and a second programme (PEACE II) committed €995 million for a further five years (2000–04) followed by an additional €120 million that extended the programme for a further two years (2005–06). PEACE II had the same overall aim as PEACE I, but two distinctive objectives to 'address the legacies of the past' and 'take opportunities arising from peace' were introduced.

While there were many difficulties, particularly in getting new political institutions operating, the EU provided a further phase of funding of €225 million for PEACE III (2007–13) with a greater emphasis on dealing with the past and future reconciliation. The reasons for this focus on reconciliation within PEACE III are discussed below.

Overall, the EU is providing consistent support of almost €2 billion to peace and reconciliation in Northern Ireland through PEACE I, II and III over a 20-year period (1994–2013). There has been some evolution in the aims and objectives of the EU PEACE programmes from an early emphasis on economic recovery and employment initiatives to more recent emphasis on dealing with the legacies of the conflict. By the end of PEACE II the weighting for 'reconciliation' in assessing whether projects would be funded had increased from 6 per cent to 20 per cent. The funding has been broad-based and supported the work of many different agencies, and has included funding for development within the education sector. In particular, much of the early work described above involving contact between schools and later curriculum development related to social, civic and political education was supported through EU funding. Importantly, and ironically, as the peace has become more secure, there has been increased appreciation by EU funders of the importance of social development:

> Indeed, while there has been a general decline in the number of deaths and incidents connected with the security situation, significant barriers to peace and reconciliation still remain. This is particularly evident given the high number of sectarian incidents that have occurred in recent years in Northern Ireland. These trends indicate a significant reduction in the overall level of violence. The trends also indicate a change in the nature of violence from incidents involving paramilitaries and security personnel, to broader sectarian violence and hate crimes. This demonstrates an underlying culture of intolerance and violence and suggests that while one of the major components of the violence data has been taken out of the equation, another component may have increased. This relates to particularly 'low-level' violence at the interfaces of residentially segregated communities. (Special EU Programmes Body, 2007, 35)

More than a decade after ceasefires and a peace agreement, there are still struggles within the society over expressions of identity through language, culture and religion. Despite a reduction in political violence and economic investment, conflict remains a reality for many local communities and there is awareness of a need to address the concerns of victims and survivors of the conflict.

There has also been some evolution in funding modalities. PEACE I was criticized for using government departments who provided matching funds as the main gatekeepers in the assessment of proposals and disbursement of funds. This approach was criticized, particularly by those who perceived government to be partial and part of the problem, for channelling funds to 'safe' projects and organisations,. PEACE II introduced the concept of channelling funds through 'intermediary bodies' and 'local partnership boards' – an innovation designed to decentralize funding decisions and bring them closer to local communities. This gave rise to challenges over the equitable distribution of funds and the possibility of funding finding its way to support paramilitary groups. The EU response was tighter audit arrangements which in turn brought complaints about community groups being overburdened with bureaucracy and administration. Other issues have included criticisms about lack of coherence across different funding streams and the emergence of a 'peace economy' with a consultancy culture, numerous jobs and newly created organizations dependent on the continuation of EU funding. However, on the positive side, sustained funding from the EU over such a long period has provided opportunities for continuity and progression in priorities and funding modalities. In development terms, Northern Ireland has been relatively insulated from a multiplicity of international donors with competing priorities and demands in terms of reporting and accountability. This has also created the possibility for institutional learning and reflection on what works, although as everywhere, the commitment to evaluation could be stronger.

PEACE III and post agreement challenges

The current PEACE III (2007–13) programme is consistent with the recommendation of the Organisation for Cooperation and Economic Development-Development Assistance Committee (OCED-DAC) Principles for Good International Engagement in Fragile States and Situations (2007) to take context analysis as the starting point. The programme undertook a detailed security, political and economic analysis and identified changes in the operating environment. These included, for example, the fact that almost a quarter of the population considered themselves to be a victim of the troubles and that sectarianism continues to be a significant problem. While an overall improvement in community relations was noted (based on findings from the Northern Ireland Life and Times Survey, a social attitudes survey administered by the University of Ulster and Queens University Belfast), a number of important challenges were identified. These included high levels of residential segregation (37 per cent of Census areas have 90 per cent or more people from one community background) and lack of shared space:

> In many cases, residential areas and public spaces are often 'marked out' with flags, emblems and graffiti to define the territory as belonging to one community, making the other community feel unwelcome. The marking of territory has impacted on the value of shared space in Northern Ireland. Evidence from the Northern Ireland Life and Times Survey, for example, shows that the proportion of respondents who believe their local shops are a neutral space 'always or most of the time' decreased from 84 per cent to 77 per cent between 2004 and 2005. In addition, the Life and Times Survey highlights that 69 per cent of respondents feel that town and city centres are generally not safe and welcoming places for all people. (Special EU Programmes Body, 2007, 15)

However, the Northern Ireland Life and Times Survey also found that respondents who preferred to live in a mixed religion neighbourhood had increased from 71 per cent in 1998 to 79 per cent in 2005. Residential segregation had also increased the number of 'interface areas' where Protestant and Catholic communities live beside each other but with little contact. Such interfaces are potential flashpoints for sectarian violence and are sometimes marked by 'peace walls', physical barriers between communities, but can also be less visible boundaries such as a road that runs between two communities. There are at least forty 'peace walls', some built since the peace agreement because of insecurity between local communities, and the challenge will be how such barriers might be removed if confidence in the peace process continues. Other social factors identified include lack of shared public services (such as community health centres, job centres, public housing and public transport), lack of cross-community contact (63 per cent said either 'all' or 'most' of their friends were of the same religion as themselves) and lack of shared schooling (less than 6 per cent of children attend integrated schools, although 61 per cent of people in 2005 said they would prefer to send their children to a mixed religion school compared to 56 per cent in 1998).

A distinctive feature of planning for PEACE III was reference to an analysis of ten theories of change (Woodrow, 2005). Particular emphasis was placed on a combination of theories of individual change in attitudes and theories about change in relationships (see Special EU Programmes Body, 2007, Appendix B, 113–14). This provided the rationale for a focus on two main priorities:

Priority 1: Reconciling communities through initiatives to build positive relations at local levels (dealing with issues of trust, prejudice and intolerance) and acknowledging and dealing with the past (hurt, losses, trauma and suffering caused by the conflict).

Priority 2: Contributing to a shared society through initiatives to create shared public spaces and shared institutional development.

PEACE III also targeted areas and groups that have been affected by the conflict (sectarian interfaces, disadvantaged areas, areas with high levels of sectarian and racial crimes and areas where economic and social development has been inhibited by the conflict with problems of exclusion and marginalization). Target groups included:

- victims of the conflict, that is the surviving injured and/or disabled people (either physically or psychologically) of violent, conflict-related incidents and those who care for or are related to them, including close relatives who mourn their dead;
- displaced persons, that is those who have involuntarily moved from areas of violence or from interface areas, and communities in which there is a concentration of such displaced persons or who are isolated by border closures;
- people who have been excluded or marginalized from economic, social and civil networks as a result of problems related to sectarianism, racism and the conflict (this includes, inter alia, a focus on young people, women, older people and minority communities);
- former members of the security and ancillary services;
- ex-prisoners and their families, that is qualifying prisoners who were or would have been released under the terms of the Good Friday Agreement; and
- public, private and voluntary sector organizations and their staff who have a contribution to make towards developing a shared society. (Special EU Programmes Body, 2007, 50).

PEACE III therefore involved a contextual assessment, an analysis of change theories and identification of two main priorities that gave more emphasis to social development, including dealing with the past and contributing to future reconciliation. It was targeted at particular areas and groups. In addition, it included quantified targets and indicators for each priority, for example, one indicator for dealing with the past was that at least 1,000 people would receive trauma counselling. Such indicators have provided the basis for a Monitoring and Evaluation Plan (ibid., 82–5).

Dealing with the past

Another distinctive feature of PEACE III was the inclusion of a definition of reconciliation developed by Hamber and Kelly (2004) as part of the previous phase. The definition refers to five interrelated strands, as follows:

- *Developing a shared vision of an interdependent and fair society:* The development of a vision of a shared future requiring the involvement of the whole society, at all levels. Although individuals may have different opinions or political beliefs, the articulation of a common vision of an interdependent, just, equitable, open and diverse society is a critical part of any reconciliation process.
- *Acknowledging and dealing with the past:* Acknowledging the hurt, losses, truths and suffering of the past. Providing the mechanisms for justice, healing, restitution or reparation and restoration (including apologies if necessary and steps aimed at redress). To build reconciliation, individuals and institutions need to acknowledge their own role in the conflicts of the past, accepting and learning from it in a constructive way so as to guarantee non-repetition.
- *Building positive relationships:* Relationship building or renewal following violent conflict addressing issues of trust, prejudice and intolerance in this process, resulting in accepting commonalities and differences, and embracing and engaging with those who are different to us.
- *Significant cultural and attitudinal change:* Changes in how people relate to, and their attitudes towards, one another. The culture of suspicion, fear, mistrust and violence is broken down and opportunities and space opened up in which people can hear and be heard. A culture of respect for human rights and human difference is developed creating a context where each citizen becomes an active participant in society and feels a sense of belonging.
- *Substantial social, economic and political change:* The social, economic and political structures that gave rise to the conflict and estrangement are identified, reconstructed or addressed, and transformed. (Hamber and Kelly, 2004)

The increased emphasis on reconciliation and 'dealing with the past' in PEACE III has very significant implications for education. If the Hamber and Kelly definition is used as a starting point then it is clear that education has a significant role in underpinning each of the five interrelated strands, particularly as an instrument to facilitate attitudinal change among new generations of children and young people. An obvious 'entry point' is through the new citizenship programme which includes a specific requirement that pupils have an opportunity to: 'Investigate how and why conflict, including prejudice, stereotyping, sectarianism and racism may arise in the community. Investigate ways of managing conflict and promoting community relations, reconciliation' (Northern Ireland Curriculum, 2006). These became statutory requirements for all schools in Northern Ireland from September 2007, although it will take time to develop a clear picture of the extent to which schools are addressing these themes through explicit reference to the conflict. However, PEACE III has provided funding for 'addressing legacy and truth in public memory' which includes the development of television programmes, web-based resources, archives, exhibitions and educational materials, training and support for teachers and youth workers, so these may be a basis to meet the curriculum requirements.

The role of education?

In broad terms the peace agreement marked a very important transition – an attempt to move away from the use of violence to bring about political change, to a commitment to power-sharing and democratic politics in the context of a deferred decision on the constitution. This change of context has meant that questions are raised about the role that education can play in reinforcing and supporting such a transition. I concentrate here mainly on schooling and formal education, but obviously this is only part of the broader contribution that also needs to be made through informal youth, community and adult education.

Now more than 10 years since the peace agreement has been signed the level of violence has subsided, but conflict remains in many local areas through tensions over territory and cultural issues such as parades. There have been challenges in terms of demilitarization through a reduction in the number of soldiers and visible security, as well as the reintegration of former combatants into civil society. There are new political structures and power-sharing arrangements and the accompanying challenge of educating people about how these operate and what it means to be a citizen within these new arrangements. There is a real shift in power relations within the society and the need for public education that promotes equality, non-discrimination and respect for differences in order to support and consolidate these changing power relationships. There are numerous victims and survivors of the conflict, many of whom still seek truth about past events or struggle with the legacies of the conflict and need recognition and support. A new generation of children has been born since the signing of the peace agreement and we no longer have any children in our primary schools with direct experience or memory of the conflict. In addition, we are approaching the point where no newly trained teachers have any experience of the conflict either – this raises questions about how we, the Northern Irish, explain our recent past to successive generations and how we remember, commemorate or acknowledge the past. We could leave this to happen by chance, through families, communities and the media or we can ask whether education also has a role to play.

There is no formal Truth and Reconciliation Commission (TRC) in Northern Ireland, but a Consultative Group on the Past (2009) was established to make recommendations on how we acknowledge and deal with the past. It recommended that education programmes be developed 'which inform young people, in a balanced way, about the nature and impact of the conflict', but provided little insight into what this might mean in practice. One research study (Magill, Smith and Hamber, 2009) that explored this was funded by the EU Peace and Reconciliation Programme. It involved interviews with 91 children and young people aged 11, 16 to 18 and 24 to 25 years in Northern Ireland and Bosnia and Herzegovina (BiH) between 2007 and May 2009. The aim was to explore, in a comparative way, children and young people's experience of conflict in their region (the Troubles in Northern Ireland and the 1992–1995 war in BiH); their awareness and understanding of the conflict and where this awareness came from; their concepts of reconciliation and views on the role of education in reconciliation. The findings (Smith and Magill, 2009) include recommendations that formal education might include areas within the curriculum that deal with the past and future challenges for the society. However, this gives rise to a series of extremely challenging questions for educators including:

- The need to clarify why such work should be included in the curriculum (is it to seek truth, to understand conflict – what are the key reasons?)
- How the task can be developed in a way that secures the support of parents and wider society. How is 'legitimacy' and 'permission' secured?
- Epistemological questions. Is truth 'objective', 'subjective', 'relative' or 'inter-subjective' – what position should educators take?
- Conceptual issues. There are many complex and contested concepts associated with educational enquiry in this area (truth, justice, amnesty, reparations, forgiveness, etc.). How can these be interrogated, clarified?
- Where does this work sit within the current curriculum? Is it part of history, social studies, peace, human rights or citizenship education?
- What is the appropriate age and stage to introduce such content to children and young people? Should content be spread across several levels of schooling or addressed at a specific level?
- What skills do children need to learn to interpret evidence or assess the authenticity and credibility of multiple versions of the past (pedagogy, methodologies, etc.)?

- Are there gender differences in the way that young men and women relate to the past? What education environment do they need to learn about these issues (shared, separate, etc.)?
- Resources. What texts, artefacts, people, sites, multiple perspectives and resources of civil society are acceptable and most useful?
- What approach should be adopted by schools in relation to memorialization, remembrance and commemoration?
- What opportunities exist to promote intergenerational learning?
- What steps need to be taken to consult, engage and be sensitive to concerns of victims and survivors when developing curriculum?
- What ethical and child protection issues (such as confidentiality, disclosure and psychosocial support) have to be considered?
- How can teachers (who have their own loyalties or may have been part of the conflict) receive intensive training and support? What form of training is most appropriate?

These questions are only just emerging in Northern Ireland and they raise a difficult challenge for educators within post-conflict societies. The complexity of addressing such questions may be sufficient deterrent for schools to avoid the challenge altogether and they make it difficult to secure political or institutional support. A common attitude among many people of all ages in Northern Ireland is to forget the past and look to the future. However, it should be possible to build on the earlier curriculum development work of programmes such as Education for Mutual Understanding that have evolved as the conflict itself has transformed. Internationally there are initiatives by organizations such as the UNICEF Innocenti Centre and the International Centre for Transitional Justice who have developed a series of papers to consider the implications of transitional justice processes for children, but there is limited experience to build upon. There are some examples of TRCs that have involved children and made recommendations for education, such as Sierra Leone (Paulson, 2006), but follow-up implementation is very weak. In other cases, such as Peru (Paulson, 2010), there have been initiatives to introduce school texts that have been thwarted by political changes. Perhaps the most successful example is post World War II reconciliation in Europe, but again insight into the role played by education in this transition is scarce.

In the case of Northern Ireland there is a strong foundation based on engagement with issues of conflict and identity. This means there is no need to create a new platform, but to build on what has gone before. From the earliest days of the conflict a range of education initiatives emerged, somewhat independently and exploring the potential of new types of schools, inter-group contact and curriculum change to promote reconciliation. Much of the early work on education for mutual understanding could be characterized as a form of intercultural learning, but as the conflict evolved and transformed, the emphasis has also changed. In the 10 years following the peace agreement there has been much more attention given to the concept of citizenship and what it means to be a citizen within a divided society that has different national and political loyalties. Many of the challenges are less about mutual understanding and more about equality and the application of human rights for all citizens irrespective of identity factors such as language, culture, religion and politics.

The new citizenship curriculum provides an obvious entry point to now begin to address issues about the past and legacies of conflict. Resources are being developed, although it is clear that teachers will require considerable professional development if they are to be used sensitively. Of particular significance is the potential for the new citizenship education programme to play an important role in the development of greater 'political literacy' among new generations. This is especially important in the context of Northern Ireland since the peace agreement in 1998 transformed the conflict (from use of violence to use of politics), but only by deferring the question about the political status of the territory (whether it is part of the UK or Ireland). This question will still confront future generations. For example, the next iconic date in Irish history is likely to be 2016, the hundred year anniversary of the Easter Rising that eventually led to Irish independence. It will also be two decades since the peace agreement that promised that the future constitutional status of the territory will be determined by the wish of the majority of the people who live there. While the peace agreement does not provide any details on how this would be determined in practice, it is not unreasonable to assume that future generations may face a referendum on this issue.

There are a number of dangers. One is that we are complacent that the reduction in violence means that the conflict has been 'resolved' and we neglect to educate new generations about the underlying political nature of the conflict. Another is that we fail to challenge the concept of citizenship based solely on ethnic (religious and cultural) identity. The implications of this are that the result of any future referendum will be based on ethnic voting, the outcome is likely to be very close and the result could carry the potential of justifying a return to violence whichever way the outcome goes. Unionists and loyalists could feel unprepared for a vote that would take them into a united Ireland; or nationalists will be disaffected and 'dissident' republicans could feel that they were right to oppose a peace agreement that has not led to a united Ireland through democratic politics. The potential for future generations from either community to be mobilized in support of a return to violence may be increased when voters have no direct memory of the consequences of violent conflict. However, a form of citizenship education that explores the implications of alternative constitutional arrangements could play an important preventative role in educating future generations about the benefits of democratic solutions, the dangers of ethnic politics and the polarizing effects of referenda based solely on dualistic questions.

It is difficult to be definitive about broader lessons learned about the role of education in peace building and reconciliation in a society that has experienced conflict for nearly 4 decades and is still in a process of political transformation. However, it is also worth highlighting the following points from the experience of Northern Ireland:

- Local efforts by parents, teachers and NGOs emerged during the conflict to meet local needs. In the initial stages many of these were emergency responses to difficult circumstances. As the conflict continued many initiatives could be perceived as creating a more favourable climate for peacemaking, and since the agreement the challenge has been how education might contribute towards future peace building. This is important because it shows that: (a) the post-conflict environment itself is not necessarily the starting point for educational initiatives for reconciliation; (b) there are very valuable resources and knowledge available locally that can be built upon by government and international donors; (c) these issues are important to people during, as well as after, conflict. Building on what is already there is extremely important for education and reconciliation initiatives.
- From a more international perspective there seems to be a key message that is consistent with the DAC principle to 'Act fast . . . but stay engaged long enough to give success a chance'. This is particularly the case in terms of the EU funding for peace and reconciliation in Northern Ireland. While the programme has had limitations in terms of generating a 'peace economy', it is an example of an international donor that has stayed engaged over a long period of time and successively re-evaluated priorities and funding mechanisms to meet the changing dynamics of the conflict itself. Perhaps most importantly, there continues to be an engagement and funding commitment for a 15-year period after the peace agreement, which acknowledges that this simply marked a transition to a period of sustained post-conflict peace building during which difficult questions of political stability and reconciliation still need to be addressed.

These developments have taken at least a generation since the height of the conflict. This suggests that there is yet much work to be done in securing agreement that education has a role to play in dealing with the past and contributing to future reconciliation, and even more to be learned about what this means in practice.

Guiding questions

Is there space for education to play a greater role in peace agreements and other conflict resolution processes?

What have been the main challenges to integrated schools in Northern Ireland?

What opportunities and challenges for curriculum are raised by the resolution of the conflict in Northern Ireland?

Reference list

BBC News (2000), 'Prison officers leave the maze', 29 September, http://news.bbc.co.uk/1/hi/northern_ireland/948161.stm (accessed 10 August 2010).

Consultative Group on the Past (2009), *Report of the Consultative Group of the Past*. Belfast: Consultative Group on the Past.

Cormack, R., A. M. Gallagher, and R. Osborne (1991), 'Religious affiliation and educational attainment in Northern Ireland: The financing of schools in Northern Ireland', in *Sixteenth Report of the Standing Advisory Commission on Human Rights, Report for 1990–1991, Annex E*. London: HMSO.

—(1992), 'Access to grammar schools', in *Seventeenth Report of the Standing Advisory Commission on Human Rights, Annex E*. London: HMSO.

Department of Education for Northern Ireland (1998), *Towards a Culture of Tolerance: Integrating Education*. Bangor, County Down, UK: Department of Education.

— (1999), *Towards a Culture of Tolerance: Education for Diversity*. Bangor, County Down, UK: Department of Education.

Fay, M. T., M. Morrisey and M. Smyth (1999), *Northern Ireland's Troubles: The Human Costs*. London: Pluto Press.

Gallagher, A. M., R. Osborne, and R. Cormack (1993), 'Community Relations, Equality and Education', in A. M. Gallagher, R. Osborne and R. Cormack (eds), *After the Reforms: Education and Policy in Northern Ireland*. Aldershot, UK: Avebury.

Hamber, B., and G. Kelly (2004), *A Working Definition of Reconciliation*. Occasional paper published by Democratic Dialogue, Belfast.

Magill, C., A. Smith, and B. Hamber (2009), *The Role of Education in Reconciliation*. Report for EU Peace and Reconciliation Fund. Coleraine, UK: University of Ulster.

Murray, D. (1992), 'Science and funding in Northern Ireland grammar schools: A case study approach', in *Seventeenth Report of the Standing Advisory Commission on Human Rights, Annex G*. London: HMSO.

Northern Ireland Curriculum (2006), *Statutory Requirements for Local and Global Citizenship*, www.nicurriculum.org.uk/docs/key_stage_3/areas_of_learning/statutory_requirements/ks3_citizenship.pdf (accessed 8 August 2010).

Northern Ireland Life and Times Survey, University of Ulster and Queens University Belfast, www.ark.ac.uk/nilt/ (accessed 8 August 2010).

Northern Ireland Office (1998), *The Agreement*, Belfast: NIO, http://cain.ulst.ac.uk/events/peace/docs/agreement.htm (accessed 8 August 2010).

O'Connor, U. (2008), *Evaluation of the Pilot Introduction of Education for Local and Global Citizenship into the Revised Northern Ireland Curriculum*, Coleraine, UK: University of Ulster. http://unesco.ulster.ac.uk/PDFs/summaryreport.pdf (accessed 6 August 2010).

OCED-DAC (2007), *Principles for Good International Engagement in Fragile States and Situations*, www.oecd.org/dataoecd/61/45/38368714.pdf (accessed 8 August 2010).

Osborne, R. D. (1986), 'Segregated schools and examination results in Northern Ireland', *Educational Research*, 28, 1, 43–50.

Osborne, R. D., Cormack, R. J. and Miller, R. L. (eds) (1987), Education and Policy in Northern Ireland. Belfast: Policy Research Institute.

Paulson, J. (2006), 'The educational recommendations of Truth and Reconciliation Commissions: Potential and practice in Sierra Leone', *Research in Comparative and International Education*, 1, 4, 335–50.

— (2010), 'Truth commissions and national curriculum: The case of the *Recordándonos* in Peru', in S. Parmar, M. J. Roseman, S. Siegrist and T. Sowa (eds), *Children and Transitional Justice: Truth-Telling, Accountability and Reconciliation*. Cambridge, MA: Harvard University Press.

Smith, A. (2001), 'Religious segregation and the emergence of integrated schools in Northern Ireland', *Oxford Review of Education*, 27, 4, 559–75.

— (2003), 'Citizenship education in Northern Ireland', *Cambridge Journal of Education*, 33, 1, 15–31.

Smith, A. and Dunn, S. (1990), *Extending Inter School Links: An Evaluation of Contact between Protestant and Catholic Pupils in Northern Ireland*. Coleraine, UK: University of Ulster Centre for the Study of Conflict.

Smith, A., and C. Magill (2009), 'Reconciliation: Does education have a role?' *Shared Space: A Research Journal on Peace, Conflict and Community Relations*, 8, 1, 5–15.

Smith, A., and A. Robinson (1992), *Education for Mutual Understanding: Perceptions and Policy*. Coleraine, UK: University of Ulster Centre for the Study of Conflict.

— (1996), *Education for Mutual Understanding, The Statutory Years*. Coleraine: University of Ulster Centre for the Study of Conflict.

Smyth, M., and Scott, M. (2000), The Youth Quest 2000 Survey. Londonderry: INCORE.

Special EU Programmes Body (2007), *Peace III. EU Programme for Peace and Reconciliation 2007–2013. Northern Ireland and the Border Region of Ireland Operational Programme*. Belfast: European Union.

Standing Advisory Commission on Human Rights (1987, 1989, 1990, 1991, 1992), *Annual Reports*. London: HMSO.

UNICEF Innocenti Research Centre (2010), *Children and Transitional Justice*. http://www.unicef-irc.org/research/207/ (accessed 8 August 2010).

Woodrow, P. 'Strategic Analysis for Peacebuilding Programs', cited by Church, C. and Rogers, M. (2005), *Designing for Results: Integrated Monitoring and Evaluation in Conflict Transformation Programs*. Washington, D.C.: Search for Common Ground.

4

Understanding Responses to Postwar Education Reform in the Multiethnic District of Brčko, Bosnia-Herzegovina

Briony Jones

Chapter Outline

Introduction

Literature on reconciliation and education often highlights the importance of contact time between students from different ethnic/racial/religious/cultural backgrounds, drawing on the contact hypothesis, which claims that increased contact will improve social relationships and promote peaceful behaviour. This is a logic that assumes that integration of conflicting or previously conflicting groups will be followed by reconciliation:

> The promotion of mutual understanding and respect for diversity through contact, alongside the empowerment of the minority Arab community language and culture are seen as the central mechanisms for achieving the coexistence values that the [bilingual/bi-national] schools promote [in Israel]. (Hughes, 2007, 421)

The assertion of a link between integration and reconciliation is supported by scholarship which suggests that integrated schooling can lead to equal status of traditions in schools, the development of mutual understanding (Salters and McEwan, 1993), the rebuilding of social capital and fostering of social cohesion (McGlynn, 2004), and minority empowerment (Hertz-Lazarowitz et al., 2008). However, other work cautions against simplistic links between the 'input' of integration and the 'output' of reconciled societies. In fact, the transmission of such policies into practice does not happen in a social vacuum free of agents and their negotiation of practice. In an analysis of integrated schooling in Northern Ireland and Israel, Donnelly and Hughes (2009) find that existing social and cultural norms can interact with policy to influence the process and outcome of contact. Integration can also be complicated by strategies teachers employ to avoid sensitive and difficult topics in the classroom (Bekerman, 2009; McGlynn, 2004), and the influence of context in terms of community attitudes and political discourse (Bekerman, 2009; Salters and McEwan, 1993). Hart, in this volume, highlights structural factors outside the classroom that impact upon, and may be more important than, education initiatives designed to foster reconciliation. Accordingly, reconciliation efforts should be seen as located in political-economic as well as cultural contexts, and pay attention to the localized experiences, perceptions and agency of children and young people.

Research thus illustrates that integration cannot be separated from wider social and political processes, and that the space of the integrated classroom is not distinct from the contexts in which students and teachers are embedded. Given this, it is problematic to assume that integration will be uniformly understood and accepted by students, teachers or the wider community, or that it will necessarily lead to reconciliation in post-conflict societies. This central question of how policies of integrated schooling interact with context and agency will be explored in this chapter through the case study of Brčko District, Bosnia-Herzegovina. In particular, the focus will be on protests by secondary school students at the time of ethno-national integration of their schools. These protests were dismissed by District Government officials and international observers as the result of manipulation by ethno-national political forces. However, looking more closely at the narratives of students who did and did not take part, it is possible to see that the protests were more than ethno-nationally motivated; they were expressions of voice in a rapidly changing social and political space, and marked a moment of contestation over the terms of membership and association in that space. It is this contestation that can illuminate more about the process of education reform and its meanings for reconciliation than a simplistic lens of ethno-national mixing versus ethno-national separation.

The Brčko District context

Brčko District 'is always an exception to politics as usual in BiH [Bosnia-Herzegovina]'. (Perry, 2003, 76). Following the 1992–1995 war, the Dayton Peace Accords (DPA) divided BiH into two ethno-national entities of the Federation of Bosnia and Herzegovina (FBiH) and the Serb Republic (RS). This established a consociational democracy based on tripartite power sharing between the three main ethno-national groups of Bosniak, Bosnian-Croat and Bosnian-Serb, with external supervision by the Office of the High Representative (OHR), an ad hoc international institution charged with overseeing the civilian aspects of the peace process and nominated by the Peace Implementation Council. Political deadlock, ethno-national veto, and constitutional crises have been hampering this state-building project ever since (International Crisis Group (ICG), 2007, 9). Brčko District, in contrast, is a unitary district established by a 'Final Award' in 1999. In a strategic position near the international borders with Serbia and Croatia, and dividing the RS and FBiH (Cigar and Williams, 1998), debate over Brčko District nearly derailed the whole peace process. It is now held in condominium by both entities (FBiH and RS) but answerable to neither. It has its own international supervisor, higher levels of economic recovery than the rest of BiH (Bieber, 2005, 430–31), and an ethno-nationally integrated political assembly, judiciary, police force and school system. High rates of return to the region have led to an ethno-national mix similar to pre-1992 (Bieber, 2006, 134) and Brčko District is seen by the OHR as an example for the rest of BiH:

> This city, which was once well-known as a 'black hole', is steadily becoming a model for the whole of BiH. When the rest of the country accomplishes what has been accomplished here, BiH will be a much more developed country. (Former High Representative Paddy Ashdown, cited in ICG, 2003, 1)

Brčko District has been seen by some as a microcosm of the international community's task in BiH, dominated as it is by different ethno-national groups in different areas. With a mixed population before the war, the District was cleansed of Bosniak and Bosnian-Croat residents by Bosnian-Serb forces from 1992. Brčko Town became almost entirely Bosnian-Serb, with newcomer Bosnian-Serb residents moving in from elsewhere in BiH, while the rural parts of the District were home to Bosnian-Croat and Bosniak residents and displaced people. The 1999 decision on Brčko District reflects multiethnic aspirations as it makes provisions for each resident to choose allegiance to either of the entities (FBiH or RS) through their electoral registration, equal status of the Latin and Cyrillic alphabets and the neutrality of symbols such as flags. Significantly, for this discussion, it also established multiethnic institutions such as the police, judiciary and schools. Education reform, as will be elaborated in more detail below, was underpinned by an assumption that ethno-nationally mixed student and staff bodies would contribute to reconciliation and the establishment of a peaceful coexistence within the District. Education reform is a central part of the Brčko District reconciliation success story, a narrative which describes the District as a multiethnic oasis capable of driving a stake through the 'heart of the ethno-political vampire of BiH' (Mujkić, paraphrased from the original Bosnian, 2008, 1) and as a 'third space' that might exceed the oppositional binaries that define postwar societies (Dahlman and O Tuathail, 2006, 655).

Research methodology in Brčko District

The empirical work on which this chapter is based was undertaken over 6 months in 2007 and 2008. In line with an interpretivist epistemology, qualitative methods were used, primarily narrative and semi-structured interviewing. In addition to these main methods, and in response to the fluid nature of 'the field', some focus groups were conducted and participant observation undertaken where possible. An employed interpreter was present at the majority of interviews, which means that most of the quotes used here have been translated from their original Bosnian/Serbian/Croatian and are thus a representation of what was said, rather than an exact replication of language and expression. Ethical guidelines were followed according to the guidelines of the Economic and Social Research Council. Respondents' quotes have been anonymized, identified only by key indicators relevant for the fieldwork context, which are used consistently across respondents. My analysis of respondents' quotes was influenced by the presence of the interpreter and my experiences in and of 'the field', but the opinions stated are my own and do not represent those of anyone else who took part in the fieldwork.

Education, reconciliation and the logic of integration in Brčko District

According to Hromadžić (2008), the current education system in BiH reflects the consequences of the destruction of the war, the paradoxes of the DPA, and the weakness of the BiH constitution. After 1995 and the establishment of consociational democracy, education in BiH has been decentralized leading to the establishment of thirteen education policy making authorities: the government of the RS; the government of FBiH; the ten cantons within FBiH and Brčko District. This has made the system difficult to coordinate at the state level (Smith and Vaux, 2002, 24) and vulnerable to ethno-national capture by leaders who in many cases see education as a means of promoting ideologies linked to politico-cultural identities (Stabback, 2004, 44).

Currently, there is no state-wide curriculum, but a core of subjects whose teaching has been agreed upon by each entity, as well as a set of 'national subjects' that are taught according to the territory where the school is based and the ethno-national identity of the student body. These national subjects: history, literature, geography, religion, language, art and music, have been controversial in the postwar period and form part of multiple projects of ethno-national citizenship (Perry, 2003, 33). Content of curricula in national subjects has been used to promote the culture of one particular ethno-national group and to support particular versions of history (Fischer, 2006, 300). While education has become a sphere in which ethno-nationalist forces oppose reform to ensure the protection and transfer of certain cultural and religious principles across generations, it has also been seen by international players as one of the layers of reform underpinning the transition of BiH towards peace, democracy and market economics. This standardization of education-for-reconciliation interventions is also critiqued by Hart in this volume, demonstrating how standardized approaches replace localized moral frameworks and can ignore the relevance of meaning constructed by children themselves.

It is because of this desire to create replicable frameworks for education reform that the integrated schools system of Brčko District is viewed as a model for the rest of BiH in terms of promoting reconciliation between ethnic groups through its ethnically mixed student and staff bodies. As stated in the Final Award which established Brčko District in 1999:

> . . . the Supervisor [of Brčko District] will integrate the District's educational system, harmonize curricula within the District, and ensure the removal of teaching material which the Supervisor considers to be inconsistent

> with the objective of creating a democratic, multi-ethnic society within the
> District. (Annex to Brčko District Final Award, 18 August 1999, point 11)

During the 1992–1995 war, Brčko District had been split into three parts each using its own education curriculum (OSCE, 2007, 6). The establishment of Brčko District in 1999, however, changed the political and financial context, making reform possible. The elimination of segregated education became a key issue for the OHR and the District Supervisor in improving relationships between the three main ethno-national groups and promoting development in the District.

In July 1999 the Brčko District Supervisor established an education department within his office, intent on pursuing reform in education (Perry, 2003). However, the new education law proposed by the Supervisor was unable to gain a majority in the District Assembly, due to opposition from the Serb Democratic Party (SDS)[1] and the Serb Orthodox Church (ICG, 2003). It only became law after intervention from the District Supervisor who used his powers to impose the Single Law on Education and Harmonised Curriculum on 5 July 2001 (Perry, 2003, 78). This law provided a strict framework for integrated schooling including specific provisions for language[2] (OSCE, 2007, 7), increased contact time between students from different ethno-national groups (Perry, 2003, 80), including in some national subject lessons (OSCE, 2007, 15), and created a new subject lesson of Democracy and Human Rights (ibid., 16).

As previously stated, education reform in Brčko District has been seen by key international agencies working in BiH as model for education reform in the country more broadly:

> In order to maintain the status quo, some in society even suggest that the
> 'integration' of schools . . . is another term for 'assimilation'. The District of
> Brčko belies this argument. There, students of different ethnicities go to
> school together, receive instruction in their own languages in the same
> classroom, and retain their individual cultural identities . . . The evidence
> suggests that, with sufficient political will, it can [serve as a model for the
> rest of BiH]. (OSCE, 2007, 5)

This is a model based on the logic of the contact hypothesis discussed in the introduction:

> . . . the goal should be to maximize the time students spend in a classroom
> together so that tolerance can be learned through the simple process of
> going to school [in BiH]. (Perry, 2003, 37)

Ethno-national integration of the secondary schools in Brčko District is particularly interesting. In 2000–2001 the mainly Bosniak school system operating in the rural parts of the District started to be integrated with the mainly Bosnian-Serb school system operating in Brčko town. This happened in two distinct phases for secondary schools. In the first phase there was a two-shift system whereby the pupils from the two ethno-national school systems would use the same school buildings in Brčko Town but at different times. Students were brought by bus into the town according to a carefully regimented schedule so that there was a limited and controlled time during which the two student bodies were able to interact. The second phase of integration occurred through the ethno-national mixing of classes and teaching staff, except in the 'national subjects' such as language, on a year-by-year basis until all years were mixed in 2006. At the time of the two-shift system (2000) demonstrations were held by Bosniak students for 1 day, which were followed by demonstrations by the Bosnian-Serb students, which lasted for approximately 3 days. Protests were followed by a previously unplanned period of approximately 1 month when the schools were closed before the second phase of integration began.

Education reform in Brčko District is now seen as a success. A survey of five hundred respondents from Brčko District and two thousand across BiH, conducted in 2004 and published by OSCE in 2007, shows that respondents from Brčko District were generally in favour of choice regarding language in which to be taught, choice of language in which to express oneself and the joint teaching of history. In comparison with the rest of BiH, respondents from Brčko District were less in favour of students attending schools or universities where one language is used exclusively and the teaching of history is done separately. According to statistics, again published by the OSCE, secondary schools in Brčko District in the school year 2006–2007 were mixed between the three main ethno-national groups in numbers roughly equivalent to the population numbers (2007, 13). These excerpts from interviews illustrate the success narrative:

> Our motto is that every student should be proud of where he comes from, of his religion and so on, but when he enters the school he becomes a student and they all have the same rights. (Interview, Bosniak, Male, Unknown Residential Status, Head Teacher, Brčko District, 14 March 2008)

> This integration process has been completed successfully and today we have quite a high level of tolerance among the students and it generally functions as it should. (Interview, Bosniak, Male, Returnee, Teacher, Brčko District, 25 March 2008).

The integrated classroom is seen as a 'neutral' space in terms of ethno-national identity, and the right of every student to access it is seen as fundamental to the ethos of integration. Its success is premised on the current ethno-national mixing which is seen as accomplished. Education reform in Brčko District was about reaching this endpoint: a modern successful education system with a multi-ethnic student body representative of the wider integration and reconciliation in Brčko District.

It is easy to look at Brčko District and to see integration as a 'job well done'. This is the approach taken by many commentators and officials interviewed in the course of my research, and can explain their approach to Brčko District as a model. In Brčko District schools are integrated and classes mixed to a greater extent than anywhere else in BiH. However, the success narrative minimizes, and in some cases even erases, the actions of people who are actually in and part of the reform process. Moreover, the measures taken in the model prioritize ethno-national identities and the relationships between people of different ethno-national backgrounds as indicators of the quality of the relationships between people. Interviews with former students and teachers challenge this focus on success and ethno-national identity as the basis for integration and reconciliation. They highlight the importance of wider social and political changes that informed the actions of the student protesters, who are agents in their own right, contesting and negotiating the terms of social and political membership.

Narratives of protest and re-thinking integration

Official accounts of the protests, of which there are few, dismiss them as the result of ethno-national manipulation by politicians, as this report by the OSCE demonstrates:

> Although this [Final Award] gave the Supervisor a clear and robust mandate to reform education in the District, it was not until after student riots in 2000 that multi-ethnic or 'integrated' education became a more immediate concern. In these riots secondary school students had protested against the introduction of such multi-ethnic schooling. It was widely suspected that politicians had orchestrated this protest and that it was only nominally about education. The riots took place just 15 days before municipal elections in the rest of the country. (2007, 7)

Here, the 'riots' are constructed as acts of deviancy interrupting the pace and structure of education reform. Ethno-nationalist politicians did protest in response to multiethnic education reform, and in October 2001 when the second phase of integration was underway, SDS politicians staged a boycott of the District Assembly (Jeffrey, 2006, 217). However, explaining the protests exclusively with reference to ethno-nationalist political agitation essentially writes out the accounts of the students who participated. Their motivations, actions and responses are absent from such accounts, which reduce the protests and protesters to a stage of reform. They are, at best, a problem that required an institutional solution through an imposed education law. The association of the protests with political views considered non-legitimate denies the possibility that they could be linked to other concerns that might be viewed as more legitimate. A focus on the experience of the protests by the protesters themselves is needed. As my interpreter put it:

> Still at that time, many people protested to us being in the same building, same city. [The official who was interviewed] skipped that part but I am part of that generation, I cannot skip that part. (Interview, Bosniak, Male, Returnee, Teacher and Interpreter, Former Student, Brčko District, 3 July 2007)

The presence of ethno-nationalism

The official narratives of the 2001 protests are missing both student voice and an interrogation of motivation. Because they explain the protests as ethno-national manipulation of an impressionable student body, details of the protests themselves are absent. Importantly, they do not mention the two stages of protest, one undertaken by the Bosniak students and one by the Bosnian-Serb students. The dynamic between the two protest groups is a feature of the student narratives and is used to explain the protests in a relational sense, to understand them as part of an active–reactive exchange. One Bosniak former student explains the buildup to the protests as he understood it:

> There was a lot of fear and we were pretty scared calling each other by our names so that someone might recognize that we are Bosniaks . . . The incident that caused the demonstration in general was the fact that two of our friends were beaten up by a boy and his sister, they were beaten up by a group of Serb students and that happened on a Friday and as a result we protested. And then after that for several days came the Serb protests where all Bosniak shops, houses, stores, where Bosniaks had already

returned by then were completely devastated by protesters. (Interview, Bosniak, Male, Teacher, Brčko District, 25 March 2008)

A Bosnian-Serb former student also notes the two stages of protest and perceives the action by Bosnian-Serb students as a response to the unreasonable behaviour of the Bosniak students during their protest:

> First the day before we came out on the streets Bosniaks came out from the technical school near OHR, and they demonstrated by going to the Catholic Church through the whole town and in the end they burnt a Serbian flag and that probably made many people angry. Serbs, all kids from all Serbs, came out onto the streets and they started demonstrating against integrated schools. (Interview, Bosnian-Serb, Male, Newcomer, Student, Brčko District, 26 March 2008)

In the official narratives the rationale for downplaying the importance of the protests is their link to agitation by Bosnian-Serb ethno-nationalist politicians who are opposed to the establishment of the District and to multiethnic reform. The students' accounts cited above contradict this as they identify that it was the Bosniak students who protested first, prompting a response by Bosnian-Serb students. The dynamic of the protest response described here places the protests in relation to each other so they can be compared, explained and potentially justified. For the Bosniak students, the Bosnian-Serb protest that followed their own was seen to be an extreme response to their own legitimate protest over concerns of actual violence that had taken place. For the Bosnian-Serb students, their protest was retaliation to the inflammatory actions of the Bosniak protesters.

In official accounts of the protests that explain them as ethno-national manipulation, the implication is that if it were not for the agitating of ethno-nationalist politicians, then there would have been no protests by the students. However, many of the former student respondents were keen to point out in their accounts the spontaneous and organic nature of *their* protest:

> The general issue that we wanted to address is the safety. We didn't feel safe at all, even the fact that our way to school and back home was done by bus . . . So we felt pressured by the whole situation, so going to school like a herd and then leaving school again like a herd . . . So there was no freedom at all, so we addressed this issue and after these two friends of ours have been beaten up we decided something has to be done. We have to be able to move freely around the city, to move freely from school and

so on. (Interview, Bosniak, Male, Returnee, Teacher, Former Student, Brčko District, 25 March 2008)

Claiming an active role for students and affirming their initiative was common in the student narratives, and important for explaining how the protests began and gained momentum:

> The protest itself wasn't something that was planned. We actually gathered in front of the school and then we heard what happened [two fellow students were beaten up] and we started gathering and decided to protest to draw the attention of the authorities . . . The authorities did not really notice the protests until they were happening, nobody was aware there were going to be protests, they just reacted when they saw a crowd of people walking down the city . . . nobody planned it. (Interview, Bosniak, Male, Returnee, Student, Brčko District, 23 March 2008)

> Those pupils from technical school came to grammar school and let's say they called us out, but the Director locked the school so we couldn't go out, but most of the students went out of the window and after that the doors were unlocked when almost no-one was left in school. So when all students were in one big crowd we started. (Interview, Bosnian-Serb, Male, Newcomer, Student, Brčko District, 26 March 2008)

However, it is also too simplistic to suggest from these accounts that the students were not aware of and reacting to wider concerns and pressures regarding ethno-nationalism:

> . . . some people might be pushed into this by their parents and adults since students are the mass that you can easily manipulate. Some people might have complaints because there are other nationalities coming to the school. (Interview, Bosnian-Serb, Male, Stayee, Media Employee, Brčko District, 29 March 2008)

> . . . it was very hard for each child to accept [integration] because many of their friends had lost someone in the war, they saw their enemies in those other kids and that's why those demonstrations started. (Interview, Bosnian-Serb, Male, Newcomer, Student, Brčko District, 26 March 2008)

However, the importance and influence of ethno-nationalism is less direct than suggested in the official narratives. The students can be seen as agents of protest in their own right and concerns over the ethno-national integration of the secondary schools interacted with the broader social and political context of which they were aware. Bekerman (2009) found that experiences of integrated schooling in Israel are influenced not only by the relationships formed at the local level, but also the immediate and distant context in which the space of the school and classroom is embedded. This is clear to see in Brčko District where rapid social and political changes formed the context in which integration was supposed to take place, a theme that is dealt with more fully in the following two sections.

Integration and international supervision

One explanation for the disjuncture between official and elite accounts of the protests and student accounts is that the protests were part of an expression of responses to postwar changes and a desire for agency. For all of the students I spoke to, the question of their ability to control the changing contexts in which they accessed their education was significant. In particular many felt alienated from the integration process and wanted to express their specific concerns that centred on timing, security and integration itself:

> That's the idea of Brčko District, complete integration. These are ideas I completely agree with, but it went too fast. One day you're told okay, you're going to go to Brčko, we didn't even feel comfortable being there. We started to protest against being pushed around. We walked round the town as a large group of people, about three thousand students, who are going through a city where you have ten Muslim families max. (Interview, Bosniak, Male, Returnee, Teacher, Brčko District, 3 July 2007b)

This quote is important as it illustrates that this former student was not opposed to integration as an ideal, but was protesting against the pace of integration and the social context in which it was taking place. He felt integration would be more difficult in a situation of high tension and that integration of the schools was problematic if it preceded integration of society more broadly. A student who participated in the Bosnian-Serb protest expressed a similar view and suggested that it was the disruptive nature of a fast-paced integration that motivated him to express anger through protest:

> Any integration cannot be done very fast and each integration makes lots of changes and for some people who are stuck in one system it's a big

> change for them and that's how I and my generation felt at that time. (Interview, Bosnian-Serb, Male, Stayee, Media Employee, Brčko District, 29 March 2008)

These quotes illustrate that the pace and timing of reform was a significant problem for the students, and that they felt disempowered by it. Opposition to reform was therefore motivated by the timing and process of reform as much as it was by the ultimate goal of the reform itself.

A sense of collective motivation and comradeship is also present in the student narratives, suggesting a shared moment of agency. This was both empowering and substantive, a desire to be heard as social and political changes occurred largely without students' consultation. An observer of the Bosnian-Serb protest said that:

> I think that was pretty shocking for let's say grown-ups because, even though maybe the cause was not right, finally students agreed about protesting about something . . . and that was maybe an issue for institutions in the town like for the school or police. (Interview, Bosnian-Croat, Female, Stayee, NGO Employee Brčko District, 13 March 2008)

There was a strong sense in the interviews of the desire for expression, of the need to be heard as youth and students with a legitimate voice. This was felt within a context in which young people were not always able to define what the 'right' causes were. As students they were told that they had to start going to school in an environment and under conditions not of their choosing, and were halted in their protests, which were dismissed as anti-integration. The momentum of reform was controlled by institutions of the international community and the District Government under the master narrative of needing to 'solve' the 'problem' of segregated education in order to achieve the end point and closure of reconciliation. This seemed to take away from the students any sense of being able to question the process itself in light of other concerns; life in Brčko District and multiethnic education came as a package. This resonates with Hart's findings in this volume that young people themselves are often seen as less important stakeholders in education aimed at reconciliation. This can have a detrimental effect on the success of initiatives, and in the case of Brčko District, the lack of awareness by those controlling education reform of the complex subject positions and perceptions of secondary school pupils was a contributing factor to the protests.

By linking the very existence of the District with multiethnic reform, and disregarding the views of citizens of Brčko District who needed to be 'educated' in the ways of coexistence, there was no room allowed for delay or compromise over integration. This was a dynamic that the students had identified:

> They [the OHR] closed school for three weeks, a reaction, and basically for the first two or three days of demonstration they just left it. They were very quiet about it but after they said you do whatever you want, multi-ethnic school will happen and that was it. (Interview, Bosnian-Serb, Female, Returnee, INGO Employee, Brčko District, 15 March 2008)

Although agency and voice were an important part of the student narratives, some also expressed a sense of ultimate powerlessness in the face of reform and external intervention:

> . . . everything that happens with integration people reject, and then they have to live with it because it is not possible to change anything . . . If someone from outside, some supervisor or something, wants to do that it will happen definitely. (Interview, Bosnian-Serb, Male, Stayee, Unemployed, Brčko District, 27 March 2008)

A school newspaper ran an article in December 1999, shortly before the protests, entitled 'Why are the Foreigners Sniffing Around our School?' In this student article, OSCE, OHR and the NATO-led Stabilisation Force in BiH (SFOR)[3] activities in the school are identified, including visits of delegations from the organizations mentioned, requests for the Universal Declaration of Human Rights to be understood by students and asking the students questions about multiethnicity. The response to such activities in this article[4] is strong:

> Frequent visits of 'democrats' and 'thoughtful people' from all over the world were probably just political acts motivated by completely different reasons and pursuing different aims. But we hope that the Gymnasium Vaso Pelagić can preserve its look, its program and all the ethnic character-istics in spite of hidden and invisible dangers . . . While I am writing this, some inspection group of foreigners is sniffing around my school, entering the classrooms and looking stealthily into our school books. (Stevanović, 1999)

These student opinions were dismissed by those spearheading the integration process as ethno-nationalist, and, once the integration was completed, it was claimed that students had reconciled to living and studying together; to being multiethnic. The narratives of former students do not discount the claim that the protests were a negative response to integration. Indeed, the excerpt from the school newspaper shows this negative sentiment clearly. However, contained within the students' narratives is a linking of the question of ethno-national integration with the pace and nature of the reform agenda. There is anger directed towards the school officials, the District Government and international observers as dominating agents in the process. The students themselves felt disenfranchised, and this was a factor in when and how they decided to protest. In this way the protests were as much about international supervision as they were about opposition to integration. There is a need to pay attention to this context in which education reform occurred, as this can inform a critical evaluation of its perceived positive (integration success) and negative (protests) effects. In a more general sense, this then furthers understanding of the nuanced, complicated and unpredictable processes through which education reform 'inputs' are transformed into reconciliation 'outputs'.

Change and contestation of social and political communities

It is important to acknowledge the coincidence of integration reform alongside already potentially destabilizing social and political changes, and how this impacted upon the timing and form of the protests. The immediate context of return to Brčko District was important in the student narratives. In general terms, for Bosniak students their attendance of the two-shift system in Brčko Town made them feel vulnerable as the population of the town was still primarily Bosnian-Serb. For the Bosnian-Serb students, there was resentment towards the returning Bosniak population and related concerns over housing and job security once returnees started to claim back their properties and look for employment. There was also an added dynamic of Bosnian-Serb residents who had come from elsewhere in BiH and settled in Brčko Town. These displacement and return dynamics formed a significant part of the context of integration and people's experiences of displacement and return affected their attitude to education reform:

> One of the problems that made the integration process even harder was the fact that not all the people lived in Brčko. At the time over 70 per cent of Bosniaks were living outside of Brčko in the property that was earlier called the Federation and almost the same number had not returned to

their previous homes, which means that the property was occupied by someone else. And you had also Serbs which were not from here but somewhere else, and this integration process had also to do with getting to know each other. (Interview, Bosniak, Female, Returnee, Head Teacher, Brčko District, 12 March 2008)

This coincidence of substantial social change at the time of integration made many students feel anxious about the effect it would have on their lives. This was expressed in the details of the actions during the protests:

People were crashing windows of the stores that were belonging to Bosniaks because at that time some of the people were coming back and opening their stores in the town . . . you know Bosniaks were coming back to the town, Croats were coming back to the town, so living together started in those times. (Interview, Bosnian-Croat, Female, Stayee, NGO Employee, Brčko District, 13 March 2008)

The fears about Bosniak and Bosnian-Croat return were fuelled by the actions of the Bosniak protests:

. . . we did chant some things like 'this is Bosnia, this is Brčko, we're from Brčko, we have the right to be here' and so on 'we want to live where we're born' and stuff like that. (Interview, Bosniak, Male, Returnee, Student, Brčko District, 23 March 2008)

Bosniak students were expressing a complex position. They wanted ultimately to return to Brčko Town but, at the same time, were angry about the hostile 'welcome' from town residents and being forced to integrate into the school system before their place in the town more generally had been secured. It was the Bosniak students who had started the protests even though they were the students who were being 'returned' to Brčko Town. For them, their lack of security was a symptom of other problems related to their current minority and displaced persons status. Their protest was an expression of a right to be in that town; to reclaim their part of that space politically, economically and socially. This was a threat to the town population:

The problem here is that Brčko, the centre of the town, was basically full of Serbs who moved into the town from different areas and they were living in the flats which were not theirs. So what happens if the Muslims return to the town? It will mean they also have to leave the flats and apartments, which means that . . . they are maybe losing their homes . . . so now the tide was changing and people were starting to return to their homes and that means also they took all the jobs which were available at that time in Brčko. And if people return to Brčko, to their home, they have also the right to work here which also means some of the others will lose their job. (Interview, Bosnian-Serb, Male, Stayee, Unemployed, Brčko District, 15 March 2008)

Teachers, students and officials alike, were all aware that integration did not just mean integration of the secondary schools. The space of the integrated classroom cannot be seen as distinct from wider processes and contexts (Bekerman, 2009; Donnelly and Hughes, 2009). Integration was, as has been discussed above, part of a multiethnic reform package underpinning the very idea of Brčko District; it was related to return, the establishment of a multiethnic police force and judiciary and to the reclaiming of property originally owned by those who had been forcibly displaced during the war. Saying 'no' to multiethnic education was also informed by concerns related to job and housing insecurity, and many of the more ethno-nationalist impulses of the protests need to be viewed with this in mind. Just because integration was a multiethnic policy does not mean that anti-integration protests were purely an expression of opposition to multiethnicity.

Integration, education and reconciliation

This chapter began with an assertion that education reform in Brčko District did not happen in isolation, and that by exploring more closely the student protests one could better understand the complex dynamics shaping the relationships between people in this particular postwar society. Taking this focus shifts the angle of view from a narrative of reform aimed at both improving education and the relationships between ethno-national groups, to a site at which other more complex social and political relationships are expressed. It was also claimed that the idea of Brčko District as a 'model' and 'success' underpinned official narratives of integration that simplified explanations of the protests to manipulation by ethno-nationalist politicians. A split is presented in this narrative: on one side is the pre-integration system captured by ethno-nationalist elites who manipulated popular opinion, and on the other is the post-integration system where people embrace what they have really wanted all along. This implies a dichotomy between pre- and post-integration and passivity on the part of those who are supposed to reconcile. Such implications are challenged by empirical insights presented here. Students have been, and are, far from passive when it comes to integration, and their actions, when explored, can tell us about how they perceive their own position in society in relation to those around them.

The importance and expression of ethno-national identities changes according to the situation. At times of stress or tension individuals may feel they need to claim a particular ethno-national identity, while at other times they behave in a way which belies the primacy of said identity. Looking closely at the response by students in the form of protest illuminates a wider picture in which their perceived place in society is mediated by war experiences, displacement and return dynamics, the influence of family, their chosen friends and their own personal aspirations for educational achievement. These threads were woven together in the narratives of each respondent in a way that is meaningful to them. The timing and form of the student protests, as well as responses to them, were linked to multiple concerns regarding return dynamics, sustainable livelihoods and who 'belongs' in Brčko. Students do not fit into a 'multi-ethnic mould'. It cannot be assumed that action and behaviour relates only to ethno-national affiliation as this risks reinforcing the narrow social lens associated with conflict in the first place.

Even after the moments of protest and when officials, teachers and students from elsewhere are visiting Brčko District to learn from the model's success, it is clear that teachers and students are actively making choices every day about how they will respond to integration. Speaking to teachers working now in secondary schools it is clear to see what integration reform means to them on an everyday basis, and how in the space of the classroom they respond to the resulting changes. One teacher spoke of the 'big burden for people who are in this process, I have to be careful of which letter I have to write the very title of my lesson in' and the sensitivity of suggesting textbooks seen as connected to one ethno-national group or another. (Interview, Bosnian-Serb, Male, Newcomer, Teacher, Brčko District, 8 May 2008). McGlynn also found in Northern Ireland that teachers had varying degrees of commitment to an integration ethos (2004, 88) while Bekerman found that teachers in Israel had to find strategies for dealing with or avoiding difficult issues when in the classroom (2009, 239). The research on Brčko District that has been presented here, together with these other examples, complicates notions that contact through education necessarily equals reconciliation. Contestations and practice mediate any effect a policy 'input' might have in terms of social transformation.

The case of secondary school integration demonstrates that it is more pertinent to ask at what times, in what ways and for whom different forms of identity and belonging are important. It also highlights how, in this case, reconciliation was not an end point achieved with the 'success' of reform but is rather an ongoing process of contestation of the terms of political and social association that teachers and students are still grappling with. Work by Evans (2008) and Hart (in this volume) highlights the importance of seeing young people as agents making choices and expressing opinions, especially in situations of conflict or tension. In work on citizenship and conflict, Gibney (2006) suggests that violence may be employed when political routes for addressing the inequalities in question are blocked. In this case the students felt that their grievances could not be articulated through formal mechanisms, partly because they would be dismissed as ethno-nationalist agitation, and partly because of the pace of reform determined by external intervention. Their protests thus contained within them a broad social and political commentary that is important for understanding how education reform takes place in pre-existing spaces that may affect the ways in which it plays out in practice.

Reconciliation in Brčko District's schools is assumed to be achieved through integrating ethno-national groups in numbers representative of their populations. Little or no attention is paid to other aspects of social and political community, which are meaningful for the citizens of Brčko District. The protests around integrated education offered a space in which concerns outside of integration were expressed including, most importantly, insecurities over the return process. This suggests that contestation over the terms of association are vitally important for constructing a reconciliation that is meaningful for those who are supposed to reconcile, and for opening up the possibility of different ways of conceiving of reconciliation. This may include socioeconomic opportunities, international intervention, state and nation-building and justice mechanisms. These possibilities serve to illustrate that reconciliation is not an endpoint that can be achieved unproblematically through policy inputs such as education reform. It is an ongoing site of contestation in which agents make sense of themselves as 'integrated' and 'reconciled' subjects.

Guiding questions

How can the student reactions to educational integration described in this chapter best be understood?

⇨

> ## Guiding questions—Cont'd
>
> Are there ways that international and local ideas and responses to integration might better be negotiated?
>
> What lessons emerge from the experience in BiH for peacebuilders and others seeking to promote reconciliation?

Notes

1 *Srpska Demokratska Stranka*, which was led by Radovan Karadžić and is associated with ethno-nationalist Bosnian-Serb politics.

2 Four rules on the use of language were stipulated in the law: the student has freedom of expression in his or her own language; school documents will be issued in the language and alphabet requested by the student or parent; the ethnic composition of teachers should reflect that of the students in the school; and existing textbooks can be used if they are harmonized with the curriculum.

3 SFOR was in operation from January 1996 until December 2005 when it was replaced with the European Union Force EUFOR.

4 The newspaper articles analysed in this section were written and printed in the language formerly known as Serbo-Croat and its translation into English by the primary interpreter hired for the duration of both periods of fieldwork is quoted here.

Acknowledgement

The author would like to thank Dr. Sam Hickey and Dr. Sara MacKian for their supervision of the Doctoral Thesis upon which this chapter is based, Julia Paulson for her valuable editorial work and finally all of the citizens of Brčko District who contributed to this research.

Reference list

Bekerman, Z. (2009), 'The complexities of teaching historical conflictual narratives in integrated Palestinian-Jewish schools in Israel', *International Review of Education*, 55, 235–50.

Bieber, F. (2005), 'Local institutional engineering: A tale of two cities, Mostar and Brčko', *International Peacekeeping*, 12, 420–33.

— (2006), *Post War Bosnia: Ethnicity, Inequality and Public Sector Governance,* Basingstoke and New York: Palgrave Macmillan.

Cigar, N., and P. R. Williams (1998), 'Reward Serbs with town of Brčko? Don't do it', www.publicinternationallaw.org/publications/editorials/Brcko.htm (accessed 7 March 2007).

Dahlman, C., and G. O. Tuathail (2006), 'Bosnia's third space? Nationalist separatism and international supervision in Bosnia's Brčko District', *Geopolitics,* 11, 651–75.

Donnelly, C., and J. Hughes (2009), 'Contact and culture: Mechanisms of reconciliation in schools in Northern Ireland and Israel', in J. R. Quinn (ed.), *Reconciliation(s): Transitional Justice in Postconflict Societies.* Montreal: McGill-Queen's University Press.

Evans, R. (2008), 'The two faces of empowerment in conflict', *Research in Comparative and International Education,* 3, 50–64.

Fischer, A. (2006), 'Integration or segregation? Reforming the education sector', in M. Fischer (ed.), *Peacebuilding and Civil Society in Bosnia-Herzegovina: Ten Years after Dayton.* Berlin: Lit Verlag.

Gibney, M. (2006), *Who should be included? Non-citizens, conflict and the constitution of the citizenry.* CRISE, Working Paper 17, www.crise.ox.ac.uk/pubs.shtml (accessed 31 July 2010).

Hertz-Lazarowitz, R., A. Mor-Sommerfeld, T. Zelniker, and F. Azaiza (2008), 'From ethnic segregation to bilingual education: What can bilingual education do for the future of Israeli society?' *Journal for Critical Education Policy Studies,* 6, 142–56.

Hromadžić, A. (2008), 'Discourses of integration and practices of reunification at the Mostar Gymnasium, Bosnia and Herzegovina', *Comparative Education Review,* 52, 541–63.

Hughes, J. (2007), 'Mediating and moderating effects of inter-group contact: Case studies from bilingual/bi-national schools in Israel', *Journal of Ethnic and Migration Studies,* 33, 419–37.

International Crisis Group (ICG) (2003), *Bosnia's Brčko: Getting In, Getting On and Getting Out.* Balkans Report No 144. Sarajevo, Brussels: International Crisis Group.

— (2007), *Ensuring Bosnia's Future: A New International Engagement Strategy,* Europe Report 180. Sarajevo, Brussels: International Crisis Group.

Jeffrey, A. (2006), 'Building state capacity in post-conflict Bosnia and Herzegovina: The case of Brčko District', *Political Geography,* 25, 203–27.

McGlynn, C. (2004), 'Education for peace in integrated schools: A priority for Northern Ireland?' *Child Care in Practice,* 10, 85–94.

Mujkić, A. (2008), 'Marginalizacija oaze multietničnosti u BiH: Pravni i politički status Distrikta Brčko u predstojećim ustavnim promjenama', www.pulsdemokratije.ba/index.php?a=pdf&l=bs&id=824 (accessed 1 May 2008).

OSCE (2007), *Lessons from Education Reform in Brčko,* Brčko OSCE Mission to BiH Education Department.

Perry, V. (2003), *Reading, Writing and Reconciliation.* Flensburg, Germany: European Centre for Minority Issues.

Salters, J., and A. McEwen. (1993), 'Doing something different: 'Integrated' parents in Northern Ireland', *Research in Education,* 49, 53–62.

Smith, A., and T. Vaux (2002), *Education, Conflict and International Development*. London: Department for International Development.

Stabback, P. (2004), 'Curriculum development, diversity and division in Bosnia and Herzegovina' in S. Tawil and A. Harley (eds), *Education, Conflict and Social Cohesion*. Geneva: UNESCO IBE.

Stevanović, R. (1999), 'Why are the foreigners sniffing around our school?' *Novi Vidik*. Brčko, 15.

5

A Cloud Over the Rainbow Nation? Language, National Reconciliation and Educational Transformation in Post Apartheid South Africa

David Johnson

Chapter Outline

Introduction

> . . . why the national units should disdain, detest, abhor one another, and that even when they are at peace, is indeed a mystery. . . . It is though when it becomes a question of a number of people . . . all individual moral requirements were obliterated, and only the most primitive, the oldest, the crudest mental attitudes were left.
>
> (Sigmund Freud, *Reflections upon War and death*, 1915)

It is 15 years since the Truth and Reconciliation Commission was set up under the Promotion of National Unity and Reconciliation Act, No. 34 of 1995, yet racial intolerance seems to prevail in South Africa's institutions of higher education; this despite the lengths to which the post-Apartheid government of 1994 went to create a democratic society and unified national institutions. It is also significant because most young people entering higher education have largely grown up in a post-Apartheid era, marked by years of non-segregationist schooling, and equal-status contact (Pettigrew, 1998; Allport, 1954). What then, in a society in which the cornerstones of forgiveness and healing had been laid, and indeed one in which the principles of non-racism, non-sexism, democracy and unity had been so carefully negotiated, would account for some of the more recently observed signs of poor racial integration and cultural unity?

The question is asked against the backdrop of increasing intolerance in institutions of higher learning. The situation has so deteriorated in some universities, particularly in the university residences of former Afrikaans-only universities, that a ministerial committee, the Committee on Progress towards Transformation and Social Cohesion and the Elimination of Discrimination in Public Higher Education Institutions, was set up to investigate the nature and extent of racism and racial discrimination in public higher education, and in particular university residences. The commission concluded that racism and other forms of discrimination 'is pervasive in our institutions' and profoundly, that 'the dehumanising acts of humiliation perpetrated and experienced daily in contemporary South Africa' have a high cost to society (Soudien, 2010).

The committee's brief was to examine how far universities have been able to adopt the 'Programme for the Transformation of Higher Education' that was set out in a white paper in 1997 (DOE, 1997). In brief, the programme includes improved access to the university for black students and staff; increased levels of participation for black students in learning and other cultural activities in the university and integration and unity (social cohesion) between black and white students and members of staff.

Given the circumstances under which the commission was established, it understood that its primary brief was to investigate racism within the framework of the South African Constitution, which defines racism as an 'ideology of white supremacy, which serves as a rationale for the unequal relations of power that exist between people in South Africa'.

The acceptance of a brief that required the committee to make appropriate recommendations 'to combat discrimination and to promote social cohesion'

(Soudien, 2010, i), suggested the need to understand racial intolerance in higher education against the backdrop of a transformation process, both in society more widely, and in its institutions.

Thus, amidst much debate about what reconciliation actually means (Cole, 2007), the chapter takes the view that it must be studied not only as a 'dynamic, complex and long term process' in which 'differences are engaged and managed' (ibid., 10), but also as 'evidence of its progression' (Dwyer, 1999). In other words, if the ultimate goal in South Africa is the democratic transformation of a previously unequal society and its institutions, what progress has been made towards it? It is beyond the scope of this chapter to assess the extent of democratic transformation in all sectors and as such it will concentrate on educational transformation.

For Dwyer, the question is how can reconciliation move beyond sentiment and idealism (that we can all live happily ever after) to an examination of the relationship between reconciliation and realpolitik. If we take the view that apology and forgiveness are merely constituent parts of reconciliation, then our task is to resolve the tensions between reconciliation and justice (Crocker, 2002) or, for others such as Barkan (2001), and this is certainly true for this paper, the relationship between reconciliation and redress or restitution. Opotow (2001) argues that this means a focus on reconciliation as social and political change. She writes:

> While reconciliation has enormous positive potential, it can disappoint when it is an empty ritual that cloaks injustice, thwarts social change, and maintains the status quo. The challenge of reconciliation after impunity and atrocity is to create a more just society. Reconciliation requires not only bringing people together to create a shared understanding, but to succeed, much more. It requires an unflinching confrontation with the underlying chronic injustices faced by a society and the mobilisation of its institutions to address these issues in ways that are distributively and procedurally just, and genuinely inclusive. (167)

There can be little disagreement that one of the most pervasive and persistent 'chronic injustices' of the Apartheid state lay in the provision of education. Separated by race and language, those institutions that catered for black students were systematically discriminated against in receipts of funding, facilities and even in a determination on what could be learned. The year 1952 marked the introduction of 'Bantu Education' (inferior education designed to restrict the upward mobility of black South Africans) and was justified by then Minister of Education, Hendrik Verwoerd, as follows:

> There is no place for [the Bantu] in the European community above the level of certain forms of labour . . . What is the use of teaching the Bantu child mathematics when it cannot use it in practice? That is quite absurd. Education must train people in accordance with their opportunities in life, according to the sphere in which they live. (Quoted in Lapping, 1987)

In the years that followed, much of the struggle against the injustices of Apartheid was played out in schools and universities. The African National Congress–led 'Congress of the People' declared in 1955 that South Africa would not be free and democratic until the 'doors of learning and culture' were open to all. In 1976, the protests for a free and democratic educational system spilled out into the streets of Soweto, a township in Johannesburg. The violent and excessive response of the Afrikaner government, which led to the deaths of dozens of students, reignited the mass democratic struggles of the 1950s and 1960s, and solidified international support in the struggle against Apartheid. The link between the struggle for a free and democratic educational system and the struggle for national liberation from other 'chronic injustices' such as the pass laws which rendered black people foreigners in their own country, or the lack of housing and clean drinking water and other basic social services, was thus clearly established. Thus national reconciliation could not be seen only as a mater of forgiveness for physical atrocities and violence committed during the Apartheid years (such as the cases brought forward at the Truth and Reconciliation Commission), but as a matter of correcting the injustices so deeply entrenched by Apartheid laws; and in this there could be no forgiveness without redress. Difficult choices were necessary to ensure historical redress while at the same time ensuring that institutions functioned in a manner fair to all. The most difficult areas would involve the language in education question, given that it was a central plank in the creation of separate institutions (also the separation of English-speaking white institutions from Afrikaans-speaking white institutions); the right for anyone to study at an institution of their choosing, regardless of race or culture (this to include language which as we shall see later remains a sensitive issue); opportunities for equal participation in teaching and learning and enjoyment of common facilities and the forging of a 'oneness', a new South Africanness.

So, how far then has a national reconciliation project that takes into account the transformation of institutions in respect of these goals come? Following

Opotow (2001) above who argues that reconciliation requires a confrontation of injustices and a mobilization of institutions to ensure fairness and justice, this chapter explores educational transformation as a facet of reconciliation.

Background

It seems that transformation and thus reconciliation remains a distant goal in some higher education institutions in South Africa. In February 2008, a video was made by four white students of the University of the Orange Free State, in which five black workers were depicted as being subjected to various mock activities. This included them being forced to consume food that appeared to have been urinated on. The video led to riots and racial strife among students at the university. According to several newspaper reports, white students were warned to leave the campus by protesting black students, who allegedly threatened that all white 'bitches' would be raped and all white farmers killed. A few white students on the campus were assaulted, and residents of Reitz and other hostels formed furniture barricades, purportedly because they were in 'fear for their lives'.

This incident in itself is extraordinary in a society that had gone to great lengths to deal with racial hatred spawned by Apartheid. More disconcerting though is the fact that it was not an isolated incident. Seven students at North West University, another former white-only Afrikaans-speaking institution were subjected to disciplinary action after being accused of being instrumental in setting up a racist group on the Facebook social networking site. The postings described black people in derogatory terms and those who posted them made it plain that they did so unapologetically (*Mail and Guardian*, June 2008). In separate incidents, black students entering their first year at the North West University were subjected to initiations (to be fair, white fresher students are also subjected to similar initiations), which they found culturally strange. For example, first year students were apparently forced to crawl in contorted positions over a piece of lawn to obtain the so-called 'grass license' before they were allowed to enter the Over de Voor residence. Those wanting to qualify for a place on the third floor had to take thirty lashes to the buttocks administered with a cricket bat. It would be difficult to argue that such 'initiations' are all racially motivated – they are deeply rooted cultural practices (some of which are humiliating for all subjected to them) – but they did seem more sinister when a black female lecturer was pulled into a shower by white students for walking on the 'forbidden grass' at the Over de Voor residence (Report of the Ministerial Task Team, 2009, 23).

The situation had become so untenable at the North West University that the Minister of Education appointed a task team to carry out an investigation into 'the causes of disruptions, instability and discontent' (Report of the Ministerial Task Team, 2009, 2). One of the terms of reference for the ministerial task team was to look at 'the extent, manner and success of enhancing social cohesion and a new institutional culture across all campuses that overcomes the apartheid-induced divide between historically white and historically black institutions' (2009, 2).

The ministerial task team reports that white students unanimously defended the initiation practices in the residences and said that the complaints made by black students were an indication that they were unable to adjust to 'our culture' or 'our campus' (Report of the Ministerial Task Team, 2009, 23). White staff interviewed by the task team seemingly held similar views. The task team reports one comment as follows – 'these non-white groups are trying to fit into our culture' (ibid., 23). The task team concludes that both white staff and white students, saw their black counterparts as 'guests and not as equals' (ibid., 24).

Indeed, the Committee on Progress towards Transformation and Social Cohesion and the Elimination of Discrimination in Public Higher Education Institutions (Soudien, 2010), which looked at the problem nationally, found strong evidence of continued opposing cultural mentalities. It asserts that:

> . . . perpetrators . . . live and operate in a world that reinforces the misconception that the best of what it means to be a human being is represented by their lifestyles, desires and aspirations. Victims are denied the opportunity – either through a lack of access to opportunities or due to outright discrimination – to realise their full potential. In the process, the country is robbed of valuable but untapped human resources. (359)

In order to make sense of the spate of incidents at former white-only universities, some explicitly intended as racist, and others, including a wide spectrum of black student protests, an assertion of language, culture and identity, we must first examine whether the 'reach' of the Truth and Reconciliation Commission, as the vehicle of national reconciliation, was sufficiently extensive. In other words, whether it was able to penetrate the institutional arrangements, particularly those formerly racially divided universities that had been compelled through a legislative process to merge. It is also necessary to examine whether the process of reconciliation was substantial enough to ensure the vision of democracy and unity upon which the Constitution and social charters before it, such as the Freedom Charter[1] of 1955, were based.

The truth and reconciliation process: The cornerstone of national transformation?

We know that in South Africa, the truth and reconciliation process was premised on the hypothesis that knowledge of the past will lead to acceptance, tolerance and reconciliation in the future. Gibson (2004) tested the hypothesis, based on data collected in a 2001 survey of more than 3,700 South Africans. His most important finding is that those who accept the 'truth' about the country's apartheid past are more likely to hold reconciled racial attitudes.

But there are many who question whether the primary purpose of achieving restorative justice has been achieved in all communities. Wilson (2001) conducted extensive anthropological fieldwork among African urban communities. He argues that the TRC had little effect on popular ideas of justice as retribution. Wilson examines how the TRC's religious-redemptive model was received in the townships around Johannesburg, in particular in Sharpeville, where the infamous Sharpeville massacre took place on 21 March 1960, and Boipathong. People came forward to testify at the TRC, less as a deep commitment to reconciliation and nation building than for more practical reasons such as the 'need of victims to clear their name, [as some had been accused of collaboration with the apartheid government] and to use a public forum to do so' (ibid., 142). The 'Reconciliation through Truth' model rarely prompted victims and perpetrators to actually come together. Rather, it seems probable the 'message was never likely to achieve more than the restoration of social relationships *between victims*, where suspicion and stigma had been wrongfully attached to one person or family' (153).

In his fieldwork, Wilson found that a strong desire for revenge persists in South Africa despite the efforts of the TRC. '[T]he TRC's version of human rights as reconciliation did little to challenge the prevalence of revenge in the townships because it could not meaningfully engage with a punitive view of justice' (ibid., 161). He examines the divergent paths of retributive justice in the neighbouring townships of Sharpeville and Boipathong. Despite the rhetoric from political leaders and the press that widely condemns retribution, Wilson finds this inconsistent with feelings among much of the public, especially as crime continues to be a highly salient issue. 'This institution [the TRC] is widely praised abroad and in international conferences on post-conflict reconstruction and reconciliation around the globe, while being largely peripheral to the lives of those living in townships wracked by revenge killings' (187).

Many in South Africa believe that the TRC process is incomplete because reparations have been so meagre and slow in coming. They argue that prosecutions are necessary for the many apartheid leaders who never sought amnesty in exchange for truth, and that the vast disparities in wealth and privilege that still exist must be addressed if South Africa is to continue a peaceful transition from apartheid to democracy and majority rule.

Nearly 10 years after the Truth and Reconciliation Commission, the conditions in South Africa's black townships have seen little improvement. By most accounts, the black economic empowerment strategy has benefited only a small section of the population. But, perhaps wealth creation and distribution, particularly in the period since the end of Apartheid is a strong measure against which to gauge the progress of the reconciliation project. Surely, though, the pace of reform and transformation in the educational institutions of South Africa has been more rapid?

Reconciliation and transformation in education

Assessing educational transformation as an outcome of the reconciliation process requires an understanding of the state before, and especially the importance of the language question.

Shortly after the Afrikaner Nationalist Party came to power in 1948, only 4.8 per cent of university students were black (Council on Higher Education (CHE), 2004a). At the time, there was no formal prohibition on black students attending universities that largely served the white population, but access was made difficult. This changed with the advent of the 1959 Extension of University Education Act which prohibited black students' access to white institutions. Now, access to higher education was deliberately divided by race and language.

White-only universities were separated into two language-of-education groups: English and Afrikaans. The universities of Stellenbosch, Pretoria, Orange Free State, Potchefstroom and Rand Afrikaans University, all of which served the white Afrikaans speaking community, are described by Mabokela (2000) as 'the nucleus of Afrikaner nationalism and cultural consciousness' (26) and Bunting (2006) adds the dual-medium University of Port Elizabeth to this group since its governing body was predominantly Afrikaans. The 'liberal universities' of the University of Cape Town, University of Natal, Rhodes University and the University of Witwatersrand saw themselves as far more autonomous than the Afrikaans universities.

Along with a university for 'coloured' students (University of Western Cape), and one for Indians (University of Durban Westville), the Extension of University Education Act 1959 created three black universities which were segregated along ethnic and linguistic lines. These institutions comprised the University of the North and the University of Zululand and the already existing University of Fort Hare, the oldest black institution in South Africa, which became the designated institution for Xhosa speakers. Three more black universities were founded in the 1980s in the 'homelands' of Bophuthatswana, Transkei and Venda (Mabokela, 2000). Despite the ideological segregation of the black universities, based on arguments of race and language, they all used English as the language of teaching and learning.

These universities grew artificially and along separate paths through 'racially motivated planning' (Badat, 2007). As Ridge argues, historically white-only universities 'have naturally served the interest of the apartheid planners, strengthening the white hold on privilege' (Ridge, 1991, 1–2, quoted in Badat, 2007, 26), while Badat, who largely concurs, adds that 'both [white-only and black-only universities] are products of apartheid planning and were functionally differentiated to serve the development and reproduction of apartheid order' (2007, 27). Indeed, Johnson, Unterhalter and Wolpe (1991) found that different institutions defined their roles in relation to the nation state in different ways. The law faculties of Afrikaans-speaking white-only universities, for example, thought it their prerogative to produce state prosecutors while the others concentrated on training the defence lawyers.

But, it was the sheer weight of the burden of Apartheid that undermined the role and status of black institutions. They were poorly funded, and mostly staffed by Afrikaner lecturers, many of whom were apologists for the Apartheid State; and the hold of the State on these institutions was severe. Student protests, of which there were many, were brutally put down by Apartheid security forces. Indeed, where protests were prolonged, the State shut down the institutions often for as long as a whole academic year, rendering indiscriminately, all work completed or time spent null and void. Little wonder that many black students in these disadvantaged institutions took almost twice as long as their white counterparts to complete their degrees.

According to the white paper 'A Programme for the Transformation of Higher Education' (DOE, 1997), years of apartheid have affected institutions, staff, students and the culture of teaching and learning in higher education. The under-funding of historically black institutions, the political struggles and actual battles for equality that took place at these institutions on the one hand, and the institutional peculiarities of the well-funded historically white institutions, left deficiencies and idiosyncrasies in the higher education system that were far reaching (DOE, 1997).

The report found that the Apartheid system of higher education had reproduced inequality in South Africa and failed to promote 'a democratic ethos and a sense of citizenship defined around commitment to a common good' [National Commission on Higher Education (NCHE), 1996, 1.2.1]. Thus the transformation of higher education would have to tackle the political, academic, economic, pedagogical and ideological deficits, which were the legacy of apartheid.

In a radical attempt to arrest the separate paths of higher education development, South Africa embarked upon a series of forced mergers of higher education institutions in order to create a more efficient, equitable and desegregated system (CHE, 2004b).[2] Identifying the majority of institutions involved in these mergers as former Afrikaans-medium institutions and former homeland institutions, Blaauw (2008) claims that it was the transformation of these two types of institution, rather than the rationalization of higher education, which was the aim. So how far has this attempt at reconciling differences between institutions served the transformation and reconciliation project? In discussing this, the chapter will look at the case of the North West University. By all accounts, this was an extraordinary merger between one of the most conservative Apartheid created Afrikaner institutions and an Apartheid created homeland institution; the characters of both could not have been more different.

The North West University resulted from a merger of three institutions in 2004. These were the Potchefstroom University for Christian Higher Education (an historically white institution (HWI) that had had a strong Afrikaner identity, according to Mabokela (2000)), the University of North West (a historically black institution (HBI), which was previously the University of Bophuthatswana), and part of the distance learning institution of Vista University, and a former white-only technical college, the Vaal Technikon. The merged university consists of three campuses – Potchefstroom (the site of the former Potchefstroom University for Christian Higher Education), Mafikeng (the site of the former University of the North West) and the Vaal Triangle. By 2008, the institution was experiencing a number of challenges, among these, widespread student discontent, mainly at the former University of North West in Mafikeng.

From the outset it is clear that a significant constraint to educational transformation and thus reconciliation in merged institutions, particularly Afrikaans language-speaking universities, is the language question. Language, culture and identity are central to any discussion of reconciliation and national transformation and crucial to three key areas that will be used as a yardstick to 'measure' educational transformation as an outcome of reconciliation: improved access to the university for black students and staff; increased levels of participation for black students in learning and other cultural activities in the university; integration and unity between black and white students and members of staff.

All South African Universities have had to engage directly with the tensions around an adoption of a language policy. In brief, most black students favour English as the medium of instruction. This is not a significant problem at the former white, English-speaking universities but has been a subject of much political debate in Afrikaans-speaking institutions. Most institutions have adopted some variant of a bilingual mode of instruction which usually means that those wishing to study through the medium of Afrikaans (mainly white Afrikaner students and 'Coloured' (mixed heritage) students for many of whom Afrikaans is mother tongue, end up in a largely white-only stream, and those wishing to study through the medium of English, end up in a black-only stream. This leads to two institutions on one campus and does very little to cement reconciliation, integration and unity.

Taking the North West University as a case study, the chapter will examine a unique language model pioneered by the university, which aims to bridge the race divide and promote access, participation and unity by teaching through simultaneous interpretation. Could such a model successfully implemented serve to minimize the disharmony between racial groups described above, and lead to true reconciliation?

A study into the simultaneous interpretation model was carried out by the author, in partnership with the director of the programme. The research was undertaken by a postgraduate student; the discussion that follows draws substantively on that work.

A case study of North West University (NWU)

The language question and access for all

When taken as a whole, NWU is a multilingual university with classes delivered across the three campuses in English and/or Afrikaans, both through dual-medium and parallel-medium instruction and in some cases (predominantly at Potchefstroom but also at Vaal Triangle) with the use of simultaneous interpretation. Furthermore, the promotion and development of African languages are undertaken; Setswana at Potchefstroom and Mafikeng and Sesotho in Vaal Triangle. At the Potchefstroom campus 'Afrikaans has an established position as the language of vertical communication within organised student life' (ibid., 6). Teaching is also mainly in Afrikaans, however NWU states that '*access and success* are facilitated by means of interpreting services, afternoon programmes in English in certain faculties, and provision to submit assignments and answer scripts in English' (ibid., 4, emphasis added). Study guides are also available in English.

With the student demographic for contact students at Potchefstroom being 80 per cent white (Van der Walt and Brink, 2005, 838), and 87 per cent of students at Potchefstroom having Afrikaans as their home language (Verhoef and Venter, 2008, 386), it would seem, following from the policy stated above, that having Afrikaans as the main language of tuition at this campus is to be expected. Furthermore, Van der Walt and Brink (2005) point out that access for non-Afrikaans-speaking students and the preservation of Afrikaans as the language of tuition are not incongruent with the transformation agenda since there is a 'breadth of language options across 3 campuses' (838).

However, the continued use of Afrikaans as the main undergraduate medium of instruction at Potchefstroom is not wholly endorsed by everyone. Potchefstroom is seen by some as the dominant campus at North West (Kamsteeg, 2008, 444). It is the best resourced and still has a predominantly white staff and student population. Indeed, the Report of the Ministerial Task Team (2009) reports a 'bullish affirmation from staff and students of Potchefstroom as being unapologetically an Afrikaans-speaking campus'. The task team finds that the language policy runs against a number of moral, political and constitutional imperatives. It goes on to say:

> The task team finds it untenable that the majority of South Africans and Africans in particular, are substantially constrained from accessing public resources in the university campus as a result of the language policy. The 'dismal student equity profile is proof of this otherwise the university would have to declare that black students are uneducable or generally unsuitable in respect of its standards'. (ibid.)

> The Afrikaans community cannot claim a monopoly on language rights at the expense of the common interests of all South Africans by claiming that they are entitled to their own language university. The logic would be a return to separate development. (ibid.)

NWU for its part is careful to point out that whatever the main language used, this is with the provision that 'access and success are not hindered' (NWU, 2007,

4). It claims success for its simultaneous interpreting services, which it insists allow access to lectures for those students for whom Afrikaans is not a first language (black students) and fends of the charge that the programme is tokenistic or that it serves only courses of marginal academic interest.

Blaauw (2008, 32) argues that those courses at NWU which are offered with simultaneous interpreting are 'of strategic importance in terms of providing highly skilled human resources for the developing South African economy' which would seem to respond to the white paper's call for transformation in higher education so as 'to equip a developing society with the capacity to address national needs and to participate in a rapidly changing and competitive global context'. (DOE, 1997, 2.25).

Furthermore, it is 'prestigious courses' which are offered with simultaneous interpreting. In 2008, Nursing Studies, Law, Pharmacy and Engineering, totalling four hundred lecture hours per week, were delivered using simultaneous interpretation. The choice of prestigious courses would seem to indicate that the language policy is considering redress and equality, thus tackling the state of affairs identified in the National Plan for Higher Education whereby 'the spread of black students across different programme areas, in particular those which generate the highest levels of private benefits for graduates, is uneven'. (NPHE, 2001, 3.1.2). The implication in the Language Policy for Higher Education (LPHE) edict that predominantly Afrikaans-medium universities 'ensure that language of instruction does not impede access, especially in high cost programmes with limited student places such as the health sciences and engineering' also appears to be addressed in the decision to simultaneously interpret these particular courses.

But the main question for this chapter is whether the model encourages access and is inviting to black students? One of the students surveyed thought not. He/she argued that he/she came to the campus because it was 'prestigious for its Pharmacy studies', but did not seem to think that providing simultaneous interpreting was the same as having the choice to study directly in English as he/she continued, 'we are forced to learn Afrikaans and we do not have a choice in the matter' (SQD, August 2009).

A large majority of the students surveyed considered the availability of bilingual education to be important to access their courses. 84 per cent of the students asked replied that simultaneous interpreting had a positive effect on their ability to take their courses at NWU. Many said that it would have been impossible for them to take their chosen courses at NWU without bilingual provision, with a large number saying that this was because they knew no Afrikaans. One student said 'I can't learn anything without interpreting because Afrikaans is Greek to me'. (SQD, August 2009). Another reported that simultaneous interpreting was important 'because it was going to be impossible learning Afrikaans, which is a new language to me'. (SQD, August 2009). Although one student expressed doubts about Afrikaans being the main language and the interpreting being in English — 'I'm not too thrilled about it' — he/she goes on to say:

> . . . but I have adapted to it and now I'm used to this method. [Interpreted lectures] are essential. . . . without a bilingual form of teaching I would not be studying the course, it would have been almost impossible. (SQD, August 2009)

More than a third of students who stated that it was important to have bilingual education had a knowledge of Afrikaans; however, they thought that they could not learn effectively in it. Thus one student said: 'Interpreted lectures are of the utmost importance to my learning. Although I understand some Afrikaans I find it difficult to learn in Afrikaans.' Another comment shows that when study material is available only in Afrikaans, a person with some knowledge of Afrikaans can use the interpreted lectures to help illuminate that material: 'without the interpreted service I would not be able to study my notes which were mostly in Afrikaans'. He/she continues that if a bilingual form of teaching were not available, then taking the course would not have been possible 'because I cannot really understand Afrikaans, particularly spoken at a very high speed' (SQD, August 2009).

Two students mentioned that although they would have taken the course without a bilingual provision, the simultaneous interpreting made it easier. Of these two, one, who had studied Afrikaans as a second language and did not feel happy with it as a language of instruction, said that since this course was available only at NWU she/he would have taken it anyway. The other student was the unique in that he/she seemed to embrace the spirit of multilingualism that the government is trying to promote; 'I always wanted to know Afrikaans. I could do the course without the interpreter, but the interpreters' service is important because it makes things easier' (SQD, August 2009).

It seems to be the case that access to the education offered at the University, particularly in some of its more prestigious courses, was facilitated by the interpreting programme. Black students were on the whole positive about the program; but, this was not necessarily the case among Afrikaans-speaking white students and some lecturers who felt that simultaneous interpretation wasted their time (Report of the Ministerial Task Team, 2009).

The language question and improved participation

While there is some agreement that the simultaneous interpretation model encourages access to learning, thus meeting at least one of the transformation goals, it is not altogether clear that it allows students to participate more fully in the educational process. One student interviewed in the study argued that: '"we" get the message late and can't correspond' and 'a question is asked in Afrikaans and it will be already answered by somebody by the time it's interpreted' (SQD, August 2009).

Another student commented that not understanding jokes made by the lecturer because they are not interpreted made him/her feel 'isolated and a dummy' (SQD August 2009). Another student explained the impact that being in the minority has on his/her ability to participate:

> It's really difficult because 99 per cent receive the class in Afrikaans. When you start to participate using other languages like English, students (Afrikaans) are getting bored to such an extent of making noise . . . some of them tend to laugh at you . . . you end up not asking questions in class, waiting to go and ask the lecturer in the office. (SQD, August 2009)

Thus, one of the most challenging issues to arise from the data was the fact that the simultaneous interpreting programme only has its use in a classroom setting. Owing to this, some students said they were unable to attend all activities concerned with their course. Three such comments were made:

> English students cannot attend functions due to the language barrier. During practicals, English students are separated into different classes or asked to stay behind afterwards for a repeat in English. In this way some important facts are left out.
>
> It really doesn't bring unity . . . we can't participate in some of the activities since it's in Afrikaans e.g. PASV [the student association for the course].
>
> . . . some other activities that are done for my specific faculty I cannot attend because I will not understand what is going on and what is being said. Most people using the interpreting service do not usually attend such functions due to language barrier. (SQD, August 2009)

The concerns raised by students are important pointers to the distance that needs to be travelled towards an institutional culture of learning that allows both black and white students the possibility to make valued intellectual contributions, but more important, that they value each others' contributions and learn from those to come to new shared understandings. This is crucial in breaking down the old dividing mentalities that blacks were of inferior intellectual aptitude, or alternatively, that whites had an innate intellectual superiority. Reaching reconciled attitudes in this case is not a matter of 'absolution', rather a process by which respect and dignity is won 'in action', or in common intellectual activity. This leads us on to the next point.

Integration and unity

Purser (2000) sees that in bilingual universities contact between different groups can 'help overcome some basic historical issues' since 'contacts between students can certainly create positive outcomes' (455). The opportunity for students to interact, learn and form shared understandings together was an area this researcher wanted to investigate since such activities might contribute in some way to the transformation of South Africa.[3] Webb (2005) suggests:

> . . . the only way in which social transformation can really occur . . . [is] through communication, and the consequent establishment of a commonality of values and norms, points of view, attitudes, loyalties and social practises. This is also the only way in which stereotypes, prejudices and misrepresentations can be broken down, and respect can be engendered for one another. (153)

While on communication Alexander points out:

> . . . the real issue in the matter of promoting national unity is not that people should all speak any one particular language (although this is clearly very helpful!), but that they should be able to communicate with one another'. (Alexander, quoted in Orman, 2008, 93)

Since parallel-medium instruction does not truly bring students of different language groups together in class it struggles in the role of 'unifying' groups. As mentioned earlier, Garigue (Garigue, 1985, 943 quoted by Du Plessis, 2006) saw parallel-medium universities as 'practically two universities in one'. Walker (2005) illuminated the importance of this in the South African context. From her research into a former Afrikaans-medium HWI, which operated parallel-medium classes in Afrikaans and English, she points out:

> . . . the University offers parallel classes in English and Afrikaans. This
> means that some students take all their classes in Afrikaans and are unlikely
> to encounter any black people at all in class, and most likely to encounter
> students of the same racial and Afrikaner cultural background. In effect
> two universities operate side by side on the same campus. (138)

It would seem then that simultaneous interpreting really has an advantage
over parallel-medium education when *trying* to promote integration and unity
between students. One of the aims of the NWU's language policy is to promote
integration and the language directorate believes that simultaneous interpreting
'contributes to unity in diversity' and that '[i]ntercultural liaison is increased by
keeping together in one class students with different language preferences'.[4]

Since the role of communication in transforming social attitudes was key to
this research, students were asked how far they felt the language barrier was
removed by simultaneous interpreting and how this contributed to unity and
shared experiences. Five comments from the sixteen received on this theme
were emphatic that the language barrier was not removed. For example one
student said,

> It doesn't remove the language barrier. I receive the lecture in English and
> they receive it in Afrikaans. It doesn't allow much interaction between
> students who speak different languages. (SQD, August 2009)

However three students felt that the language barrier was removed, with one
saying 'at least we are able to respond to our fellow classmates' (SQD, August
2009). The other two linked the removal of the language barrier to the ability to
participate in class discussions or understand other students' questions. These
comments lean towards the pedagogical gains of the programme, which, as with
the comments on participation, demonstrates the students are reflecting generally on the classroom mechanics of the programme rather than on potentially
broader themes. However, these pedagogical gains are obviously of great importance to the students since a further five comments dealt exclusively with how
the removal of the language barrier helped them understand the course or the
lecturer, while only one student reflected on the difference between removing
the language barrier altogether and removing the language barrier between student and lecturer. That student noted: 'It does not necessarily remove the barrier
but it helps to understand the course' (SQD, August 2009).

Only three students approached the question from the angle of removing the language barrier to aid communication between classmates and build relationships. They said:

> It doesn't fully remove it [the language barrier], you sometimes feel like you're in a world of your own.
>
> [The language barrier is removed only] to a small extent because outside of the class I still cannot chat to my other class members because of the language barrier.
>
> There are still some students in class who can't speak English so as a result I can't work with them. But it has nothing to do with race. (SQD, August 2009)

When it came to unity the students overwhelmingly said that they did not feel that simultaneous interpreting helped achieve classroom unity. Twelve out of sixteen students answered that there was no unity, or that they did not feel the class was integrated. Many of these comments pointed out specifically that language was the force that divided the class and that the inability to communicate with each other did not seem to be helped to any real extent by the use of interpreting. Students pointed out:

> Simultaneous interpreting is just for the benefit of English students. No mixing and mingling, for example class groups will *always* be English or Afrikaans and not a mixture . . . due to the language barrier (student's underlining).
>
> It doesn't help achieve class unity at all, the earphones put you in another dimension and it makes one feel isolated. The people that require interpretation are still mostly black people and this can make one feel marginalized.
>
> . . . we are always divided by according to the language you speak. (SQD, August 2009)

Three students felt that simultaneous interpretation helped to achieve classroom unity, but again this seemed to be linked to the pedagogical gains rather than anything deeper. Thus one student said:

> [Simultaneous interpreting helps achieve class unity] . . . to a very large extent, we can all participate in class discussions and activities. (SQD, August 2009)

The remaining student said he/she did not know if the simultaneous interpretation helped unity but it 'really helps to achieve an understanding of the course' (SQD, August 2009).

This data raises questions about how important building a sense of unity in the classroom is for students. Perhaps students view the classroom as a place to learn and nothing else, and furthermore, as a place to learn from the lecturer since learning from each other was only reported by four out of sixteen students. Or perhaps they feel that their educational experience is diminished by a lack of unity, and although they did not mention it in the questionnaires, it is important to them.

Discussion and conclusions

Using access, participation and integration as a yardstick by which to measure reconciliation as progress, we have seen that the language policy at NWU takes access seriously, and by adopting a policy of multilingualism it provides classes in both English and/or Afrikaans through a variety of methods across its three campuses. At the Potchefstroom campus where Afrikaans is the main language of tuition, simultaneous interpreting is used in the prestigious courses to allow access for non–Afrikaans-speaking students. The student data showed that students consider simultaneous interpreting as vital not only to their access to NWU, but to the opportunity to take the courses of their choice. However, there is not widespread support of the model, notably from some Afrikaner academics and students, and from some members of government who feel that the whole language question needs to be revisited.

The answer to the question of whether simultaneous interpreting offers opportunities for meaningful interaction in an academic setting which, in turn, might improve integration, is unclear. Although students being together in one class presents more opportunities for interaction between language groups than parallel-medium education, the absence of any real feeling of unity in the classroom or interaction between students and the frequent comment that the class was divided along linguistic lines must be acknowledged. However, it should also be pointed out that the students' desire for parallel classes in English suggests that being integrated with students of another language group was not the major concern for them.

Neither the negative answer to this question nor the students' belief that they would gain more from separate classes in English should be allowed to detract entirely from the programme's ability to promote the transformation agenda, which was the main question of the research.

The model holds promise, not only for its ability to present academic content to a multilingual class, but because it may help with the wider South African and institutional transformation agenda. At present, unity and integration do not seem to be fostered in the simultaneously interpreted class; however, the students *are* educated together, access has been widened and participation in learning does occur. Therefore, despite the data showing that simultaneous interpreting is not the students' 'first choice', and that their reflections on unity and integration are couched in the pedagogical, the simultaneous interpreting programme does still have worth. That worth lies in its potential to affect change and push forward the transformation agenda. However, what the institution has to do now is to look for other ways to enhance communication and build unity between its student groups. Recognizing that more has to be done in terms of ensuring that non-Afrikaans-speaking students have not only an opportunity to learn, but that they actually feel they belong and have an equal experience to their peers, is the key.

The effect of apartheid on South African higher education cannot be under-estimated, nor should its legacy. The political functions of the universities, the divisions and segregation along ethno-linguistic lines and the huge inequalities and disparities in the funding of institutions and the opportunities they afforded their students continue to shape South Africa today. As was shown, even after the end of apartheid, access to and participation and success in higher education remained major issues for the black population. Simply removing the official barriers to access has not been enough to ensure redress and equality in the system, and in particular, access to a comparable education with the same chance of success and opportunities has not yet been afforded to the black population. Furthermore the education system cannot be said to have truly desegregated given the concentration of black students in certain courses and modes of study-ing which have in fact not transformed the campuses of some HWI.

Achieving reconciliation in education is a complex and difficult process. The legacies of apartheid in the South African higher education system can still be seen. Inequalities in access and success are still evident, while integrating black students at some previously white institutions remains a challenge. At the heart of this is the language question, which presents a barrier to all three transforma-tive goals discussed here. It is hard to see how this can be overcome if the section of the South African Constitution on language rights, which recognizes the importance of giving each language group the opportunity to study in the lan-guage of their choice as far as is practicable, is upheld – and it should be! Of all the options to work with this principle, itself an important facet of reconcilia-tion, the NWU simultaneous interpretation model holds some promise but has a long way to go if the cloud that hangs over South Africa's rainbow nation is to evaporate. In the short term there are likely to be more racist inspired incidents such as those described above. In the long term, reconciliation as an outcome of education is only possible in a culture of learning in which blacks and whites can learn to bury the past misconceptions in respect of intellectual aptitude through a common valuing of each others' contributions and a forging of a new common intelligence. In this, much hangs on the evolving language in education debates.

Guiding questions

What important components of reconciliation emerge from the chapter's discussion of education in post-apartheid South Africa?

Language is introduced in this chapter as a key issue and potential challenge for reconciliation– in what other ways might language be important for reconciliation processes?

This chapter offers insights into ways that reconciliation might be measured as progress – what other indicators of reconciliation as progress might be developed?

Notes

1 The Freedom Charter was an outcome of a door-to-door campaign in which the people of South Africa were asked what their vision for society was. It was adopted, clause-by-clause at a 'freedom rally' organized by the Congress of the People (an alliance of anti-Apartheid groups) in Kliptown, Johannesburg, in 1955. In its preamble, it states that 'South Africa belongs to all who live in it, Black or White', and sets out a number of demands such as 'there shall be houses for all'.

2 This policy in itself has been an area which has attracted great deal of research (see Jansen (2004)) and is not something that can be covered here.

3 This supposition ties in with Allport's 'contact theory' as explained by Slavin (1999, 49).

4 Beukes and Pienaar (2006) make the point that intercultural liaison in the simultaneous interpreted classroom has important pedagogical gains too, since much can be learnt from classmates with differing experiences to their own.

Reference list

Allport, G. W. (1954), *The Nature of Prejudice*. Reading, MA: Addison-Wesley.

Badat, S. (2007), Higher Education Transformation in South Africa Post 1994: Towards a Critical Assessment. Johannesburg, South Africa; Centre for Education Policy Development.

Barkan, E. (2001), *The Guilt of Nations: Restitution and Negotiating Historical Injustices*. New York: W. W. Norton.

Beukes, A. M., and M. Pienaar (2006), 'Some factors influencing the use of simultaneous interpreting as an alternative to parallel-medium teaching in tertiary education', *Journal for Language Teaching*, 40, 2, 127–39.

Blaauw, J. (2008), 'Sourcing and maintaining a pool of suitably skilled interpreters for educational interpreting at a tertiary institution', *Southern African Linguistics and Applied Language Studies*, 26, 3, 301–13.

Bunting, I. (2006), 'The higher education landscape under apartheid', *Transformation in Higher Education*, 10, 1, 35–52.

Cole, E. A. (2007), (ed), *Teaching the Violent Past: History Education and Reconciliation*. Lanham, MD: Rowman & Littlefield Publishers, Inc.

Council on Higher Education (CHE) (2004a), Higher Education and Social Transformation: South Africa Case Study. University of Cape Town. www.che.ac.za/documents/d000066/H EandSocialTransformationReport_25Feb2004.pdf (accessed 3 July 2010).

CHE (2004b), *The Governance of Merger in South African Higher Education: Research Report for the Council on Higher Education*. Pretoria: CHE.

Crocker, D. A. (2002), 'Punishment, reconciliation, and deliberative democracy', *Buffalo Criminal Law Review*, 5, 509–49.

Department of Education (DOE) (1997), 'A Programme for the Transformation of Higher Education, General Notice 1196 of 1997', white paper. Pretoria, South Africa.

Du Plessis, T. (2006), 'From monolingual to bilingual higher education: The repositioning of historically Afrikaans-medium universities in South Africa', *Language Policy*, 5, 1, 87–13.

Dwyer, S. (1999), 'Reconciliation for realists', *Ethics & International Affairs*, 13, 1, 81–98.

Freud, S. (1915), *Reflections on War and Death*. New York: Moffat Yard.

Gibson, J. L. (2004), *Overcoming Apartheid: Can Truth Reconcile a Divided Nation?* New York: Russell Sage Foundation.

Jansen, J. D. (2004), 'Changes and continuities in South Africa's higher education system, 1994 to 2004', in L. Chisholm (ed), *Changing Class: Education and Social Change in Post-Apartheid South Africa*, Johannesburg: HSRC.

Johnson, D., E. Unterhalter, and H. Wolpe (1991), 'Formal and non-formal structures of human resource development for a post apartheid South Africa', in *Human Resource Development for a Post-Apartheid South Africa*, London: Commonwealth Secretariat, Mimeograph.

Kamsteeg, F. (2008), 'In search of a merged identity: the case of multi-campus North West University, South Africa', *TD: the Journal for Transdisciplinary Research in Southern Africa*, 4(2), pp.431–51.

Lapping, B. (1987), *Apartheid: A History*. New York: George Braziller, Inc.

Mabokela, R. O. (2000), *Voices of Conflict: Desegregating South African Universities*. New York: Routledge.

Mail and Guardian (2008), 'Racism at universities "alive and well"', 20 June.

Opotow, S. (2001), 'Reconciliation in times of impunity: Challenges for social justice', *Social Justice Research*, 14, 149–70.

Orman, J. (2008), *Reviews of National Policies for Education: South Africa*. Paris. OECD

Pettigrew, T. H. (1998), 'Intergroup contact theory', *Annual Review of Psychology*, 49, 65–85.

'Promotion of National Unity and Reconciliation Act – Act 95-34' (1995), Online: www.fas.org/irp/world/rsa/act95_034.htm (accessed 5 August 2010).

Purser, L. (2000), 'The bilingual university: General reflections on its origins, mission, and functioning', *Higher Education in Europe*, 25, 4, 451–59.

Report of the Ministerial Task Team (2009), Investigation by the Ministerial Task Team into the North-West University, Notice 136 of 2009. www.info.gov.za/view/DownloadFileAction?id=95665 (accessed 3 July 2010).

Republic of South Africa Department of Education (2008), *Report of the Ministerial Committee on Transformation and Social Cohesion and the Elimination of Discrimination in Public Higher Education Institutions*.

Slavin, R. D. (1999), 'Comprehensive approaches to cooperative learning', *Theory into Practice*, 38, 2, 49.

Soudien, C. (2010), 'The reconstitution of privilege: Integration in former white schools in South Africa', *Journal of Social Issues*, 66, 2, 352–66.

Van der Walt, C. and Brink, C. (2005), 'Multilingual universities: A national and international overview', *South African Journal of Higher Education*, 19, 4, 822–52.

Verhoef, M., and T. Venter (2008), 'Functional multilingualism at the North-West University as part of the institution's transformation agenda', *Southern African Linguistics and Applied Language Studies*, 26, 3, 379–92.

Walker, M. (2005), 'Race is nowhere and race is everywhere: Narratives from black and white South African university students in post-apartheid South Africa', *British Journal of Sociology of Education*, 26, 1, 41–54.

Webb, V (2002), *Language in South Africa: The Role of Language in National Transformation, Reconstruction and Development*. Philadelphia: J.Benjamins.

Wilson, R. A. (2001), *The Politics of Truth and Reconciliation in South Africa: Legitimizing the Post-Apartheid State*. New York: Cambridge University Press.

6

Reconciliation Through Educational Reform? Recommendations and Realities in Peru

Julia Paulson

Introduction

In Peru, education has been widely identified as a factor that contributed towards a violent conflict that lasted 20 years, from 1980 to 2000 (CVR 2003, 2004; Ansión et al., 1993; Degregori, 1990). The conflict in Peru, between the Maoist group Shining Path (*Sendero Luminoso*) and the Peruvian armed forces fed upon the long-standing inequalities and exclusion in Peru that have led the country to be described as made up of 'many Perus' (Paulston, 1971). Those who lived in rural, indigenous, poor *mestizo*, Andean, jungle and urban slum 'Perus' were those who suffered most violently during the armed conflict. These same groups are among those who have long been excluded from the political and social 'development' of the Peru imagined by those who govern it.

Education's role in maintaining these many Perus was highlighted by the Truth and Reconciliation Commission (CVR, *Comisión de la Verdad y Reconciliación*) when it sought to explain the causes of conflict between 2001 and 2003. Early in the CVR's final report we find the following:

> Among the thousands of testimonies collected by the CVR, it is common to find phrases that highlight the feelings of exclusion and indifference experienced by the individuals and communities who were the principal victims of the internal armed conflict. Many of them felt that for the rest of the country, and especially for the main centres of political and economic power, what was happening in their towns, homes and families was happening in 'another country'. (CVR, 2004, 20)

The reform of education, therefore, is seen as critical in order to address the legacies of that conflict, to promote reconciliation and to prevent future conflict. The CVR (2003, 2004) identifies education as one of four 'essential areas' for institutional reform, and makes recommendations to guide a comprehensive reform of the education sector in the post-conflict context.

Since in many cases education is only marginally on the agenda of transitional justice initiatives, such as truth commissions, which aim, among other things, to promote reconciliation, Peru offers an interesting case in which to explore issues around education and reconciliation. Arguably, the Peruvian truth commission has engaged more explicitly with education – its role in conflict and its reform post-conflict – than have the many truth commissions that preceded it around the world.[1] This chapter looks at progress towards the recommendations for educational reform made by the CVR 5 years after the release of the CVR's final report.[2] In doing so, the chapter adopts a double focus. It first asks whether, and how, the Peruvian truth commission has been able to contribute towards post-conflict educational reform in the country. In establishing the limitations of the truth commission's contribution and the lack of actual transformation that has occurred in Peru's educational system since the conflict, the chapter then focuses on the possibilities for reconciliation that have been opened and, at least temporarily, closed in this process.

What emerges from this exploration is a complex picture of momentum and inertia, discursive consensus and political inaction that have frustrated not only efforts at reconciliation through education, but also much needed educational reform in the country. Behind a general perception that the educational recommendations of the CVR have gone unimplemented lie several moments in which the recommendations have been mobilized for specific political intentions – intentions that often do not align with the vision of reconciliation put forward by the CVR.

The truth commission was clear that meaningful reconciliation would need to include the transformation of the profound inequalities that characterize Peru and of the racist, regionalist and linguistic discrimination that enables such inequality. The CVR insisted that a critical and encompassing national reflection on the conflict and its causes should be one part of a reconciliation process (CVR, 2003, 2004). Indeed, the CVR insists that the process be a national and inclusive one, '. . . a mandate from the absent and forgotten to the entire nation' to take responsibility for the conflict and to ensure the conditions that enabled it are transformed. As this chapter shows, these components that are necessary (though certainly not comprehensive) for reconciliation have thus far not been enabled through educational reform. The interpretation of the CVR's educational recommendations by Peru's Ministry of Education (*Ministerio de Educación*, MED) have not led to the reduction of inequality within the educational sector or beyond it, or to the systematic introduction of educational processes and content that address pervasive stereotype and discrimination, or to reflexive teaching and learning about Peru's history and its recent conflict.

To make these arguments, this chapter draws on research conducted in Peru over an 8-month period in 2008. In addition to interviews with former members of the CVR, MED officials, NGO representatives and international donors, I spent time in the CVR archives (held by the national ombudsmen's office, *Defensoria del Pueblo*) and analysed education policy documents. I conducted my interviews and analysis in Spanish; the translations in this chapter (and any errors in them) are my own.

Conflict and education in Peru

Publicly provided education in Peru – a country with one of the highest levels of inequality in Latin America (the most unequal region in the world between 1950 and 1995) – is described by researchers as 'an education for the poor' (Balarin, 2005), and as such has been systematically neglected for decades. Those families that are able to do so ensure that their children attend one of an ever-growing number of private schools (Figueroa, 2008). However, since close to 50 per cent of Peruvians live below the poverty line (CIA World Factbook, 2006), state schools are the only option for most; 85.2 per cent of children attend state schools (Rivero, 2007).

Despite the strong commitment of families to children's education in the country, Peru's educational system has largely failed to enable the aspirations for social mobility that accompanied its massification to indigenous, *campesino* and urban poor communities post-independence (Crivello, 2009; Degregori, 2005, 1990; Bing Wu et al., 2000). Since the mid-twentieth century, strikingly low levels of public investment in education, economic crisis, corruption and neglect combined to create an educational crisis that finally exposed itself in students' poor performance in national standardized tests and in the OECD's PISA (Organization for Economic Co-operation and Development, Programme for International Student Assessment) examinations in the early 2000s. Indeed, following the publication of these examination results, Peruvian publicly provided education was declared by the MED to be in a 'state of emergency' (Frisancho and Reátegui, 2009). The ensuing plan to address the 'educational emergency' became the guiding policy framework for the Ministry of Education from 2004 to 2006 and therefore, as will be discussed below, also configured the Ministry's response to the CVR's recommendations.

While the effects of conflict on the educational sector were likely to have played a part in the decline of Peru's educational system, as the CVR identified, the education system itself was a factor in sparking and sustaining violent conflict in Peru. The Shining Path subversive group, to which the CVR attributes responsibility for 54 per cent of the approximately 69,000 deaths during the conflict (CVR, 2004, 17), was described in 1993 as a group that 'feeds itself off the Peruvian educational system' (Ansión et al., 1993, 11). Shining Path began as one of many splinter groups that emerged from disputes in the Peruvian Communist Party and concentrated itself in a public university in the poor, highland department (province) of Ayacucho. Here, the group spread its Maoist/Marxist ideology among students, eventually extending its influence to other state universities in the country.

In addition to capturing the sympathies of many university students, Shining Path gained followers among state school teachers, particularly through a focus on controlling several teacher training institutes and a presence in the national teachers' union. *Sendero Luminoso* was also able to gain support among many young people in rural, *campesino* and indigenous communities, those same communities long excluded from full participation in Peruvian society and economy that Sinesio López (1997) called 'imaginary citizens'. Though for many these loyalties would fade as *Sendero Luminoso* violence became increasingly arbitrary and brutal, the group initially offered an 'illusion of absolute coherence' (Degregori, 1989 in Ames, 2009, 371) for young people whose involvement with education set them apart from their traditional communities, yet promised few avenues for future employment in a society that rejected their indigenous and/or rural backgrounds. For these young people caught in 'a no-man's land between two worlds' (ibid., 368), *Sendero* seemed as though it might offer a 'path towards social mobility' (Degregori, 2005, 131). It helped that Shining Path indoctrination mirrored the authoritarian, didactic and unquestionable peda-gogical style that had long characterized teaching and learning in Peru's state schools (Frisancho and Reátegui, 2009; CVR, 2003; Ansión et al., 1993).

The teaching profession, which had become one of the few options for edu-cated young people from rural communities in Peru, was marked by Shining Path's influence. Juan Ansión and colleagues (1993) describe the options availa-ble to rural young people as: teaching, small-scale farming, migration, coca production, *Sendero Luminoso*, the army or petty crime (41). Teaching declined in prestige due to the proliferation of teacher training institutes following policy change in the 1990s, the admittance of uncertified teachers into the profession and consistent wage cuts. This, along with the increasingly desperate socioeco-nomic conditions in which teachers worked, led many to leave the profession. Those who remained teaching, particularly those who worked in impoverished rural areas, tended to be under-qualified, under-paid and disgruntled (ibid.). Whether through their presence in the national teachers' union and in teacher training institutes, or through their actual coercive presence in schools and com-munities, Shining Path recruited or intimidated a number of teachers (as well as a number of students) into their ranks.

There is no doubt that many within the public education sector resisted the increasing influence of Shining Path. Indeed, in many communities teachers and students became expert at complying with the demands of insurgents when they were present in their schools and carrying on relatively normally when they were not (ibid.). Resistance in the teachers' union was often outspoken and for some was met with lethal violence (CVR, 2003, Volume 3). This resistance was not helped by the increasing perception outside the sector – especially from state forces – that public education and public universities were a 'terrorist nest' (CVR, 2003, Volume 5, 610). In some cases, the schools that resisted Shining Path incursions had to do the same when the armed forces arrived in their communities (Ansión et al., 1993).

During the 1983–1985 'scorched earth' policy, *Sendero Luminoso* militants and innocent people alike were killed by the armed forces, which used violence to subdue entire regions. Teachers, students and the university community especially were treated with intense suspicion by the police, army and navy and were disproportionately victims of state violence (CVR, 2003). Indeed, teacher and terrorist were often synonymous terms to members of the armed forces and teachers were the first suspects when the military entered a new community. Ansión and colleagues (1993) heard reports of teachers being threatened, abused, raped, disappeared and killed by the armed forces. They describe a 'vicious cycle' in which the state presumption that teachers were *Sendero* terrorists under-pinned human rights violations, which then caused teachers to reject the armed forces' efforts to protect civilians and to increase their sympathy towards *Sendero*. The CVR's investigations found the armed forces to be responsible for 37 per cent of deaths during the conflict. The CVR also assigned 'serious respon-sibility' to the Peruvian state for its equation of educators and students with ter-rorists, for its neglect of the educational system and for the failure to ensure that education enabled the aspirations of the young people within it (CVR, 2004).

Education in the CVR

The leader of the Shining Path, Abimael Guzmán, was arrested in Lima in 1993. Although then-President Alberto Fujimori heralded this as the end of the conflict, and although *Sendero*'s capacity to continue waging war against the Peruvian state decreased very substantially, the CVR was mandated to investigate the period from 1980 to 2000. This was because Fujimori continued to use the conflict and national security to justify increasingly authoritarian policies and practices, which included dismantling the legislature, ignoring the constitution, enforcing the sterilization of indigenous women and disregarding due process in the justice system (CVR, 2003a). When a corruption scandal led to Fujimori's hasty exit in 2000, several transitional processes began in Peru – among these a post-Fujimori transition back to democracy, a transitional justice process that began with the CVR[3], and a period of 'telling the truth' about the nation's educational crisis.

The CVR's focus on education in its work and recommendations is one of the points at which these different transitional processes have overlapped. The CVR operated over a 2-year period from 2001 to 2003, producing a 9-volume final report that drew on testimony from over 17,000 survivors, participants, victims (and their relatives) and witnesses of conflict. From the CVR's final report emerges a narrative in which long-standing inequality, exclusion and racial, regional and linguistic discrimination enabled a complacency and indifference among those whose political power might have prevented or minimized the massive human rights violations of tens of thousands who came predominantly from the country's most marginalized regions and communities (CVR, 2004, 2003). Eighty-five per cent of those killed or disappeared in the conflict came from the Andean or jungle departments of Ayacucho, Junín, Huánuco, Huancavelica, Apurímac and San Martín; 55 per cent of victims depended on agriculture and/or fishing for their livelihoods. While only one-fifth of Peruvians speak an indigenous language as their mother tongue, more than 75 per cent of victims fit this profile. Sixty-eight percent of victims did not have a secondary education (while nationally around 40 per cent of Peruvian have not completed secondary schooling) (CVR, 2004, 20–24).

As already mentioned, the CVR listed education among the 'factors that made the conflict possible' (2004, 333). It therefore made recommendations for educational reform, which are presented in Table 6.1.

In short descriptions provided around each of the above recommendations, the CVR stressed the importance of: intercultural and bilingual education; linkages with other sectors in addressing the needs of the most vulnerable children; the need for scientific education, and a move away from dogmatic teaching (especially given its linkages with *Sendero Luminoso* ideology); early childhood education; and local educational management (CVR, 2003, Volume 9, Chapter 2, 134–38). The recommendations are presented without guidance as to how, by whom or by when they are to be implemented. The decree that established the CVR, however, states that CVR recommendations are to be 'processed and attended to through legislative, political or administrative initiatives' (Decreto Supremo No. 065–2001-PCM, 2001); thus obliging the Peruvian government to carry out and implement the CVR's recommendations, an obligation to which the government further committed itself with President Alejandro Toledo's acceptance of the CVR's final report in 2003.

Table 6.1 The educational recommendations of the CVR

Principles that should guide action in the educational sector

D.1 Emphasise educational policies aiming to transform the school into a place where the human condition of the student is respected and a place that contributes to the holistic development of the student's personality. Achieve a conscientiousness of peace and affirm education as its instrument.

D.2 Establish a Study Plan that stimulates learning and orients knowledge towards wellbeing in order to achieve a holistic formation and a distancing from the proclivity to violence; reformulate simplistic and distorted visions of the Peruvian historical reality.

D.3 Promotion of education that includes respect for ethnic and cultural differences. Adapt all aspects of the school to the ethno-linguistic, cultural and geographical diversity of the country.

D.4 Strengthen instances of participation and the democratization of schools .

D.5 Discipline: . . . The CVR proposes prohibiting all forms of physical punishment or humiliating practice against boys and girls as a form of discipline and drastically sanctioning these as the exercise of violence.

Recommendations towards a 'special programme' for rural schools, especially in the areas most affected by violence

D.6 Urgent attention to the most vulnerable populations: beginning with the youngest in the most needy areas.

D.7 Develop a literacy plan with priority given to adolescent girls and women in rural areas.

D.8 Redefine educational content, methodology and provision in function with capabilities to access the labour market, with particular emphasis on rural populations.

D.9 Give quality to and return the dignity of the rural school.

Source: CVR, 2003, Volume 9, Chapter 2, p. 134–138.

'The recommendations are not new': Arriving at the educational recommendations

In this sense [making educational recommendations] the Commission didn't do original work, no? They repeated the advice that had more or less been developing at this time about the necessity of an educational reform . . . The recommendations don't seem to be original to me . . . They are more less what had been developing as a consensus. (Interview, former Minister of Education 2001–2002, 26 February 2008)

. . . in one way or another, even if it we don't say it explicitly, in the CVR we were supporters of working as has been done – and as now needs to be applied – on the National Educational Project [*Proyecto Educativo Nacional*,

PEN] that the National Education Council [*Consejo Nacional de Educación*, CNE] developed. (Interview, former president CVR, 30 January 2008)

So, here, in this sense, I think that what the CVR proposes is absolutely correct. The PEN proposes exactly this. Here we need a structural reform. We don't want to improve what we have in education; we need to re-think it. We aren't the only ones who think in this way, it isn't an outlandish thought. There is a lot of consensus. (Interview, member of the CNE, 4 March 2008)

As these interview quotations demonstrate, actors from within and from outside the CVR felt that the truth commission's educational recommendations drew on and lent momentum to existing proposals for educational reform in Peru.[4] A respondent recalled that since Fujimori's self-exile there had not only been a justice-focused process of truth telling, but also a period of telling the 'truth about education' (interview, *Tarea* Programme Officer, 6 October 2008). The dire situation of state education in the country, which Fujimori had done his best to cover over, had come vibrantly to light at the turn of the century.

This educational crisis – obvious to students, parents and teachers in the 1990s – became a major public issue. There was greater public awareness of previously unpublished educational outcomes, the results of Peru's participation in PISA, and with the launch, by Valentín Paniagua's (2000–2001) transitional government, of a nationwide consultation on education. Translating the findings of the national consultation 'that mobilized thousands of Peruvians' (CNE, 2008, 12) became the task of the National Education Council (CNE) through the development of the National Educational Project (PEN) that laid out a proposal for the institutional reform of the educational sector in 2006 (ibid.).

In parallel, therefore, with Peru's transition back to democracy (after Fujimori's dismantling of the democratic apparatus) and towards peace (after two decades of conflict) emerged a consensus among education actors of the need for a wide reform – a 'restructuring' and 're-thinking' (interview, member of CNE, 4 March 2008) – of Peruvian state education. This was particularly the case among those working relatively independently from the MED, for instance in the CNE or in education NGOs. Key principles in this consensus were eventually articulated within then PEN and revolved around quality, relevant, decentralized, culturally appropriate and value-centred education for all, delivered by professional, competent teachers and managed by an efficient, forward-looking Ministry of Education (ibid.). The PEN drew attention to the unequal nature of education in Peru and to the fact that the poorest students, and especially those in rural locations, received the poorest quality education and demonstrated the lowest learning outcomes.

The principles guiding the educational reform envisioned by the PEN, and its prioritizing of rural education in particular, are understood to be consensus themes that the CVR picked up on and repeated in its own recommendations for educational reform. Although the final version of the PEN was not yet published when the CVR presented its final report in 2003, the CNE was already articulating the consensus emerging from the national consultation on education. Though the CVR never explicitly mentions the PEN in its recommendations towards education, actors from both the CNE and the truth commission perceived their reform proposals to be in agreement in terms of key educational problems and their solutions in Peru. As will be seen in later discussions, this perceived consensus had particular consequences for the possibilities of educational reform in the country.

Since the CVR: Educational reform in the post-conflict context

Nearly 3 months after the presentation of the CVR's final report, President Toledo addressed the nation in order to express the government's position on the CVR's work. Toledo paid tribute to the report, apologized to all the victims of the 20 years of violence and accepted the CVR's message that social exclusion and state abandonment contributed to the conflict. Toledo was less open in acknowledging the role of the armed forces outlined in the CVR report and tended instead to highlight 'terrorist' violence.

In 2004, the MED's Vice-Minister of Institutional Management stated that: 'The agenda of the educational sector coincides with the recommendations of the CVR' (Oficina de Prensa y Comunicaciones, Ministerio de Educación, Républica del Perú, 2004). Speaking to a group of representatives from conflict affected areas, the vice-minister continued:

> No recommendation of the Commission is, in essence, different from what the Ministry of Education requires of itself in its normative framework. There is no difference encountered for us in working together for quality education, whose absence affects the marginalized and the excluded. (ibid.)

The vice-minister went on to state that the MED, operating under the 'educational emergency' framework at this time, had outlined the following 'concrete actions' that aligned with the CVR's recommendations. These included:

- Scholarships for orphans and victims of political violence
- Incorporating the CVR's recommendations in Regional Educational Projects
- Promoting the CVR's recommendations with regional educational authorities
- Developing a 'special project' with children in regions affected by violence to promote a culture of peace
- Distributing educational materials, including materials in indigenous languages
- The creation of library modules in 7,300 secondary schools
- Professional development for teachers
- Educational decentralization based on a strategy that reflects the context of rural and *campesino* children (ibid.)

With this 2004 announcement, and Toledo's 2003 formal reception of the CVR in mind, I was interested in 2008 in tracing whether and how the CVR's educational recommendations had in fact been implemented by the Ministry of Education, along the lines outlined above or in other ways. Since the High-Level Multi-Sectoral Commission (*Comisión Multisectoral de Alto Nivel*, CMAN) charged with following up on the CVR's recommendations and eventually given a budget in 2005, focused its work almost exclusively on collective and (eventually) individual reparations under the CVR's reparations plan (CMAN, 2010; interview, Executive Secretary, CMAN, 20 October 2008), the CVR's recommendations themselves were largely left to the discretion of the sectors and Ministries towards which they were addressed to implement, with virtually no guidance, monitoring or coordination.

Perhaps unsurprisingly, studies into the implementation of CVR recommendations as a whole suggested limited progress (Macher 2007; Oelschlegel, 2006). While Sofía Macher (2007) found that some advances had been made, she noted 'insufficient social compromise' and 'fragile and derisive political will' towards the recommendations (8). She also found that where progress towards CVR recommendations had been made, it was not generally due to explicit commitment and action on CVR goals (ibid.).

Within the MED's response to the CVR recommendations, the vice-minister's announcement above was the first of several examples in which commitment to the CVR's recommendations was used discursively to lend momentum to certain policy initiatives already underway within the Ministry of Education. Notably, however, and in line with Macher's findings, the impetus for these initiatives usually did not spring from commitment to implementing or complying with the CVR's educational recommendations.

The sentiment expressed by several respondents above – that the CVR's educational recommendations were not new and drew on a relatively broad consensus around the necessary direction of educational reform in Peru – was echoed in the MED in a slightly different way. Ministry officials repeatedly claimed (publicly and in interviews for this project) that the CVR recommendations aligned with their existing priorities. This claim was made despite the fact that the MED has been criticized for its failure to commit to and act upon the consensus around educational reform in Peru (CNE, 2008; Balarin, 2005). Furthermore, the Ministry continued to claim that the CVR aligned with Ministry priorities as these priorities (at least superficially) continued to change. For instance, when the educational emergency framework was dropped entirely as the Toledo administration was replaced by that of Alan García in 2006, the CVR's recommendations were still reported to echo the Ministry agenda. The MED's insistence on resonance between the CVR's recommendations and their 'agenda' and 'normative framework' enabled a stance in which no specific actions related uniquely or directly to the CVR's recommendations were necessary.

Looking in detail at three themes that have emerged from my analysis around the progress towards the CVR's recommendations can illuminate several of the issues raised thus far. First emerged a general perception among those interviewed for this project that little progress has been made towards the CVR's educational recommendations. Second, behind this general perception is evidence to suggest that the CVR's educational recommendations have in fact been used in particular ways to generate momentum and inertia at different times and around different issues. Upon exploring these two themes, the chapter will close with a third theme that asks what these findings mean for the possibilities of post-conflict educational reform and reconciliation in Peru.

'[Sighs] No.' Perceptions of non-implementation

The range of responses to my questioning around implementation of the CVR's educational recommendations is displayed in Table 6.2.

The frequency of response is not presented numerically in Table 6.2 because, in several cases, respondents would straddle between responses – generally this

Table 6.2 Range of responses to questions re the implementation of CVR recommendations

Response	Reasoning / Justification	Respondents
No.	Because of lack of political will.	Former CVR Commissioners and staff. Former MED officials. Members of the educational community. Members of the human rights community. Regional educational authorities
	Because of the nature of the Ministry of Education, politics and bureaucracy in Peru.	Former CVR Commissioners and staff. Members of the educational community.
Maybe somewhat.	But not in a planned or coordinated way	Former CVR Commissioners and staff. Members of the educational community. Former MED officials
	Only because the recommendations pick up on themes already being worked on.	
Of course.	The MED is doing all these things anyway.	Current MED officials.

Source: Interviews conducted in Peru, 2008.

would happen as a respondent would begin by answering that no, little progress had been made towards the recommendations, and then in explaining their response would recall some initiative or occurrence that aligned with the common justifications given for a 'maybe somewhat' response. Therefore, taken as a whole, the interviews show that for most respondents their immediate perceptions around the implementation of the CVR educational recommendations tend to discount the recommendations as unimplemented. As respondents elaborate, however, they tend to offer either or both an explanation for non-implementation and/or a qualification of a limited, incomplete and unplanned implementation. For instance, the Director of the NGO, *Tarea*, initially responded, 'Hmm. No, no, no. The Ministry hasn't taken these on board in a systematic way', before going on to describe unsystematic implementation around themes important to certain areas within the MED (interview, 7 February 2008). Education officials tended to be exceptions to this general pattern of response, echoing the refrain described above around how the recommendations are in line with the actions and priorities of the MED.

For the majority of respondents, who felt there was very little progress towards meeting the CVR's educational recommendations in practice, the reasons for this lack of tangible action were to be found in lack of political will and/or in the (dysfunctional) nature of the Ministry of Education itself. Those who blamed political will tended to be critical of both the Toledo and García administrations for falling short on their commitments to the CVR and drew attention to García's own and his administration's conflict legacy. Alan García was also president of Peru from 1985 to 1990, a period during which a series of human rights violations were carried out by the armed forces. Respondents felt this must dissuade the current administration from volition to engage with the CVR.

> Julia: Do you think that the CVR has had an impact in the educational sector in Peru?
> A relative impact, no? The same as it has in the population generally. I think that, as has happened with other truth commissions, we have to wait a time – it is a relatively sensible but long time – especially with the impatience that one has, but it is a short time from an historical perspective – to see the effects of a truth commission. . . . At the moment there is a President who is judged by the CVR, right? Alan García, who had or has political and ethical responsibility, maybe even criminal responsibility. So, it is difficult that a government led by him will be very friendly towards the truth commission.
> Julia: Hmm. And, did you see the previous government taking –
> The previous government, yes, it is a frustration. Because Toledo was the one who could have done the most for the CVR. Simply because he isn't, he isn't one of the cases that we studied – we studied the governments of Belaúnde and García and Fujimori – and also because he belongs to those *campesinos* and indigenous groups who were worst affected. But I think he was lacking vision and grandeur (*grandeza*). At least he didn't interfere in the work of the commission, he didn't involve himself, but he didn't do much more with respect to the CVR. (interview with former CVR president, 30 January 2008)

Those who referred to political will tended to coincide with other assessments of CVR progress (Laplante and Theidon, 2007; Macher, 2007) that point to Toledo government lethargy – even in a climate where international organizations very much encouraged CVR follow up (Macher, 2007) – and to García government efforts to avoid or even to discredit the CVR.

Those respondents who pointed to the Ministry's own shortcomings as factors preventing the implementation of the CVR's recommendations highlighted lack of leadership, the fragmentary nature of the Ministry with various units that fail to cooperate, and rigid bureaucracy.

> The problem with this is that in the Ministry there are people who are totally committed, who share the vision of the recommendations of the Commission, but these are like individual efforts. Even though they are responsible for a team or an area in the Ministry of Education, they are an

> island, every single one of them. And I think the big drama in this Ministry is that there isn't – you can't feel or establish a single path and work together on this with strength. So, you have on one side that yes, someone is reinforcing or highlighting rural education. On the other side you have a person who is interested in curriculum content and can include the CVR, on the other side [laughing] you have . . . [trails off]. But as a Ministry in reality there is no policy that says it is following the recommendations in a holistic way. So, in the end the efforts of units within the Ministry dilute themselves, no? It seems to me they are too small to produce an impact. (interview, former CVR Commissioner, 28 February 2008)

Such diagnoses of the MED in Peru resonate with research (Balarin 2008; 2005) that found 'discontinuity, or the impossibility of consolidating policy proposals' at the core of Peru's educational administration (Balarin, 2005, 92).

Several respondents who moved towards a 'somewhat' response in terms of the implementation of recommendations, reflected upon an uncoordinated, unplanned or even instrumental implementation of CVR recommendations by the MED. These were responses that indicated that while perhaps some policy efforts were in place to address the CVR's recommendations, the motivation behind these did not originate from the need to fulfil CVR recommendations.

> I don't think that the Ministry of Education has . . . the current Ministry of Education has a specific program to implement educational measures regarding the TRC. However, I think that recent education measures taken by the current Ministry in a way are trying to tackle down a couple of the problems that are well known regarding the poor educational system in our country . . . The specific recommendations regarding the TRC have not been put into practice but other government policies could be seen, in a way, as tackling that problem without saying we're fulfilling the TRC rec-ommendations. (interview with Judicial Advisor, *Comunidad Andina de Juristas*, 5 February 2008, interview conducted in English)

These perspectives provided a somewhat different take on the Ministry's own rhetorical approach towards the CVR's recommendations outlined above in which the recommendations are seen to be perfectly in line with the Ministry's already determined course of action. A member of the CNE argued that this kind of MED behaviour was not new or unique to the CVR. He explained that this approach enabled the MED to take on board and express commitment towards various educational proposals (including the PEN, which the MED adopted in 2007) without having to alter the existing structures and imperatives of education in Peru in the slightest.

> So, what the Ministry has done, or is doing, let's say, is taken politics and institutional dynamics that are basically inert, that come from long ago and that it doesn't know how to revert or restructure and it is simply renaming them. In other words, they give them the label of new demands . . . This hasn't just happened with the recommendations of the CVR, it happened with the Education for All plan, it happened with the PEN. So the Ministry of Education salutes and congratulates all of these plans and incorporates them into its discourse, but its agenda remains very flat. (interview with Member of CNE, 4 March 2008)

Hence the vice-minister's statement that the CVR's recommendations 'coincide' with and are 'no different from' the MED's own agenda and the affixing of educational interventions conceived under the framework of the educational emergency with the CVR's label (Oficina de Prensa y Comunicaciones, Ministerio de Educación, Républica del Perú, 2004). Again these diagnoses reflect scholarship on the education system in Peru. Balarin (2005) describes '[c]hanges in governments and policy-making teams hinder the application and development of policies and programmes over time, producing a kind of zero sum game that leads to inaction in spite of the permanent action that is involved in the constant redefinition of what needs to be done in Peruvian education' (3).

Finally, MED officials themselves, when it was possible to secure interviews with them, tended to point to ongoing or planned activities (like those listed by the vice-minister in the 2003 speech quoted above) that coincided with and therefore addressed the CVR's recommendations. Interestingly, the initiatives to which they referred sometimes differed quite substantially in vision, justification and ultimate intention and often did little to favour the kind of reconciliation envisioned by the CVR, a reconciliation that insisted on acknowledging and transforming the inequalities at the root of Peru's conflict.

Momentum and inertia: The use of the CVR's recommendations within the MED

Elsewhere I have suggested that truth commission educational recommendations can be seen to lend a certain momentum and legitimacy to particular post-conflict educational reform initiatives (Paulson, 2006, 2009). In Sierra Leone, the Truth and Reconciliation Commission provided momentum for the largely World Bank-led reform of the educational sector, even though several of its recommendations (such as a recommendation for free secondary education for girls) called for changes beyond the scope of the reform package (Paulson, 2006). In Peru, where a coherent programme of post-conflict educational reform is absent (despite CVR recommendations for one), the phenomenon of momentum takes on a particularly political nature. This section demonstrates how the CVR's educational recommendations have been presented as 'coinciding' with distinct educational initiatives (led by distinct political actors) towards a variety of distinct aims – aims which do not necessarily coincide with those that CVR put forward for educational reform and do not necessarily enable a contribution towards reconciliation. Indeed, what is sometimes enabled is more aptly described as inertia that maintains the status quo than as momentum towards policy reform. Inertia in an educational system whose status quo is characterized by inequality, immobility and authoritarianism does not bode well for the potential of education to contribute towards reconciliation. Three particular 'moments of momentum/inertia' are described here.

The educational emergency and the CVR recommendations

As described earlier, the MED's first reaction to the CVR and its educational recommendations was to declare their coincidence with its own agenda – an agenda that at the time revolved around addressing Peru's recently declared educational emergency. The vice-minister laid out a series of activities, already contemplated for within the emergency framework, which would demonstrate the MED's compliance with the CVR's recommendations. First, it is important to remember that the CVR's recommendations called for a large-scale institutional reform of the educational project in Peru and not for a series of discrete activities. The vice-minister's statement was in many ways a skirting around the CVR's recommendations and the Ministry's responsibility to consider them seriously.

Additionally, the educational emergency had already been criticized by CVR actors for its lack of coincidence with the messages of the CVR's final report. When the MED announced the 'most marginalized and excluded' schools (Oficina de Prensa y Comunicaciones, Ministerio de Educación, République del Perú, 2004) that would be privileged under its emergency programme, one of the CVR commissioners spoke out against the criteria for selection of the schools, which did not include the degree to which schools and communities were affected by Peru's conflict (Macher, 2004). Schools were selected based on socioeconomic poverty levels and rural and urban location. While, as the commissioner acknowledged, it is likely that some of the schools selected were seriously affected by the conflict, the legacies of conflict were not contemplated in the selection process or in the interventions designed for what the MED labelled as Peru's most marginalized schools. Since the CVR had explicitly called for the privileging of rural schools and, especially, of those schools most affected by conflict (CVR, 2003, Volume 9, Chapter 2), the Ministry's failure to contemplate conflict in its 'emergency' selection criteria was far from in line with the CVR's recommendations.

The Ministry would later distribute CVR-based materials only to those schools privileged within the educational emergency under the logic that those poor and rural schools selected for the emergency programming were the most likely to be sites for future political violence (interview, Executive Coordinator, Technical Team for EFA, Ministry of Education, 18 February 2008). Again, this decision was far from in line with the CVR's messages, which highlighted precisely this kind of stereotyping as having played a role in sustaining the conflict. Further, the CVR's final report stressed that for reconciliation to be possible it was important that every Peruvian reflect upon and take responsibility for the armed conflict.

In many ways, the emergency education framework within the MED is well-described by Balarin's (2005) account of ministerial policy making below:

> . . . the lack of a more structured bureaucracy and, generally, of a 'thicker' set of institutions means that ministerial elites have almost absolute power to impose their will and views over policies. It is the ministers and their close set of advisers who define whether new policies are to be introduced and whether existing policies are to be continued or not, and . . ., such decisions often respond to personal views and agendas. (152)

The educational emergency, an initiative of one of Toledo's Ministers, which was initiated rather suddenly in response to the poor international performance of Peru's educational system, certainly had elements of a publicity event. And, when it was firmly discontinued by García's incoming administration much of the MED's (already rhetorical) focus on the CVR's educational recommendations were discontinued with it, as a MED official explains below:

> Because the CVR materials were part of the 'educational emergency' framework and because the national programme for the educational

emergency was an initiative of the previous administration, well, today nobody speaks about the educational emergency at all. (interview, Executive Coordinator, Technical Team for EFA, Ministry of Education, 18 February 2008)

The CVR and PEN

While the activities outlined by the vice-minister in 2004 under the educational emergency framework represent the MED's most explicit policy making around the CVR's educational recommendations, they do not represent the only 'moment of momentum' the CVR generated within the MED and beyond it. As described above, the CVR's educational recommendations were seen to have drawn upon and captured a broader consensus around the need for and features of educational reform in the country – a consensus articulated within the National Education Project (PEN). The CVR recommendations and the PEN share a commitment towards improved rural education, relevant education for Peru's diverse population, value-centred education for citizenship, improved learning outcomes and equality. Although the recommendations themselves do not mention or explicitly endorse the PEN, it appears that at least some CVR commissioners, including the CVR president, saw the recommendations as an opportunity to lend momentum and legitimacy to the PEN.

When the García government questioned the existence of the CNE beyond the end of its first term in 2008, the former president of the CVR wrote an opinion piece in the newspaper *El Comercio* arguing in favour of CNE and the PEN. The CVR president argued that in the face of the lack of 'real public policies' in Peru, the CNE's process towards the creation of the PEN was 'an interesting lesson in the art of 'policymaking'. He called for the implementation of the PEN, which he described as 'proposing a route towards what should be a common direction, but what, curiously, actually signals a genuine revolutionary turn in the sector' (Lerner Febres, 2008, a4). The CVR president also noted the 'negligible attention that successive governments pay' to comprehensive and holistic long-term policy proposals like the PEN (ibid., a4).

The CVR president drew attention to the positive elements of the PEN beyond and despite its non-implementation to date. He described the PEN more as an example of policy-making possibility than as a soon–to-be-implemented package for education reform, indicating the degree towards which hopes for the PEN's implementation have been frustrated. Behind Peru's strong educational consensus articulated by the PEN and reinforced by the CVR recommendations lies stagnation in terms of actual educational change as the PEN remains yet another policy adopted by the Ministry on paper but absent in practice. In this way the CVR provided momentum for an inert movement. It added a strong, legitimate claim towards already strong and legitimate claims for the need for educational reform in Peru; claims that the Ministry continues to agree with rhetorically, and to incorporate by claiming consistency with its own agenda, claims that in practice the Ministry continues to ignore. In this way then, the fact that the CVR's educational recommendations were not new and that they aligned with a strong existing prerogative within Peru's extra-Ministerial educational community acted to decrease the likelihood of educational reform following from the CVR's recommendations. While the CVR's recommendations likely gained legitimacy among members of Peru's educational NGO community thanks to their resonance with the PEN, and while the PEN's legitimacy in the human rights community was likely bolstered by the CVR's tacit support, this mutual reinforcement did little towards the implementation of either the PEN or the CVR's reform programmes.

Stagnancy in policy making around issues highlighted by both the CVR and the PEN, such as the persistent poor quality and irrelevance of state education for young people from poor, indigenous and/or rural communities is indicative of the degree to which educational reform in Peru has failed to respond to the conflict and its causes. Without explicit policy making that is followed with concrete actions to address the ways in which the educational system maintains inequalities, fails to provide meaningful pathways towards livelihoods for the majority of young Peruvians, and continues to lack relevancy in the lives of many learners (Cuenca, 2010) a real contribution towards reconciliation via education reform is not evident in Peru.

The CVR in curriculum

The congruence of the CVR recommendations with the PEN led to a sort of stalled momentum and ignored legitimacy within the MED and to inertia around actual post-conflict educational reform. The third 'moment of momentum' considered here occurred through initiatives to insert the CVR's narrative of Peru's conflict (the 'truth' produced by the truth commission) into national curriculum. There were two demonstrative incidents in which CVR content about Peru's recent conflict was put forward as potential national curriculum content (discussed in more detail in Paulson, 2010). Each of these incidents lent momentum towards currents fundamentally in discord with the CVR's findings and message.

The first, as mentioned earlier, resulted in the selective use of conflict-related educational materials in communities considered to be prone to conflict. In this way, the MED demonstrated an attitude that placed blame for the conflict on poor, rural and/or indigenous communities – those that already bore the brunt of the violence of the conflict – and also implied that they shoulder the responsibility for ensuring that similar violence never reoccur. This attitude contradicts the CVR's insistence that Peruvian society as a whole holds responsibility for the nation's conflict and the entrenched social exclusion that enabled it, and accordingly for ensuring peace in the country through reflection upon the conditions that led to violence in the first place. The MED decision also maintains intact group distinctions and stereotypes that the CVR insists must be dismantled should reconciliation be possible within the country.

The second curriculum incident enabled a political attempt by García's APRA party to delegitimize the CVR and to call into question its findings. Many interpreted APRA's insistence on the scandalous nature of the curriculum content – described by an APRA Congresswoman as an 'apology for terrorism' (Libros, 2008) – as a part of a political attempt to displace the CVR's narrative of conflict, particularly those parts that highlight armed forces and APRA responsibility. As the incident spiralled into a media frenzy, APRA seemed intent to silence teaching and learning about Peru's conflict in the nation's schools, with little resistance from the MED. Again, the momentum generated around the CVR here went in an opposite direction to that intended by the educational recommendations and the CVR's message more generally that encouraged the reform of history education and insisted upon the need to reflect upon and learn about the realities of Peru's conflict.

Conclusion

> If public education is an education for those who are excluded, for those who do not matter, for the country's 'imaginary citizens' (López 1997), then inaction in this sector is of little consequence for the country. (Balarin, 2005, 209)

> 'The Peru' that Mr. García invokes has a responsibility to engage in dialogue, the responsibility to ask for forgiveness for its indifference during the years of internal armed conflict. It must recognize the racism and ethnic abasement that exists in this society and reconcile itself with it marginalized compatriots. (Theidon, 2004, 258)

These two quotes are useful in describing the relationship between education and reconciliation in post-conflict Peru. State education remains 'education for the poor', reaching the most marginalized and offering knowledge of questionable relevance that leads to little opportunity for social integration or economic advancement (Cuenca, 2010; Crivello, 2009; Balarin, 2008, 2005). While this situation certainly existed before Peru's armed conflict and played a role in the production and reproduction of violence in the country, the fact that it remains so in the post-conflict context is telling in terms of the possibilities for reconciliation in the country.

The ways in which the CVR's educational recommendations were alluded to but never implemented within the Ministry of Education are indicative of a broader attitude towards reconciliation on behalf of 'the Peru' of its political and economic elites. This attitude visible upon the presentation of the CVR's final report when many, including the current president (not in office at the time), declared reconciliation to be an impossible project given the actions of the 'Senderista assassins' (Alan García, 2003 as quoted in Theidon, 2004, 225). It was also clearly visible in educational decisions that cast the conflict as relevant only to those communities whose profiles match the Senderistas', and is below the surface in the status quo that fails to reform the ways in which education maintains inequality and exclusion in the country. This approach maintains the 'many Perus' that make up the nation, and makes clear those Perus and Peruvians that matter and those that do not. Until this long-standing attitude changes – one indication of which would certainly be that persistent inaction in the educational sector would begin to matter and to matter a lot – possibilities for national reconciliation remain limited.

Guiding questions

Is there greater potential for linkages between education and transitional justice initiatives? How might these contribute to reconciliation?

How should curriculum about the recent violent past be developed and introduced?

Should educational reform be a part of transitional justice processes?

Notes

1 A truth commission in Canada has since undertaken an explicitly education-focused process, investigating crimes committed under the residential schooling of indigenous children in the country (Indian Residential Schools Truth and Reconciliation Commission, 2009).

2 The CVR released its final report in August 2003. Data gathered for this chapter was collected in 2008, a year that included a celebration to mark the 5-year anniversary of the

presentation of the CVR's final report. Comments on educational policy making and educational reform in Peru in this chapter, therefore, refer to developments prior to the end of the calendar year 2008.

3 A reparations programme based on the CVR's proposed plan has since been initiated (with considerable delays and challenges) (Laplante and Theidon, 2008). Several domestic prosecutions have taken place including the trial and conviction of former President Fujimori on charges of grave human rights violations (Burt, 2009). An initiative is currently underway to establish a permanent 'Museum of Memory' (Cuenca, 2010).

4 This is not unlike the situation that I describe in Sierra Leone in 2006 (see Paulson, 2006).

Reference list

Ames, P. (2009), 'La escuela es progreso? Antropología y educación en el Perú', in C. I. Degregori (ed), *No Hay País Mas Diverso: Compendio de Antropología Peruana* (3rd edn). Lima: Red para el Desarrollo de las Ciencias Sociales en el Perú, 356–91.

Ansión, J., D. Del Castillo, M. Piqueras, and I. Zegarra (1993), *La Escuela en Tiempos de Guerra: Una Mirada a la Educación desde la Crisis y la Violencia* (2nd edn). Lima: Tarea.

Balarin, M. (2005), *Radical Discontinuity: A Study of the Role of Education in the Peruvian State and the Institutions and Cultures of Policy Making in Education*, unpublished doctoral thesis, University of Bath, http://opus.bath.ac.uk/15102/1/MBalarin_PhDthesis_Final_version_(March_2006).pdf (accessed 7 December 2009).

— (2008), 'Promoting educational reform in weak states: A case of radical policy discontinuity in Peru', *Globalisation, Societies and Education*, 6, 2, 163–78.

Bing Wu, K., P. Arregui, P. Goldschmidt, A. Miranda, S. Parandekar, J. Saavedra, and J. P. Silva (2000), in F. Reimers (ed), *Unequal Schools, Unequal Chances: The Challenges of Equal Opportunity in the Americas*. Cambridge, MA: Harvard University Press, 376–99.

Burt, J. M. (2009), 'Guilty as charged: The trial of former Peruvian president Alberto Fujimori for human rights violations', *International Journal of Transitional Justice*, 3, 384–405.

CIA World Factbook (2006), 'The World Factbook – South America: Peru', www.cia.gov/library/publications/the-world-factbook/geos/pe.html (accessed 10 May 2010).

Comisión de la Verdad y Reconciliación (CVR) (2003), *Informe Final*, volumes 1–9, www.cverdad.org.pe/ifinal/index.php (accessed 11 October 2008).

— (2004), *Hatun Willakuy: Versión abreviada del Informe Final de la Comisión de la Verdad y Reconciliación, Perú*. Lima: CVR.

Comisión Multisectoral de Alto Nivel (CMAN) (2010), 'CMAN', www.planintegraldereparaciones.gob.pe/portada.php?Id=1&opcion=CMAN (accessed 25 May 2010).

Comisión Nacional de Educación (CNE) (2008), *CNE: Balance y Perspectives 2002–2008*. Lima: CNE.

Crivello, G. (2009), *Becoming Somebody: Youth Transitions Through Education and Migration: Evidence from Young Lives Peru*, Young Lives Working Paper 43, www.younglives.org.uk/

our-publications/working-papers/2018becoming-somebody2019-youth-transitions-through-education-and-migration-2013-evidence-from-young-lives-peru (accessed 25 May 2010).

Cuenca, R. (2010), 'Is reconciliation possible in a country that seeks homogeneity among its citizens?' OTJR Debates, Transitional Justice and Reconciliation in Peru, www.csls.ox.ac.uk/otjr.php?show=currentDebate11 (accessed 25 May 2010).

Decreto Supremo No. 065–2001-PCM (2001), Lima: Presidente de la República, www.cverdad.org.pe/lacomision/nlabor/decsup01.php (accessed 26 November 2009).

Degregori, C. I. (1990), *El surgimiento de Sendero Luminoso*. Lima, Peru: IEP.

— (ed) (2000), *No Hay País Mas Diverso: Compendio de Antropología Peruana*. Lima: IEP.

— (2005), 'Harvesting storms: Peasant *rondas* and the defeat of Sendero Luminoso in Ayacucho', in S. Stern (ed), *Shining and Other Paths: War and Society in Peru, 1980–1995*, (2nd edn). Durham: Duke University Press, 128–57.

Figueroa, A. (2008), *Education, Labour Markets and Inequality in Peru*, CRISE Working Paper 48. www.research4development.info/PDF/Outputs/Inequality/wp48.pdf (accessed 25 May 2010).

Frisancho, S., and F. Reátegui (2009), 'Moral education and post-war societies: The Peruvian case', *Journal of Moral Education*, 38, 4, 421–43.

Indian Residential Schools Truth and Reconciliation Commission (TRC-CVR Canada) (2009), 'Indian Residential Schools Truth and Reconciliation Commission', http://www.trc.ca/websites/trcinstitution/index.php?p=26 (accessed 25 September 2009).

Laplante, L. J., and K.S. Theidon (2007), 'Truth with consequences: Justice and reparations in post-truth commission Peru', *Human Rights Quarterly*, 29, 1, 228–50.

Lerner Febres, S. (2008), 'La urgencia de la continuidad', *El Comercio*, http://elcomercio.pe/EdicionImpresa/pdf/2008/02/22/ECOP220208a4.pdf (accessed 6 May 2010).

López, S. (1997), *Ciudadanos Reales e Imaginarios: Concepciones, Desarollos y Mapas de la Ciudadanía en el Perú*. Lima: Instituto de Diálogo y Propuestas.

Macher, S. (2004), 'La emergencia de la educación', *Ideele Politica*, www.agenciaperu.com/columnas/2004/jul/ideele2.htm (accessed 14 April 2009).

— (2007), *Recomendaciones vs. Realidades: Avances y Desafíos en el Post-CVR Perú*. Lima: IDL.

Oelschlegel, A. (2006), *El Informe Final de la Comisión de la Verdad y Reconciliación en el Perú. Resumen crítico a los avances de sus recomendaciones*, unpublished thesis, Biblioteca Jurídica Virtual del Instituto de Investigaciones Jurídicas de la UNAM, www.juridicas.unam.mx/publica/librev/rev/dconstla/cont/20062/pr/pr31.pdf (accessed 7 June 2010).

Oficina de Prensa y Comunicaciones, Ministerio de Educacion, Republica del Peru (2004), 'Agenda de sector educación coincide con recomendaciones de la CVR', www.minedu.gob.pe/noticias/index.php?id=1211 (accessed 27 October 2008).

Paulson, J. (2006), 'The educational recommendations of truth and reconciliation commissions: Potential and practice in Sierra Leone', *Research in Comparative and International Education*, 1, 4, 335–50.

— (2009), *(Re)Creating Education in Postconflict Contexts: Transitional Justice, Education, and Human Development,* Research Unit, International Center for Transitional Justice, www.ictj.org/en/research/projects/research5/thematic-studies/3254.html (accessed 7 June 2010).

— (2010), 'Truth commissions and national curricula: The case of Recordándonos in Peru', in S. Parmar, M. J. Roseman, S. Siegrist and T. Sowa (eds), *Children and Transitional Justice: Truth-Telling, Accountability and Reconciliation.* Cambridge, MA: Harvard University Press, 327–64.

Paulston, R. G. (1971), *Society, Schools and Progress in Peru.* Oxford: Pergamon Press.

Rivero, J. (2007), *Educacíon, Docencia y la Clase Política en el Perú.* Lima: Ayuda en Accíon/ TAREA.

Theidon, K. (2004), *Entre Projimos: El Conflicto Armado Interno y la Política de la Reconciliación en el Perú.* Lima: IEP.

7

A Unified Rwanda? Ethnicity, History and Reconciliation in the *Ingando* Peace and Solidarity Camp

James Kearney

Chapter Outline

Introduction

Discussions of genocide and ethnic conflict, and their aftermaths, will nearly always provoke emotions and memories that make navigating the subject difficult. Equal sensitivity can lurk in discussions of how reconciliation and lasting peace can best be sought in the volatile post-ethnic conflict environment. The Rwandan Government's primary *Ingando* Peace and Solidarity Camp is being utilized to strengthen citizenship and connection to the identity of 'being Rwandan' by undermining the historical basis for the three traditional, ethnic groups of Hutu, Tutsi and Twa, which played such a fundamental role in igniting and sustaining the genocide of 1994. The present Rwandan government has sought to rewrite history and has cultivated the idea that Rwandans were split into ethnic groupings as a result of the machinations of various colonial powers. The idea of a unified Rwanda and the new history that accompanies it are promoted through the *Ingando* solidarity camps. This approach may help bond the different groups together in the short-term, but the question remains, does a top-down, unequivocal approach to disseminating history and reconstructing ethnicity enable meaningful reconciliation?

In this chapter I will discuss how the *Ingando* phenomenon is being utilized by the Rwandan National Unity and Reconciliation Commission (NURC) as a method of establishing unity and social cohesion at the expense of reconciliation; the chapter shows how this is reflected in the teaching and content of the work at the camp, where a single view of the past is being promulgated at the expense of open debate.

Rwanda genocide and rebuilding society

The 1994 Genocide in Rwanda resulted in the deaths of between 500,000 and 1,000,000 people[1] mainly, but not exclusively, from what was then regarded as the Tutsi tribe. Arguably, Rwanda's tragedy and continuing troubles spring from societal divisions dating back to at least the colonial period and most probably before[2] (Eltringham, 2004; Pottier, 2002; Mamdami, 2001). Imperial reinforcement of group division, the dominance of one group during and after colonial rule, corruption, land issues and geographical restrictions have all played a role in cementing social and ethnic division (Prunier, 1995 [2008]).

Rwanda is a country the size of Northern Ireland with a population more than five times as great. Soil conditions vary greatly in quality from region to region, a point of some importance when one considers that most of the ten million people in the country are subsistence farmers and thus urban centres are small and few in number (CIA World Factbook, 2009). For the researcher or 'peacemaker' seeking a point of origin for the 1994 tragedy in an effort to begin promoting 'reconciliation with the past', it would be tempting to focus purely on the Habyarimana pre-Genocide regime (1973–1994) and how it manipulated the education system in order to sustain division and reinforce its Hutu power base.[3] Indeed, this contributed greatly to division and the sense of ethnic difference, but Habyarimana and Rwanda's educational system under him reinforced and sustained internal tension by utilizing what had come before, namely, the perceptions of ethnic division that ordinary people already held (Hintjens, 2008).

It is commonly assumed that education can indeed contribute towards reconciliation, though it is unclear exactly how this is meant to happen (Zorbas, 2004). Unpicking this assumed relationship between education and reconciliation, while identifying how it can facilitate a new sense of society, can be difficult but not impossible (Volkan, 2004). In an attempt to reconfigure the collective memory of a population and thus open the way for reconciliation, education can play a vital role only if it openly tackles the past by questioning conventional knowledge of it (Buckley-Zistel, 2006; Cole and Barsalou, 2006; Kelman, 2006, 1999; Minow, 1998). In short-sighted, uninspired or overzealous hands – and under the pressure of having to bring ethnic groups together quickly, perhaps even artificially – education can also bring difficulties and create problems for the future. It is for this reason that a comprehensive picture of the past should be opened up and debated, for the benefit that the discussion brings and the short, medium and long-term historical clarity that it promotes.

The genocide of 1994 had been pre-planned, instigated by elements within the Presidential Guard, other military units and police, and spearheaded by the *Interahamwe* and other militia groups (Mamdami, 2001). Crucially, however, the killings were often largely carried out by ordinary people:

> [T]he main agents of the genocide were the ordinary peasants themselves. This is a terrible statement to make, but it is unfortunately borne out by the majority of the survivors' stories. The degree of compulsion exercised on them varied from place to place but in some areas, the government version of a spontaneous movement of the population to "kill the enemy Tutsi" is true. (Prunier, 1995 [2008] 247)

The role of ordinary Rwandans is a key point for consideration, particularly with references to questions of collective memory and history education in the post-conflict context. With 90 per cent of the country's post-genocide working population engaged in subsistence farming and with high levels of illiteracy (CIA World Factbook, 2009), the Rwandan government has focused much of its political and educational attention on the next generation of 'elite' – the University-bound youth – and has chosen a unique approach in trying to tackle the problem of ethnicity as a perceived stumbling block to reconciliation. On the one hand, the government is seeking to imbue this potential elite with leadership qualities and the capacity to think critically, and thus create a bulwark against any future mass, violent movement. However, the manner of the education and training available at *Ingando*, with its emphasis on military training, group bonding and dictatorial teaching, is at odds with the notion of a free-thinking elite. In addition, the government has created a 'blank slate' upon which to re-write history; it has attempted to draw all ethnic groups together by dissolving the notions of Hutu, Tutsi, and Twa – formerly the main ethnic groups in the country – in favour of a solidly Rwandan citizenship, which imagines a shared, amicable culture prior to the arrival of the European colonial powers in the 1800s (Eltringham, 2004; Zorbas, 2004; Pottier, 2002). Educated, university-bound youth – Rwanda's likely future civil servants, teachers and lawyers – are the spearheads through which this idea of national unity is being promulgated and the *Ingando* camps are the principal sites at which the new version of Rwandan history is taught to these young people.

Ingando

According to the NURC, *Ingando* is taken from the Rwandese verb *Kugandika* that refers to a stopping of normal activities to reflect on, and tackle national problems (NURC, 2010). The problem is, although few admit this in public, the original practice of *Ingando* is unlikely to have straddled different ethnic groups historically, as it would have normally taken place within ethnically bound communities (Mgbako, 2005). Moreover, it is likely that the practice was reinvented by the Rwanda Patriotic Front (RPF, currently Rwanda's ruling government[4]), during their exile in Uganda, as a means of fostering unity among the rebel troops. Though the exact history of *Ingando* as a practice is unclear, the doubt surrounding its history as a trans-ethnic institution is not (Purdekova, 2008, Mgbako, 2005).

The NURC (2010) – the primary engine behind *Ingando* – describes *Ingando* as:

> . . . a tool to build coexistence within communities. The first beneficiaries were ex-combatants from the DRC. The programme later expanded to include school going youth and students at secondary and tertiary levels. By 2002, the training was extended to informal traders, and other social groups including survivors, prisoners, community leaders, women and youth.

Other than internal evaluation reports, the scheme has received little attention as a tool for reconciliation, unlike other schemes aimed to promote justice and reconciliation such as the *Gacaca* community-court[5] system. To date, this author is aware of only four studies that have attempted to analyse *Ingando* in detail – Thompson[6] (forthcoming 2011), Purdekova (2008), Paquin (2007) and Mgbako (2005) – all of which have been, to varying degrees, somewhat critical of the part *Ingando* has played in attempting to foster reconciliation. Of equal scarcity has been information on the level of detail and agreement concerning the history and composition of *Ingando*. Its origins are shown by the RPF government to be pan-Rwandan, yet there is very little evidence to show that *Ingando* historically straddled the ethnic groups. Indeed, others have argued that it is a very Tutsi-specific cultural device, that was revisited and renewed by Tutsi groups in exile in Uganda (ibid.). An appropriate definition of *Ingando* is further confused by the notion that there are at present *Ingando* exercises aimed at promoting 'solidarity' among the present and future educated classes such as students and politicians; and *Ingando* exercises that tackle the 're-education' of *genocidaires* and those on the fringes of society (Thompson, forthcoming 2011; Purdekova, 2008). *Ingando* itself is a non-physical institution that, according to Mgbako (2005), began in 1996, and initially catered for Tutsi-returnees, followed by all ex-combatants – whether Tutsi or Hutu, *genocidaires*[7] or otherwise. As Mgbako (2005) comments:

> In 1999, the NURC took over management of solidarity camps throughout the country. Since the initial Ingandos for Tutsi returnees, there have been separate government-run solidarity camps for politicians, church leaders, community leaders . . . Ingandos run from several days to several months, and although the syllabus is adapted depending on the group participating, there are similarities across the curricula . . . including lessons on unity and reconciliation, history classes that highlight the defects of the genocidal regime, and lessons on present government programmes. (209)

Throughout this study when I refer to '*Ingando*', I shall be alluding to the purpose-built facility at Nkumba, in the north west of the country, and the activities that occur there. This facility's primary role is now the teaching and training of students destined for university, though it does on occasion cater to other groups such as university professors and teachers. The Nkumba camp is the largest, purpose-built facility for the teaching and training of Rwandans in peace studies, reconciliation and solidarity. It is now the hub for national peace programmes and is as much a tangible signal to the wider world of[8] the government's commitment to societal cohesion and peace as it is a practical facility for bringing a divided population together.

The flagship *Ingando* camp near the Congolese border in Ruhengeri is used to educate between 500 and 900 pre-university students for one month in leadership, peace studies, civic education and history. United Nations Development Programme (UNDP) and the UK Department for International Development (DFID) have together invested $10,670,000 in the NURC, a large portion of which goes towards *Ingando* (DFID, 2007). The UNDP (2004) project profile describes *Ingando* as a platform to:

> [S]ensitize people of Rwanda to the need for a shared vision of reconciliation and unity; advocate for social transformation through attitudinal change to achieve durable national cohesion; enhance the analytical capability of decision makers to address the issues of unity, and reconciliation and to influence public policy and mobilize positive public opinion in support of social and economic change while restoring amicable relations among nationals.

Like Dennis and Fentiman (2007), I highlight the importance of understanding an ethnic conflict in terms of its context and the history that enabled it. On the surface at least, it seems clear that the Rwandan ruling administration has a similar idea. Through *Ingando* the Rwandan government is eager to engage its future leaders in a discussion of recent history in order to promote concepts of national unity and citizenship. Given the role of civil servants in the genocide (Prunier (1995 [2008]) it appears the current administration is using *Ingando* as an attempt to fill the crucial roles of the local, regional and national government machinery with bright, free-thinking individuals – crucial bulwarks in any resistance to ethnic forces that might seek to tear the country apart once more. Two important ways it is seeking to achieve this are first by propounding one inalterable historical account which reinforces the idea that the people of Rwanda are ethnically identical, and secondly, by bonding the young students together through tough, military training. Among the risks of this approach is that bonding the students together in such a way actually limits their capacity and willingness to act singly. A further risk is that by creating and dictating a one-version-only variety of history, attempts at fostering a sustainable culture of critical analysis will be undermined.

Inside *Ingando*

In 2008 I was granted unprecedented access to the NURC archives and staff and most importantly, to the Rwandan Government's flagship *Ingando* camp. I spent three months living there with the university bound students who were spending four weeks at the camp before beginning their studies. While there, I conducted interviews and informal discussions with *Ingando* students and lecturers and I also administered 1,100 questionnaires to approximately 900 students in order to understand more about what they were learning at *Ingando*.

Isolated and reachable only by dirt roads, the flagship *Ingando* Peace and Solidarity camp was utterly hidden from most Rwandans (and from outsiders) and had the sense of a retreat. This remoteness reinforced its detachment from the daily proceedings of Rwandan society and, writing in retrospect, bolstered the authority of the teachings and way of life promoted there. The camp's location was not chosen randomly. Before the 1994 Genocide, Ruhengeri district was a Hutu heartland, and more crucially, between 1994 and 1997, it was through and from Ruhengeri district that many Hutu militia groups launched attacks against the new Tutsi-led administration. The Nkumba-based *Ingando* camp thus became a statement of intent by the new Kagame-led RPF government – a stamp of authority on this previously rebellious area.

To an extent, *Ingando* certainly goes some distance in attempting to achieve goals of unity. Indeed, the lectures and classes that I observed gave no preference to one ethnic group over another. Everyone was now understood to be Rwandan – as they had been before the arrival of the Europeans according to the new history. The president of the NURC explained in an interview:

> In my own opinion, instead of thinking that he or she is a Hutu, Twa or Tutsi, first of all he should think that he is Rwandese. The reason being those kind of divisions . . . brought our country to a disaster like that in 1994. (Interview with NURC President, October 2008)

This raises several questions, first how can identities – which provided sustenance to Rwanda's ethnic conflict – be so quickly dismantled? And, indeed, perhaps more pertinently, should they be dismantled? This dilemma was neatly described by a student at the *Ingando* Peace and Solidarity camp when he asked a lecturer:

> My question is that Hutus, Twa and Tutsi existed even before, in the past, but they taught us in history that these were just social classes. I am asking myself these days, these words are not used. I think it is not easy to forget this in people's heads. Even using them can bring effects. Is it possible to remove these from people's heads, as it was removed from the national identity cards? (Male student, Nkumba, October 2008)

Although not overtly stated, there is an unwritten rule in Rwanda that the former ethnicities – Hutu, Tutsi, Twa – are not referred to (Freedman et al., 2008; Buckley-Zistel, 2006; Freedman et al., 2004). This meant that I could not directly gauge how strongly the students were attached to the terms that they, in one way or another, had to have at least some connection to. In this simple way, this stifling of debate and silencing of certain terminology, demonstrates itself in the students' lack of variety and near-identical answers during verbal questioning. Interestingly, these standard answers were at odds with the answers they gave to confidential, written questionnaires as will be seen below. Although the government, the instructors and lecturers at *Ingando*, and the students themselves never failed to communicate the concept that 'everyone felt one now', it was virtually impossible to probe deep enough to discover if individual students had abandoned all sense of ethnic or group affiliation.[9] Many other researchers have commented on the same phenomenon:

> In Rwanda, the policy of denying the reality of ethnicity and the inability to discuss ethnicity comfortably make it hard for everyday citizens to process what happened during the genocide and to talk about lingering fears and dangers. Unless the policy is addressed and remedied, the teaching of Rwanda's history will be flawed, the potential for further destructive conflict will remain. (Freedman et al., 2008, p. 685)

Indeed, as I shall discuss later, any reference to the terms Hutu, Tutsi and Twa can have repercussions. As one student told me at *Ingando* when I attempted to question whether it would be possible to talk openly about the different ethnic groups: 'You will end up in prison' (Female student, Nkumba, October 2008).

Ingando sessions were remarkably consistent in content, and especially in the form in which they were delivered. This extract from my field notes describes the setting of a typical lecture:

> A large octagonal hall represents the setting for this afternoon's lesson. At least five or six hundred students are crammed into the hall, all dressed in army fatigues, a large majority sporting Wellington Boots (part of the 'uniform'), and all are equipped with notebooks, though it is an even split between those who are taking notes and those who are struggling to sustain any kind of focus.
>
> The lecturer (I am told he is an 'official from the Ministry') reads from his script deliberately, only stopping at times to ask the student audience a question which they all respond to in unison. Occasionally he also passes the microphone to a student who had either responded to the lecturer or volunteered him or herself. In any case their comments are short.

After an hour or so (and only a third of the way into the lesson), the students' concentration seems to be wavering. Only occasionally do they become animated when the lecturer makes (what seems on the surface at least) a witticism or a more controversial point. A soldier walks around part of the time, stopping to prod a sleeping student (of which there are surprisingly many) or ensuring, at random that someone is sitting correctly. (Observation Notes, Lecture 1, Nkumba, 23 September 2008)

The one or two daily lectures lasted anywhere between two and four hours each and began around mid-morning and finished by approximately 6 p.m. Ostensibly designed to cover a framework which had been discussed and drawn up in partnership with the joint funders (UNDP and DFID), the lectures covered a plethora of subjects that were formulated to promote unity and reconciliation among the students, so that they might reproduce such efforts within their own communities. In one fortnight period, for example, the following topics were covered: General History of Rwanda; Philosophy; Social Consciousness; Patriotism; Genocide Ideology; *Gacaca* (community courts); Domestic Conflict; Human Rights; History of Rwandan Tribes; Education; Health; Technology; the Role of the Army; Citizenship; the RPF's mission; and Conflict Resolution. Between one quarter and one third of all subject matter covered the history of Rwanda, which encapsulated discussions of ethnicity and the 1994 Genocide. Even subjects that ostensibly related to peace and unity had an historical aspect at their core – the content of which has been criticised outside Rwanda for its rigidity and assumptions (Lemarchand, 2008; Hodgkin, 2006; Eltringham, 2004; Pottier, 2002). Critics have argued that the *Ingando* accounts of Rwandan history do not reference modern scholarship that, for the most part, characterizes the foundations of Rwanda as complex and multi-dimensional. As an example, a lecture on human rights on 3 October 2008 was almost completely focused on the history of Rwanda's tribes and on the readjustment of student's ideas of belonging:

You were taught the history of Rwanda. If you talk to an old man in Rwanda about his tribe he will say, 'I am Umugesera, Umukono, Umushambo, Umosinga', etc. But today if you talk to a young man about his tribe, he will say, 'Hutu, Tutsi or Twa'. When you analyse properly, tribes did not exist in Rwanda, because a tribe has a different language, different government etc.

We had Hutus, Tutsis and Twa before the coming of the Europeans. But [up until] the end of the 1800s and into the 1900s there was much social development. There was the development of etymology. What colonizers did was to say that Rwandans were not the same. They divided Rwandans

> into groups, calling certain groups arrogant; others were short and very strong. Another group was considered as very, very short people who were pot-makers [and] they had big noses.
>
> Another bad thing they did was to say that Tutsis came from Ethiopia because he had seen people raising cattle in Ethiopia similar to those they saw in Rwanda. Another white man went to Chad [and] saw string men – very short – with big nose[s] and they are Hutus. They said that the Twa had come from Ituri forest. The very big mistake is that even Rwandans believed in this. So you have to be taught and change your beliefs. (Lecture by Kayumba Deo, Rwandan Human Rights Commission, Nkumba, 3 October, 2008)

That history is taught is not in itself deleterious to reconciliation, in fact the opposite is possibly quite true. However, for a history to be prescribed as irrefutable – particularly in light of the many conflicting assessments of Rwandan history within and outside the country – is troubling (Lemarchand, 2008; Eltringham, 2004; Mamdami, 2001). That this one version should be actively promoted and dispersed through subjects other than history is also of concern. This indicates a top-down approach that has excluded many societal players from the debate over the past, and has presented an uncompromising, unsophisticated, single-lens glance at the past that suits the message of unity and stultifies any detached, critical assessment.

Within the Nkumba camp's main hall, the students, passive and silent for most the lectures,[10] had the opportunity to ask questions of their lecturers at the end of each session. A handful would come forward and ask questions, with most questions being rather general and uncontroversial in nature. However, sometimes a student's curiosity would challenge the attempts that most lectures made to dissolve notions of ethnicity. For instance, one student asked:

> Since the coming of the Europeans, all the conflicts we are facing today were caused by these 3 groups – Hutus, Tutsis and Twa – but today you are telling us to leave these groups. Concerning remembering [the] Tutsi Genocide, what shall we explain to our children in [the] future? For example, the Hutus killed the Tutsi, how shall we explain this? (Male Student, Nkumba, 3 October 2008)

This dichotomy between the 'official line' of unified Rwandans and the students' views and memories, which continue to include ethnicity, is borne out starkly by the findings from a the questionnaires I carried out between September and November 2008 with almost 900 students, who took part during 3- to 4-week periods.

The questionnaires enabled me to ask more generally what importance the students attached to the former ethnicities and how the single version of history promoted in *Ingando* had been received. Seeking to determine how successfully students were adhering to 'non-ethnic' views and whether there was a disparity between what was being taught and what students still believed, I set out a number of basic but fundamental questions in written questionnaires[11] that were explained in English and Kinyarwanda.

The statements in both Figures 7.1 and 7.2 – 'The Best Way to Stop Genocide is to Look Closer at Our History,' and 'People Who Do Not Agree with One Version of History are Dangerous' – were formulated after observing that *Ingando* instructors were consistently expounding to the students that the key to their teaching and the point of their subject matter was to encourage students to become critically minded and thoughtfully independent. Yet, with no exposure to alternative versions of Rwanda's history, and with no sessions where critical probing or open discussions occurred, it seemed that *Ingando* was based on a contradiction: that students should feel that they are being taught to think critically while being exposed to a pedagogy and content where the opposite was true. A section removed from a lesson plan shows the exactitude with which a particular history of Rwanda was being propounded, without reference to historiography, and how this definite view of history was intricately linked to attempts to foster cohesion:

> Rwanda as a nation has a long history of over 1000 years . . . Rwanda is a nation-state composed of one people (Banyarwanda) sharing the same clan system, culture, myths, values and language. It is not a colonial construct like Congo, Uganda, Tanzania, etc. On the other hand colonialism completely re-engineered Rwanda into different 'races' (Tutsi-Hamites, Hutu-Bantu, Twa-Pygmoids). This racism was the root-cause of Rwanda's tragedy that culminated into the 1994 genocide. (Copied from 'Amateka y'y Rwanda', 'History of Rwanda', PowerPoint Presentation, Nkumba, 2 October 2008)

The reformation of a country's history in the aftermath of war or revolution, and in an attempt to foster unity, is a common method aiming at instilling political control, stability and a sense of national identity. Ahonen's (2001) study of Estonian history-curriculum change in the aftermath of the Soviet collapse shows this neatly:

> In Estonia, the conversion of history took place as one master narrative replaced another and not as a conversion from one mode of knowledge to

another, e.g. from mono-perspectivity to multi-perspectivity. The new narrative was useful for the remaking of a nation-state, but, at the same time, inevitably excluded a large ethnic minority from any role in the task of nation-building. (183)

It is quite telling that the lecturer of *Amateka y'y Rwanda* quoted above, accepts that the formation of a 'Rwanda' a thousand years ago was the result of 'a joint project of Rwandans created through their chosen institutions', and yet such a collaboration, though central both to government and *Ingando* funders' narratives, is difficult to find historically (Hintjens, 2008). The students were regularly reminded that the history of Rwanda must be probed, and yet they were warned that not adhering to the 'official' history was an obvious symptom of 'divisionism' (see Figures 7.1 and 7.2).

Whereas Figures 7.3 and 7.4 seem to demonstrate an adherence to the notion that debate and multiple views are important, they are at complete odds with the high percentage of students, who, in Figure 7.2 see people who do not agree with the one version of history as 'dangerous'. In essence, the students seemed to be regurgitating almost word for word, the teachings at *Ingando* – that students

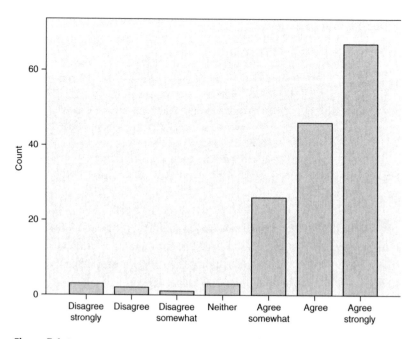

Figure 7.1 Best way to stop genocide . . . look more closely at our history

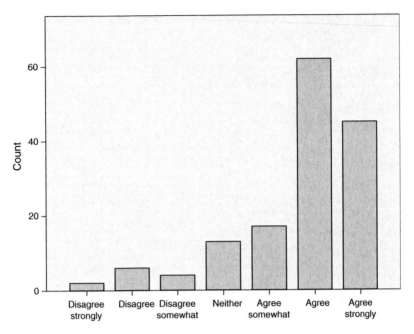

Figure 7.2 People who do not agree with one version of history are dangerous

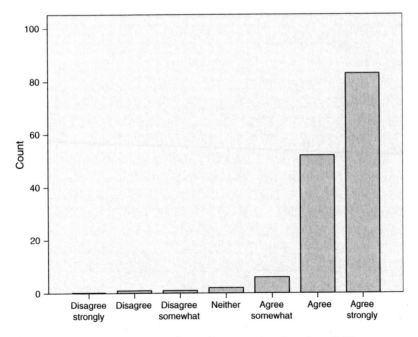

Figure 7.3 What is important is to discuss the past and analyze all possibilities

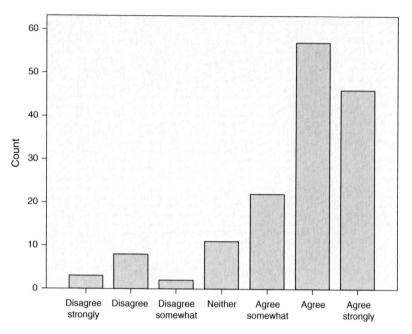

Figure 7.4 It is impossible to find one version of history

must think critically, but within the bounds set for them by the instructors, thus, eliminating true critical analysis. They were taught to relay sound bytes of critical thought that were not supported by questioning them in terms of contexts removed from *Ingando.*

Figures 7.5 and 7.6 show the results of questions designed to probe whether the students were accepting *Ingando*'s 'one version of history and ethnicity', or if they merely repeated it while at the camp in order to stay out of trouble.

Figure 7.6 shows again the verbatim response to the message expounded during every lesson ('People who want to be considered Tutsi, Hutu or Twa are dangerous'), and the predictable, comprehensive agreement. Yet, Figure 7.5 shows a strikingly different response to the actual issue of the ethnic groups historically. What is most striking here is that, with most students opting for the most extreme edges of the opinion spectrum, the ethnicity issue is still divisive, despite the presence of *Ingando* instructors, under whose watchful gaze the surveys were carried out. Equally striking is the number of students in Figure 7.5 who opt for the safe middle ground – the 'neither agree nor disagree' part of the spectrum. Might this be the students seeking to 'play it safe'? This seems like the only plausible reason as nearly every other question is answered emphatically.

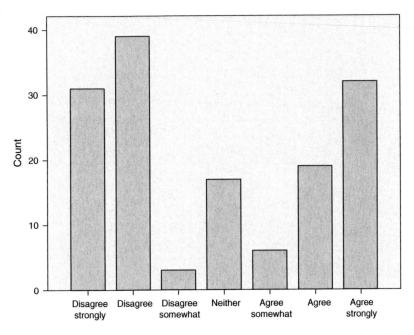

Figure 7.5 There was no such thing as Tutsi, Hutu and Twa before the arrival of colonists

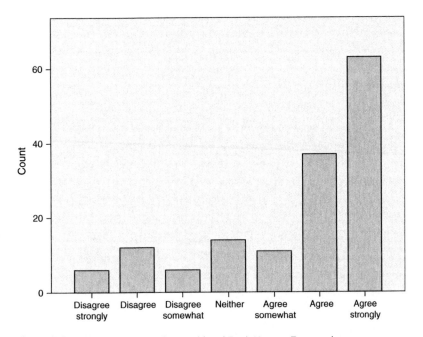

Figure 7.6 People who want to be considered Tutsi, Hutu or Twa are dangerous

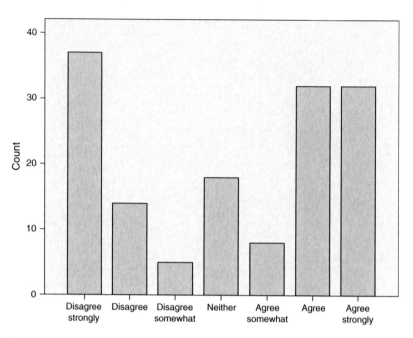

Figure 7.7 The Tutsi, Hutu and Twa were different ethnic groups before the arrival of colonists

In an attempt to bolster the material from Figure 7.5, the question concerning ethnicity was reconfigured to ascertain whether the responses could be replicated. The statement, 'There was no such thing as Tutsi, Hutu and Twa before the colonists arrived', was inverted to read, 'The Tutsi, Hutu and Twa were different ethnic groups before the Colonists arrived', for Figure 7.7.[12]

The similarity between responses to Figures 7.5 and 7.7 is unmistakable. This suggests a degree of consistency with regards the question of students' understandings of ethnicity in post-genocide Rwanda. It also suggests that although the students professed oneness with their neighbours and fellow students regardless of ethnicity and that they adhered to the ethnic history of Rwanda presented in their lessons, their individual opinions on the historical origins ethnic groups' still vary greatly. Figure 7.7 shows this, with 28 per cent 'disagreeing strongly' with the idea that 'The Tutsi, Hutu and Twa were Different Ethnic Groups Before the Colonists Arrived', while 23 per cent 'agreed strongly'. If the students showed an eagerness to support the government view that 'People who Want to be Considered Tutsi, Hutu or Twa are Dangerous' (Figure 7.6), and yet dispute or are uncertain about the government line that Rwanda as a united society and nation pre-dated the colonists' arrival, does this hint at a degree of contradiction?

At the very least, it shows a healthy confusion about the past among students that is not locked in to the party line steadfastly promoted in *Ingando*.

Unity versus reconciliation

In the surveys, the sense that reference to alternate histories and thus to ethnicity was potentially dangerous, correlates with other questions I asked referring to the more general debate surrounding Rwanda since 1994 – the debate on reconciliation. For Dwyer (1999) reconciliation is a process dependent upon and consisting of tensions:

> Reconciliation is not something we seek for its own sake. And in particular, any imperative to attempt reconciliation depends upon the existence of normative ideals to which we are independently attached. I suggest we think of human reconciliation quite generally in terms of tensions – tensions between two or more beliefs; tensions between two or more differing interpretations of events; or tensions between two or more apparently incommensurable sets of values – and our responses to them. (85)

The importance of these tensions is to enable perceptions or beliefs to meet and, through their exposure to one another, develop in relation to opposing views. Thus, an amicable, or at least workable, status quo can be reached (Cole, 2006). If that point of contact, that focus for friction and tension, is a point on a line, the point will move backward and forward with debate and revelation. It is for this reason that tension is necessary, it provides the resistance to one overarching viewpoint of an event that would hang over proceedings, dominating instead of enlightening – something to be obeyed rather than questioned. The NURC in Rwanda, through the *Ingando* Peace and Solidarity camp, is in danger of stifling that creative, emancipative tension in its eagerness to dissolve ethnicity and to enforce one version of history. Moreover, by cultivating this new history, with its lack of flexibility, the students' views – assuming they adhere to the new history – may be utterly at odds with those of their wider communities. This in itself is not necessarily a problem, but a problem may manifest itself if the one version is clung to as a fundamental principle – unalterable and uncompromising.

In a sense, the heavy use of nationalistic mechanisms and devices to foster oneness within a formerly divided people is eroding any possibility of friction and difference of opinion. While both the nationalist discourse and the promotion of a single historical narrative are employed with unity and reconciliation in mind, they are in fact disabling one of reconciliation's key features according to

Dwyer (1999) – tension, discussion and debate. At *Ingando* every 'peace-related' or 'reconciliation-related' lecture or class includes some degree of nationalist sentiment. The students were exposed to a consistent and unquestionable line of thought and were not given a space in which to think freely, think for themselves or even discuss issues with one another.

Instead of facilitating a debate around the role played by ethnicity in bringing people to violence, which might in time foster reconciliation by enabling tensions and their resolution, the Rwandan administration is creating a grand, national narrative, without a 'point of contact' where other perspectives might engage (Purdekova, 2008). This approach makes *Ingando* a less than effective scheme that does not contribute as much as it could towards reconciliation as envisioned by Dwyer and instead might possibly fuel resentment in the long-term. Indeed, the signs of increasing tension regarding Rwanda's one-party domination and the monopoly the RPF has on the 'historical narrative' are becoming clear (Human Rights Watch, 2010, 2008; Hodgkin, 2006; United States Department of State, Bureau of Democracy, Human Rights and Labor, 2005; Freedom House, 2005). This increasing hostility towards people questioning the regime was exemplified with the expulsion of Human Rights Watch's most high-ranking official within Rwanda – Carina Tertsakian – on 24 April 2010 on grounds of VISA irregularities (Afrique Avenir, 2010).

In essence, the Rwandan government is rewriting Rwanda's history and omitting details that might highlight the ethnic identities that played such a disturbing role in 1994 and before. By seeking to reinforce the notion that colonial powers in the 1800s and 1900s created ethnic division rather than manipulated it to their ends, as many historians argue (Prunier, 1995, [2008]; Mamdami, 2001), the government is taking a risk with the nation's future. Despite the teachings they received, the *Ingando* students – well-educated and about to enter tertiary education – indirectly displayed some strong associations with their former ethnicities. In 1994, most of these students were aged between four and six, yet they still sense ethnic difference – and perhaps even hold these distinctions within themselves – because their families and communities, active participants in the 1994 genocide, must too, at least to a degree, maintain an association with their ethnic identities. Therefore, one must wonder whether *Ingando* can dismantle that association, and indeed, whether it should. And, what are the consequences if *Ingando* succeeds in silencing but not erasing an individual's ethnic associations?

Ingando students were eager to talk about the camp, but it quickly became apparent that every question asked received an almost identical response that echoed *Ingando* teaching – something I would notice again and again during my time at Nkumba. Below is a typical response to a question on ethnicity and division in Rwanda given by a female student soon to graduate from *Ingando*:

> Yeah, it has changed my attitudes, like other teachers in Rwanda have been telling you these things of the tribes that come in Rwanda, where these things had come from. Because at a certain time the tribes were united, we didn't have this segregation. We have come to know that we are one just. It's the colonies that brought the divisionism. (Female student, Nkumba, 20 September 2008)

As to the purpose of education provided at the *Ingando* Peace and Reconciliation Camp, the same student commented that:

> When I go out I also try to pass on what I have learned and tell them, like, there are some people who just take things for granted, they don't know the background of this country. So I think I will have to tell them the background of this country, such as the history of this country, because we have learned it very well and we know were everything came from, to know where the country's taking us . . . and we are to analyse this because there are some people who have a low capacity of understanding, so we shall try to pass onto them. (Female student, Nkumba, 20 September 2008)

Both students and *Ingando* administrators shared the notion that an enlightened elite would pass on a sense of cohesion to other people in the country and reconcile them to the new Rwanda. Indeed, the ever-present threats of 'divisionism'[13] – any attempt to promote any or all of the former ethnicities prevalent within the country before 1994 – and 'genocide ideology';[14] – any ideas that lead to Genocide – were consistently reinforced at the *Ingando* camp and students were encouraged to combat these in their communities in order to unify the population and reinforce a new bond with the state.

The ruling party insists that 'divisionism' and 'genocide ideology' still pervade people's minds in Rwanda and must be stamped out, as an RPF political strategist and analyst was keen to tell me:

> I think since 2002 and 2003 when we had the elections we sort of deceived ourselves that the Genocide Ideology was declining. But recently, in 2007, that's when we realized that even among the young people, who were very young during the Genocide . . . now have Genocide Ideology . . . so that brings about a possibility that these young men and women are being

contaminated by their parents. (Karinamaryo Theogene, RPF Mobilizing Officer, 15 October 2008, Kigali)

Regardless of its prevalence among Rwandans, genocide ideology is not a reason to stifle discussion and impose a singular vision of history, and hence, of reconciliation. Yet, teaching and training at *Ingando* continue to emphasize critical thought on paper but to enable the opposite in the actual teaching and learning process.

Observing *Ingando* in practice, the first priority seemed to be to bond the students together in one group and emphasize equality and nationality. Indeed the leader of every activity regularly called out the word 'Quoss'. To which students immediately replied, '*Moja!*' A direct translation is difficult to arrive at, but my translator and I, after much discussion found that *Quoss* generally meant 'class' or 'group'; *Moja* could be regarded as 'oneness'.

This frequent *Ingando* refrain goes some distance in highlighting the pedagogical method and the content of the history lessons at the camp. For Cole and Barsalou (2006) pedagogy itself is central to educational and curriculum reform efforts. They argue that '[a]pproaches that emphasize students' critical thinking skills and expose them to multiple historical narratives can reinforce democratic and peaceful tendencies in transitional societies emerging from violent conflict' (1). Clearly the authoritarian pedagogical style used at *Ingando*, combined with the singular and unquestionable approach towards history (a single perspective presented as a truth rather than a perspective) do not enable the kind tendencies Cole and Barsalou envision.

Similarly, the history curriculum can play a vital role in encouraging openness.

> History taught in schools is highly susceptible to simplified and biased presentations, and this is even more likely after conflicts . . . How schools navigate and promote historical narratives through history education partly determines the roles they and those who control the schools play in promoting conflict or social reconstruction. (Cole and Barselou, 2006, 1)

The history lessons at *Ingando* were consistent in every way with the government of Rwanda's attempt to dissolve ethnic division and mould and mingle aspects of the country's history in order support the idea that Hutu, Tutsi and Twa were, and are, one people. This approach is not wholly negative and is certainly a significant departure from previous administrations' intentional exclusion of certain ethnic groupings' history and culture, but it is limited and limits possibilities for reconciliation as described above. In the context of the Nkumba camp, which was run along military lines, the already limited pedagogy and absence of critical debate, was further compounded by military training that encouraged obedience and personal effort for the greater good of the group – qualities similar to those that played a powerful role in the 1994 Genocide.

This obedience of authority was bolstered by six hours or more of military training each day which the students, male and female alike, took part in. This involved AK-47 assault weapon firing, parade-yard drill, fitness training and collective punishment, which often involved rod-whippings (see Image 7.1) of an entire platoon if even one member failed in a task or showed poor quality performance in drill.

Again, the collective punishment was a further reinforcement of the group dynamic. I often asked the students about the importance of the military aspect and responses were, to varying degrees, always positive. For example:

> They make us put on uniforms to make us think about the military because they know that during the genocide those people who were soldiers used uniforms in a bad way like scaring people or torturing people. So they make us put on uniforms like our usual clothes to make us feel like they are just something useful. (Female student, Nkumba, October 2008)

There was no getting away from the military side of *Ingando*. Every aspect of the student's lives was regimented including their classroom activities. I asked the same student quoted above about the other prominent aspects of the 5 to 6 hours of daily military training (compared to the 3–4 hour lectures on peace, civic

Image 7.1 Punishment at *Ingando*

education, history and other subjects), including the use of automatic assault rifles:

> Like teaching us how to shoot? In case something happens you can have a gun you can fire yourself. And like they make us crawl, like rolling and what, so you get self-defence. And when they bring us together we learn more things like the rebel history, because most of us do not know about the rebel history. They bring us together so we get united. This genocide and its ideology – some people have genocide ideology in them – but when we talk more about it, it changes your mind, like those who are Hutu or Tutsi, you forget about that – we feel like we are all Rwandans. (Female student, Ingando, October 2008)

The Ingando camp was partly run as a military training facility. From approximately 5 a.m. to 10 a.m. the students learned to fire weapons, were parade drilled and took part in intensive physical training that might involve running laps, belly-crawling and other exercises. This military aspect crept into the lectures, as all students were expected to respond in unison to questions asked by either the *Ingando* supervisors or visiting lecturers. The core ideas behind the military aspect were that through hard graft, and regimented daily routines, young Hutu, Tutsi and Twa would be bonded together and cease to see each other as different. What is somewhat peculiar however, is the fact that of nine or ten duel-sex platoons formed up for drill and marching one was entirely formed of the shortest students. It is entirely possible that many of these students were Twa or of Twa extraction.

It is of little surprise that after such military graft in the early morning, the exhausted students were noticeably compliant and intellectually docile during their afternoon lectures, a gruelling schedule that allowed little physical or mental energy left for critical analysis.[15] This may also partly explain the general acceptance of the potent concoction of regimented political concepts, ideas and principles on offer at *Ingando*. Not one student out of the 3,000 that I worked alongside over three months in 2008 ever described himself or herself as anything other than Rwandan or Rwandese.

The test, however, is to ascertain how much of this unity is borne out of a reconciliation with the past, how much has been instilled out of coercion, and how much is facilitated by intellectual apathy. Until an open debate regarding ethnicity and the past takes place, however, it is difficult to answer that question effectively.

Conclusion

The obvious problem – which the joint funders are seemingly unaware of or are just ignoring[16] – is that *Ingando* may be very good at forging short-term social cohesion, but may be storing up resentment for the future by failing to enable the productive tensions necessary for reconciliation. In addition to this, the peculiarity of the Rwandan Genocide poses a further problem – ordinary people, who knew their victims, obeyed instructions to the letter and killed in melee. If there was ever a situation in which attempts at fostering social cohesion ought to be carefully tempered with a pedagogy that encourages, indeed, demands the use of critical thought, it is surely in Rwanda.

Ingando is an open and complex contradiction. On the one hand, the NURC maintain that it is through *Ingando* that students will be taught to think critically and therefore ensure that a malignant authority will be questioned and not obeyed. On the other hand, my research has shown no sign of that critical thinking either being distilled or absorbed in *Ingando*. The military training aspect of *Ingando* set the tone for the Nkumba camp as one that privileged respect, obedience and adherence to the group. In other words, solidarity and belief were being promoted at the expense of judgement, reason and critical thinking. Bearing in mind the history of Rwanda, this is a desperately dangerous tactic that may be reinforcing the group dynamic over the individual voice.

In addition, the notion of 'reconciliation' has now become so deeply subsumed into the idea of 'unity' in Rwanda – and in organizations working in the country – that it is difficult to see how the two can be disentangled. For many, unity now equates to reconciliation, and that reconciliation has been accomplished is evidenced by the fact that no one refers to the former ethnicities or has a different view of history than the one promoted by the government at *Ingando*. Yet, in an environment where differing viewpoints are not promoted, this is hardly worth celebrating. Indeed, research into the role of history education in the post-conflict context tends to highlight the importance of multiple perspectives and debate in enabling possibilities for reconciliation (Freedman et al., 2008; Cole and Barsalou, 2006).

DFID and UNDP have made the decision that the local approach to reconciliation – in this case *Ingando*, despite the questions around its origins – must almost certainly be the most effective way of fostering reconciliation in the aftermath of genocide. The trouble is that neither UNDP nor DFID seemed to have defined what this reconciliation might look like beyond generalized assumptions and have, themselves, allowed for the confusion of 'reconciliation' with 'unity'. In fact, the two are not the same, and unity does not necessarily equate to reconciliation, peace or even cohesion and stability; nor is an extensively top-down approach to unity, like the one employed in Rwanda, likely to be sustainable. Instead of obsessively seeking to erode identities in an effort to bond people together, surely an open discussion of the past must finally begin in Rwanda. With the distribution of the country's first post-Genocide history textbook due in 2010, the debate may begin to open in any case, regardless of the content of the textbook.

When *Ingando* students asked me to define critical thinking, I used the example of reading a book. Of equal importance to the content of the book, is the way in which the book is read. In a sense, reconciliation can be thought of in the same way: the mechanism and the journey are more important than the end result, for this represents the process of reconciliation, not the goal of social cohesion, and only comes with time and openness.

Guiding questions

What are the repercussions of the Rwanda government's decision to teach a particular version of the country's history?

What is the role imagined for young people in Rwanda's process of reconciliation by the Rwandan government? How do young people themselves feel about this role?

Should *Ingando* continue? Why or why not?

Notes

1 The general figure agreed upon by most UN agencies lies in the region of 800,000 deaths. The Rwandan government has recently increased its estimate to over 1,000,000 deaths.

2 The debate concerning the formation of the Hutu, Tutsi and Twa ethnic distinctions is ongoing. Within Rwanda, the government actively promotes the notion that the European Imperial powers allowed for the solidification of these distinctions during the nineteenth and early twentieth centuries. The government, and many other governmental and academic institutions within Rwanda, also hold that, although 'clan' distinctions existed before the arrival of the European powers, these were fluid, mainly economically based and people were united as one people. For more see Mamdami (2001) and Eltringham (2004).

3 For more on the manipulation of the education system prior to 1994, see Prunier, (1995, [2008]) and Mamdami (2001).

4 Rwandan Patriotic Front or *Front Patriotique Rwandais,* formed in 1987 by the Tutsi refugee diaspora in Uganda.

5 For more on *Gacaca*, see Clark and Kaufman, 2008, 297 ff.

6 The author would like to thank Susan Thompson for allowing him to read and cite her forthcoming work.

7 Those guilty of carrying out acts of genocide in 1994 in Rwanda

8 More often than not, foreign delegations are taken to the *Ingando* camp at Nkumba to witness Rwanda's 'peace in action'. In early 2010 the BBC were the first major media group to be allowed in, while during my time at the camp in 2008, a high-level delegation from a South African province visited.

9 For example, without being able to ascertain the ethnic background (however tenuous this may have been) of the student, it was not possible to ascertain whether certain responses were group-specific. Equally, I was unable to determine that one group (for example, Hutus) questioned more rigorously the government's picture of the country's shared history. See Freedman et al., 2004, 260.

10 Many students were 'hit awake' by patrolling soldiers and made to sit straight. After a 5.30 a.m. start and 4 hours of military exercise, it is unsurprising that so many students were weary.

11 With the extensive aid of my translator and interpreter, the questionnaires were prepared in English and Kinyarwanda and were explained to the students in written detail and orally – each question being discussed in an open session with the students so that the meaning was clear and precise. To ensure consistency and reliability, questions were 'doubled-up', that is, each question's content was reworded and rewritten to effectively make another question, even though it was substantively the same. The emphasis of the responses was then cross-examined for consistency.

12 Table and statistical information based on preparatory written questionnaire completed by 150 students at *Ingando* Peace and Solidarity Camp on 2 separate days in October 2008.

13 According to Human Rights Watch (2008), Divisionism was made a crime in 2002 and is defined by Rwandan Law no. 47/2001, article 3. As: 'The crime of sectarianism occurs when the author makes use of any speech, written statement or action that causes conflict that causes an uprising that may degenerate into strife among people'. For more see Law N. 47/2001 on Prevention, Suppression and Punishments of the Crime of Discrimination and Sectarianism available at www.unhcr.org/refworld/pdfid/4ac5c4302.pdf.

14 'Genocide Ideology' was adopted as an offence in Rwanda in 2008. Both Genocide Ideology and Divisionism have come under much international criticism for being vague and easily exploitable by a ruling administration. (Human Rights Watch, 2008)

15 At its most extreme end, denying someone of the physical capacity to think while bombarding them with information in an educational context is regarded, at least in many Western academic circles, as a form of 'brainwashing'. See Taylor, 2004, 63 ff.

16 Since an initial email discussion with the Head of DFID Rwanda and Burundi, Elizabeth Carriere, in early 2010 – when it was stated that DFID would investigate activities at the

Nkumba *Ingando* camp – no further information has been forthcoming. UNDP Rwanda has not responded in any way.

Reference list

Afrique Avenir (2010), '*Rwanda defends expulsion of Human Rights Watch representative*', www.afriqueavenir.org/en/2010/04/28/rwanda-defends-expulsion-of-human-rights-watch-representative/ (accessed 30 April 2010).

Ahonen, S. (2001), 'Politics of identity through history curriculum: Narratives of the past for social exclusion – or inclusion?' *Journal of Curriculum Studies*, 33, 2, 179–94.

Buckley-Zistel, S. (2006), 'Remembering to forget: Chosen amnesia as a strategy for local coexistence in post-Genocide Rwanda', *Africa*, 76, 2, 131–50.

CIA World Factbook (2009), 'Rwanda', www.cia.gov/library/publications/the-world-factbook/geos/rw.html (accessed 1 March 2010).

Clark, P., and Z. Kaufman (eds) (2008), *After Genocide: Transitional Justice, Post-Conflict Reconstruction and Reconciliation in Rwanda and Beyond*. London: Hurst and Company.

Cole, E. (2006), 'History education and socio-political reconciliation after mass crimes'. http://www.ceri-sciencespo.com/themes/re-imaginingpeace/va/resources/history_education_cole.pdf (accessed 1 March 2010).

Cole, E., and J. Barsalou (2006), *Unite or Divide? The Challenges of Teaching History in Societies Emerging from Violent Conflict*, Special Report. US Institute of Peace, Washington, DC.

Dennis, C., and A. Fentiman (2007), *Approaches to Education in Countries Emerging from Conflict*. London: DFID.

Department for International Development (DfID) (2007), 'The UK and United Nations Join Forces to Support Good Governance in Rwanda', www.dfid.gov.uk/Media-Room/Press-releases/2007/The-UK-and-United-Nations-join-forces-to-support-good-governance-in-Rwanda/ (accessed 20 November 2009).

Dwyer, S. (1999), 'Reconciliation for realists', *Ethics and International Affairs*, 13, 81–98.

Eltringham, N. (2004), *Accounting for Horror: Post-Genocide Debates in Rwanda*. London: Pluto Press.

Freedman, S., H. Weinstein, K. Murphy, and T. Longman (2008), 'Teaching history after identity-based conflicts: The Rwanda experience', *Comparative Education Review*, 52, 4, 663–90.

Freedman, S., D. Kambanda, B. Samuelson, I. Mugisha, I. Mukashema, E. Mukama, J. Mutabaruka, H. Weinstein, and T. Longman (2004), 'Confronting the past in Rwandan schools', in E. Stover and H. Weinstein (eds), *My Neighbour, My Enemy: Justice and Community in the Aftermath of Mass Atrocity*. Cambridge, MA: Cambridge University Press.

Freedom House, (2005), *Country Report: Rwanda*. www.freedomhouse.org/template.cfm?page=363&year=2005&country=6819 (accessed on 20 February 2010).

Hintjens, H. (2008), 'Post-Genocide identity politics in Rwanda', *Ethnicities*, 8, 1, 5–41.

Hodgkin, M. (2006), 'Reconciliation in Rwanda: Education, history and state', *Journal of International Affairs*, 60, 1, 199–212.

Human Rights Watch (2008), *Law and Reality: Progress in Judicial Reform in Rwanda*. New York: Human Rights Watch.

— (2010), *Rwanda: End Attacks on Opposition Parties*. www.hrw.org/en/news/2010/02/10/rwanda-end-attacks-opposition-parties (Accessed 10 February 2010).

Kelman, H. (2006), 'Interests, relationships, identities: Three central issues for individuals and groups in negotiating their social environment', *Annual Review of Psychology*, 57, 1–26.

Kelman, K. (1999), *Transforming the Relationship Between Former Enemies: A Social-Psychological Analysis*. In: R. L. Rothstein, ed. After the Peace: Resistance and Reconciliation. Boulder and London: Lynne Rienner.

Lemarchand, R. (2008), 'The politics of memory in post-Genocide Rwanda', in P. Clark and Z. Kaufman (eds), *After Genocide: Transitional Justice, Post-Conflict Reconstruction and Reconciliation in Rwanda and Beyond*. London: Hurst and Company.

Mamdami, M. (2001), *When Victims Become Killers: Colonialism, Nativism, and the Genocide in Rwanda*. Princeton: Princeton University Press.

Mgbako, C. (2005), 'Ingando Solidarity Camps: Reconciliation and political indoctrination in post-Genocide Rwanda', *Harvard Human Rights Journal*, 18, 201–224.

Minow, M. (1998), *Between Vengeance and Forgiveness*. Boston: Beacon Press.

National Unity and Reconciliation Commission (2010), 'Ingando', www.nurc.gov.rw/index.php?option=com_content&view=article&id=50&Itemid=12 (accessed 7 March 2010).

Paquin, F. (2007), *Le Rwanda après le Genocide: Gacaca, Ingando et Biopouvoir*, unpublished master's thesis, Université du Quebec à Montreal.

Pottier, J. (2002), *Re-Imagining Rwanda: Conflict, Survival and Disinformation in the Late Twentieth Century*. Cambridge: Cambridge University Press.

Prunier, G. (1995, [2008]), *The Rwandan Crisis: History of a Genocide*. London: Hurst and Company.

Purdekova, A. (2008), *Repatriation and Reconciliation in Divided Societies: The case of Rwanda's 'Ingando'*, Refugee Studies Centre working paper.

Taylor, K. (2004), *Brainwashing: The Science of Thought Control*. Oxford: Oxford University Press.

Thomson, S. (forthcoming 2011), 'Re-education for reconciliation: Participant observations on the Ingando camps', in S. Straus and L. Waldorf (eds), *Reconstructing Rwanda: State Building and Human Rights after Mass Violence*. Madison, WI: University of Wisconsin Press.

UNDP (2004), *UNDP Country Cooperation: 2004–2008*. Project Profiles. Kigali: UNDP. http://www.undp.org.rw/proj_profiles_2004.pdf

United States Department of State, Bureau of Democracy, Human Rights and Labor (2005), *Rwanda Country Report*. www.state.gov/g/drl/rls/hrrpt/2005/61587.htm (accessed on 27 February 2010).

Volkan, V. (2004), *Blind Trust: Large Groups and Their Leaders in Times of Crisis and Terror*. Charlottesville, NC: Pitchstone Publishing.

Zorbas, E. (2004), 'Reconciliation in post-Genocide Rwanda', *African Journal of Legal Studies*, 1, 1, 29–52.

Conclusion: Assumptions and Realities

Julia Paulson

The assumption that education can and does contribute towards reconciliation is at the core of this book. Its contributors have taken this assumption as a starting point and have looked at the ways that it has been put into practice around the world. In exploring how particular educational initiatives have been imagined as reconciliatory, or in looking at the implicit reconciliatory intentions and outcomes of education in a given context, contributors have deepened understandings of the education/reconciliation equation with empirical evidence.

The chapters in the book, however, do not offer straightforward accounts of education fostering reconciliation. Though there are certainly demonstrations of particular forms of educational action contributing towards processes of reconciliation within these pages, the themes that emerge most strongly from the book cloud and add complexity to the assumption that education contributes towards reconciliation. They do not disprove this 'core assumption' that guides much of the work done under the name of education in emergencies, but taken together these chapters do insist on the need to think carefully about how education (of what kind) might best serve the needs and process of reconciliation in a given context, rather than simply assuming that it will.

In this conclusion I discuss six themes that emerge from a consideration of the chapters in this volume as a whole.

Context

Comparative educationalists are largely agreed that 'context matters' (Crossley with Jarvis, 2001). That despite increasing international convergence around the goals and even the processes of education, the discrete and distinct contexts in which educational initiatives are carried out are of central importance to how these educational endeavours will play out, and should be afforded central importance in planning and delivering them. Perhaps unsurprisingly, given the profound importance of this insight, the contributors of this volume show that it certainly applies to the potential of education to contribute towards reconciliation.

From the first chapter by Jason Hart, the senselessness of applying 'pre-cooked' approaches that do not take into account the lived experiences and ongoing injustices faced by those intended to participate, emerges as a poignant insight. The chapter by Briony Jones also shows how the very real concerns and constraints of the post-conflict context raise concerns for those expected to integrate and reconcile, despite their general acceptance of integration as an end goal. Like the realities of lived experience, the practicalities of security (both personal and economic) and the pace of change exert real influence on the participation in and possibilities for reconciliation through education.

In Julia Paulson's chapter the politics of educational policymaking and the politics of education within the broader context of post-conflict governance profoundly affect (and even determine) the ways in which potentially reconciliatory education proposals are used discursively and in practice. Paulson's chapter shows how these contextual, political factors can shape and even undermine reconciliatory intentions. Even where education can clearly be seen to be fostering reconciliation, as in Sarah Dryden-Peterson's chapter, the broader context, in this case of structural violence against black and migrant communities, impinges on the possibilities for 'full' reconciliation.

Children and young people

Although they are the most frequently intended beneficiaries of most educational endeavours, children and young people and their perspectives and experiences, are often left out of much educational planning. Most of the chapters implicitly describe these processes as they detail the planning and implementation of, for instance, the *Ingando* camps in Rwanda, integrated schools in Northern Ireland and educational policymaking in Peru, all undertaken largely without the input from those young people intended to participate. Some chapters show more explicitly the effects of a lack of attention to children and young people both on those young lives and on the ultimate success and impact of educational initiatives. Jones describes how at least some of the impetus for student protest at the integration of schools in Brčko was an expression of agency by those expected to enact a process over which they had little control and no consultation. Like Jones' work, James Kearney's chapter explores how young people, again burdened with the task of enacting a reconciliatory project, respond to messages and mandates imposed upon them. He paints a nuanced and complex picture in which the effects of government imposed unity are by no means certain, particularly within the young people meant to create a unified Rwanda. And, Hart shows how educational initiatives divorced from the experiences of young people can at best seem irrelevant and uninteresting and can at worst deepen antagonisms.

As funding for education in emergencies grows, this need to genuinely involve children and young people is particularly important in order to develop educational programming that offers realistic opportunities for reconciliation.

Historical narratives

One of the 'usual' activities of those promoting educational reconstruction in situations affected by conflict is the revision of curriculum (see for example Buckland, 2005; Sinclair, 2004). History curriculum (or subject curriculum through which history is transmitted in cases where history is not itself a taught subject) is of importance here, with some efforts aiming at imparting a 'neutral,' 'unbiased' or 'fair' version of history, including recent conflict (see Sinclair, 2004). While the contributors in this volume would likely discount the possibilities of ever achieving such accounts of history, their chapters do certainly draw attention to the importance of historical narrative in processes of reconciliation, particularly where education is involved.

Rather than demonstrating how a 'neutral' history can be created and deployed for reconciliatory purposes, these chapters show the deeply political nature of history in conflict-affected situations, and the weight of political interest in monitoring, if not controlling, the version(s) presented. Kearney's exploration of the *Ingando* camps in Rwanda presents an extreme case of history imposed from above and shows some of the contradictions between the 'official' version and the lived experiences of those expected to take it on. Paulson's chapter looks at the trajectory of another 'official' version of history – the Peruvian TRC's account of Peru's conflict – within the educational sector. Military pride, the political undesirability of full accountability for past crimes, and refusal to acknowledge any legitimate basis for the Shining Path insurgency led politicians to attempt to block the entry of the TRC's version of conflict into the national curriculum.

Contact and integration

When detail is given as to how education might contribute towards reconciliation one of the most common suggestions is via programmes that offer opportunities for contact between conflicting or previously conflicting groups or via the integration of previously segregated education systems. Again, the chapters in this book do not disprove these avenues as potentials, but they do highlight the fallaciousness in assuming that contact and/or integration will necessarily lead to reconciliation or to a transformation in relationships. David Johnson's work on integration in higher education in South Africa shows how formal integration (in policy and in formal practice at institutions) can mask a still very divided reality. A single issue like language continues to make full integration and unity within a single institution difficult, while the apartheid legacy is still present in racially motivated incidents on several university campuses. Johnson calls for reconciliation that acknowledges past injustices and present inequalities by policies that move beyond formal integration towards redress.

Alan Smith's chapter also asks pertinent questions about integration and integration policy. In Northern Ireland where integration at school has been voluntary, those families who choose to send children to integrated schools demonstrate a high degree of commitment to the principle – however, with only 6 per cent of students studying in integrated schools they are still a minority. Both Kearney and Jones illustrate the problems of more forced integration in the *Ingando* camps of Rwanda and the internationally heralded multiethnic district of Brčko. These empirical examples resonate with Hart's observation about the unlikeliness of meeting the high expectations of inter-group contact – peace, unity and reconciliation – without seeking to transform dynamics of power and inequality that also feature in the relationships between conflicting groups.

Changing attitudes

A second way in which education is often proposed to contribute towards reconciliation is through the changing of attitudes. Peace, citizenship and human rights education aim to change negative attitudes and stereotypes towards the other and to instil peaceful attitudes that privilege coexistence and human rights. Again, Hart is sceptical of the power of such educational initiatives in situations where human rights are in fact not guaranteed and where inequality and vast differentials in power persist. Smith highlights the difficulties of meaningfully incorporating such learning in the post-conflict context. Education for Mutual Understanding in Northern Ireland was difficult for teachers to grapple with and incorporate into their teaching without additional training. Citizenship education is hard to conceptualize in a divided society where nationhood and national identity is still much contested. Kearney looks at the employment of principles of human rights and unity in an environment where critical thinking is actively discouraged, questioning along certain lines disallowed and military discipline imposed. These contradictions do not go unnoticed by those young people expected to carry forward the peaceful and unified attitudes that will reconcile Rwandans and build a peaceful Rwanda.

Values and universal frameworks

These examples throw into question the applicability of universal frameworks that often underpin human rights, peace and citizenship education in situations affected by conflict. Hart is particularly sceptical, drawing attention to the contradictions between rhetoric and reality that young people are certain to perceive. Smith sees more potential, proposing that given the difficulty of citizenship education that relies on nation and nationhood, perhaps drawing on universal human rights and seeking to develop values of peace and coexistence, offers greater possibility. Dryden-Peterson's work offers a refreshing take on such matters – here personal change happens not through the learning of particular concepts, but instead with the help of enabling conditions (a caring school, caring teachers) that foster individual reconciliation with the self, the building of new relationships and some degree of societal reconciliation. What is novel in the reconciliation Dryden-Peterson describes is that education's role it is not prescribed according to particular values, frameworks or concepts but instead is enabling in its ethos.

Conclusion: The nature of reconciliation

Taken together, these chapters can offer some insights into the nature of reconciliation, and into education's role within it. Akin to the first theme – that context matters – the process of reconciliation in a given location and the ways in which education might contribute to it will be deeply affected by the present and past dynamics (political, social, economic etc.) of that location. Education programming that is not only sensitive to, but based on these dynamics and the lived experiences of those who shape and confront them, particularly children and young people, is most likely achieve its reconciliatory ends.

These chapters suggest that such programming, based upon and responding to contextual dynamics and the needs and lived experiences of the children and young people it seeks to engage, might be best not to envision particular static outcomes such as attitude change or mixed classrooms as indicators of reconciliation. Likewise, relying on the acquisition of certain universal concepts and values to indicate progress towards reconciliation might not best harness education's reconciliatory potential. An ethos of education that gives space for those participating in it to determine, experience and create the needs behind reconciliation and the process towards it appears to offer potential to capture education's ability to foster reconciliation.

These chapters demonstrate profoundly, though, that behind this ethos must be an effort towards greater transformation of the dynamics of inequality that sustain conflict and division. Even in Dryden-Peterson's chapter, where the practices within a school were actively fostering reconciliation, a context of structural violence limited these possibilities. Not only should educational initiatives and education policy actively seek to challenge and transform inequalities and social divisions, they should be embedded in broader social, political and economic processes that seek to do so.

Reference list

Buckland, P. (2005), *Reshaping the Future: Education and Postconflict Reconstruction.* Washington D.C.: World Bank.

Crossley, M., and P. Jarvis (2001), 'Introduction: Context matters', *Comparative Education*, 37, 4, 405–08.

Sinclair, M. (2004), *Learning to Live Together: Building Skills, Values and Attitudes for the 21st Century.* Paris: UNESCO.

Index